hot chefs • hip cuisines • top tables • signature recipes

gourmetchic ■asia

For regular updates on our special offers, register at
www.thechiccollection.com

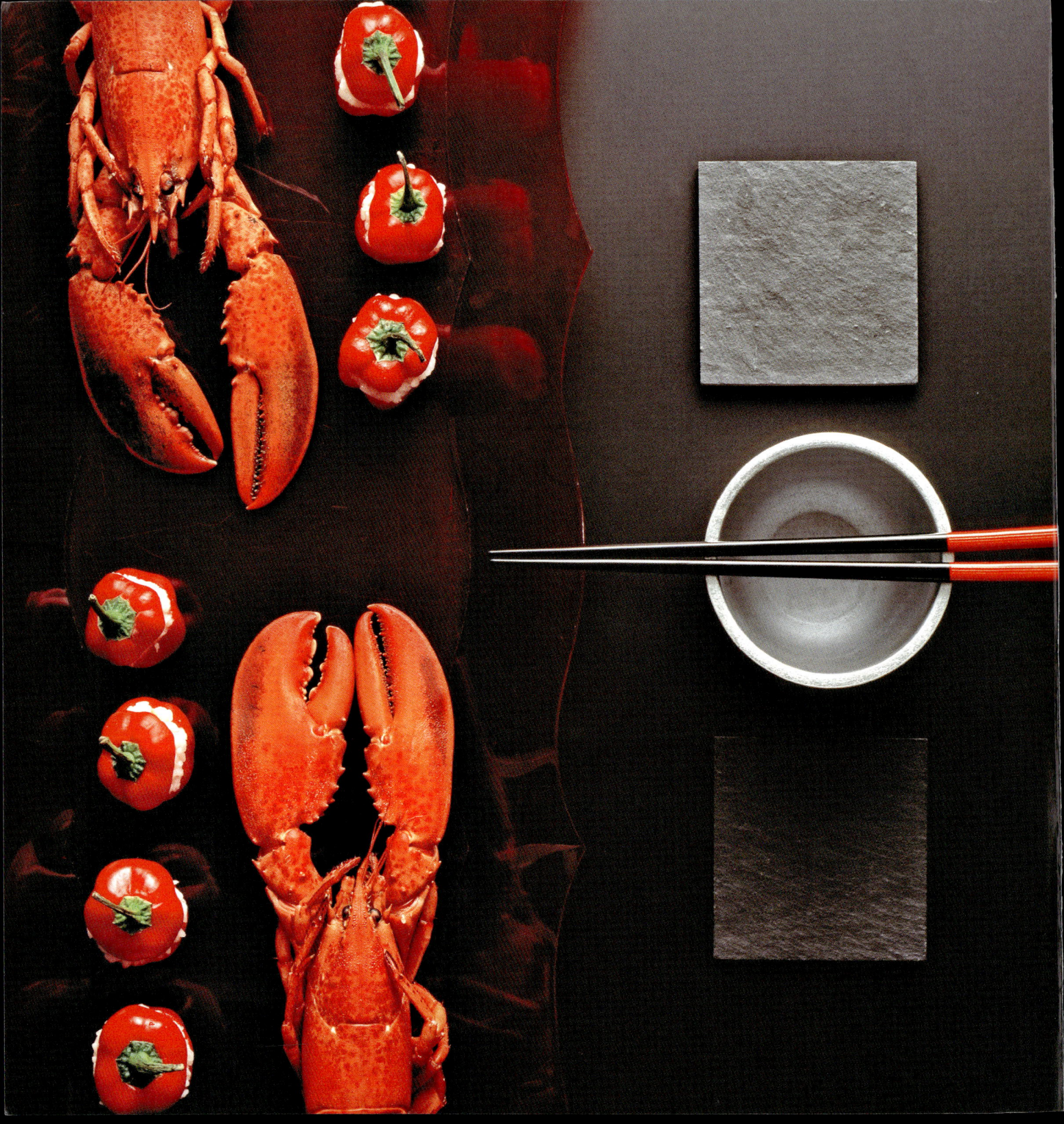

hot chefs • hip cuisines • top tables • signature recipes

gourmetchic asia

text pauline d loh • sylvia tan • amy van

thechiccollection

managing editor
francis dorai

editor
valerie ho

assistant editor
keh pei shan

designer
chan hui yee

production manager
sin kam cheong

sales and marketing director
antoine monod

sales and marketing managers
rohana ariffin
new bee yong
catherine gay paras
meliana salim
suresh sekaran
daniel tolentino

sales and marketing consultants
carolyn bickerton
beverly jangkamonkulchai

editions didier millet pte ltd
121 telok ayer street, #03-01
singapore 068590
telephone : +65.6324 9260
facsimile : +65.6324 9261
enquiries : edm@edmbooks.com.sg
website   : www.edmbooks.com

©2010 editions didier millet pte ltd

Printed by Tien Wah Press (Pte) Ltd, Singapore.

All rights reserved. No part of this publication may be reproduced, stored in a retrieval system, or transmitted in any form or by any means, electronic, electrostatic, magnetic tape, mechanical, photocopying, recording or otherwise, without prior written permission from the publisher.

isbn-13: 978-981-4260-20-6

THIS PAGE: *Crab, tuna, caviar, mango and avocado timbale—a feast for both the eyes as well as the senses.*

OPPOSITE: *Dinner on the rocks, above the crashing waves, at Banyan Tree Bintan.*

PAGE 2: *Lobster dinner for two.*

PAGES 10–11: *Plating food is as important as the flavours on the dish.*

PAGES 186–7: *The warm cheery dining area at the Raffles Culinary Academy.*

PAGES 192: *Dinner at the Conrad Bali.*

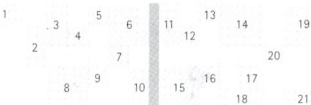

COVER CAPTIONS:

1: One of Tippling Club's cocktail, *Negroni*.
2: A French goat cheese dessert, perfect for tea, by Chris Salans.
3: Simple elegant plating focuses the diner on the food.
4: An appetising steak tartar dish by Gray Kunz.
5: Enjoy a cocktail at the St Regis Bali.
6: A romantic dinner can be enjoyed here at the Conrad Bali.
7: Gingerbread men fresh from the oven.
8: Plating creates visual appeal and speaks also of a chef's style.
9: A warm pot of tea is always welcome.
10: The kulfi dessert at The Song of India.
11: Flavoured salts add finishing touches to a dish or dessert.
12: An example of a tower-style plating.
13: Organic food need not be boring, as can be seen from the presentation here.
14: Dinner set-up under the starry sky on a beach at Banyan Tree Bintan.
15: A chic restaurant interior makes for an unforgettable dining experience.
16: "The Passion that Lasts, Knows No Bounds" by Sam Leong.
17: A mouthwatering chocolate dessert by Master Pâtissier Gianluca Fusto.
18: An assortment of bite-size treats at the Six Senses Resorts & Spas.
19: Mixologist Matthew Bax of Tippling Club.
20: Chocolate truffles.
21: Dine at the water's edge at Banyan Tree Bintan.

contents

gourmetstyle 10

introduction: the art of eating in asia 12
evolving food trends 18
leading chefs 24
signature dishes 34
chefs' tips + secrets 40
restaurant interiors 48
high-altitude dining 54
romantic escapades 60
organic food + spa cuisine 64
plating + food styling 70
gourmet summits + food festivals 74
cookery schools 78
gourmet foods + specialist markets 84
new latitude wines 88
gourmet cocktails 94

gourmetrestaurants 98

china + hong kong
Café Cha, Shangri-La Hotel, Beijing 100
Nishimura, Shangri-La Hotel, Beijing 102
Senses, The Westin Beijing Financial Street 104
Mandarin Grill + Bar, Mandarin Oriental, Hong Kong 106
T'ang Court, The Langham Hong Kong 108
Fresh, Mandarin Oriental, Sanya 110
Kathleen's 5 Rooftop Restaurant + Bar 112
Simply Thai 114

indonesia
Bale Sutra, Hotel Tugu Bali 116
Beduur, Ubud Hanging Gardens 118
glow, COMO Shambhala Estate 120
Kemiri, Uma Ubud 122
Maya Sari Restaurant, Maya Ubud Resort + Spa 124
Nelayan Restaurant, Jimbaran Puri Bali 126
nutmegs restaurant – dining at hu'u 128
Raja's, Nusa Dua Beach Hotel + Spa 130
RIN, Conrad Bali 132
Restaurant Dewi Ramona, Matahari Beach Resort + Spa 134
The Restaurant, The Legian 136

japan
Citabria 138

malaysia
Bijan Bar + Restaurant 140
Gobo Chit Chat, Traders Hotel, Kuala Lumpur 142
SkyBar, Traders Hotel, Kuala Lumpur 144
Kogetsu, The Saujana Hotel, Kuala Lumpur 146
The Restaurant, The Club at the Saujana 148
NEO Restaurant + Luxe Lounge 150
Sao Nam 152
Tamarind Springs 154
Top Hat Restaurant 156
Indulgence Restaurant + Living 158
The View, Hotel Equatorial Penang 160

maldives
FISH, W Retreat + Spa – Maldives 162
Vilu, Conrad Maldives Rangali Island 164

singapore
Carousel, Royal Plaza on Scotts 166
Cherry Garden, Mandarin Oriental, Singapore 168
Inagiku, Fairmont Singapore 170
Peach Garden 172
The Song of India 174
Yan Ting, The St Regis Singapore 176

thailand
Bed Supperclub 178
Cotton, Shanghai Mansion Bangkok 180
Minibar Royale 182
Floyd's Brasserie, Burasari 184

gourmet recipes 101

appetisers
Torched Nigiri Sushi 103
Marinated Salmon with Orange and Sichuan Peppers 105
Pan-fried Crab Claw with Celery and Bell Peppers 109
Marinated Blue-shelled Yabbies 111
Sesame-coated Crab Claws 117
Raw Green Curry 121
King Prawn, Orange and Pomelo Salad 123
Caramelised Sea Scallops on Organic English Spinach Purée with Sour Cream and Crispy Parma Ham 127
Marinated Barracuda in Beetroot with Capsicum Flan 135
Bagna Cauda (Anchovy and Garlic Dip with Miso) 139
Tori Teriyaki (Chicken Teriyaki) 147
Lobster Custard, Butter Poached Lobster and Cauliflower Purée 149
Crispy Snakehead Fish 155
Mediterranean Caesar Salad on Truffled Parmesan Custard with Olive Tapenade and Air-Dried Chicken Floss 161
Ikura Salmon Sushi 163
Smoked Salmon, Crabmeat Salad with Pistachio, Lime and Argan Oil Dressing 165
Garlic-scented Soya Sauce King Prawns 169
Hot Pot with Kyoto Winter Radish and Sweet Miso 171

main courses
Slow-braised Udon Noodles with Soya Sauce 101
Pork Loin with Croqueta, Apple Jelly and Mushroom Quinoa 107
Braised Lamb Shanks with Gremolata 113
Green Curry Chicken 115
Coriander Chicken with Pineapple Fried Rice in Red Sambal Coconut Sauce 129
Balinese Bebek Betutu (Balinese Roasted Duck) 131
Slow-cooked Petuna Ocean Trout with Marinated Fennel and Parsley Oil 137
Masak Lemak Udang Dengan Nenas (Prawns and Pineapple in Spicy Coconut Milk) 141
Char Kway Teow (Fried Rice Noodles) 143
Pan-roasted Lamb Loin, Pumpkin Mashed Potatoes in Balsamic Reduction with Lavender Infused 151
Vit Sot Tom (Duck in Tamarind Sauce) 153
Chicken and Mushroom Pie 157
Cressy Lamb Tenderloin 159
Oven-roasted Fillet of Cod, Celeriac Mousseline with Sautéed Porcini, Orange Beurre Blanc 167
Baked Fillet of Sea Perch with Preserved Duck Egg Yolk and Scrambled Egg White 173
Lahsooni Jhinga (Jumbo Prawns Stuffed with Spiced Crayfish and Shrimps in a Tandoor Marinade) 175
Dong Bo Rou (Pork Belly Stew) 177
Croque with Home-smoked Salmon 183
Lobster Thermidor 185

desserts
Passion Fruit Crème Brûlée 119
Balinese Vanilla, Coconut and Kaffir Lime-scented Pannacotta with Brûléed Mango and Coconut Wafers 125
Sake Kasu Pannacotta 133
Almond Daquoise with Berries 179

cocktails
Kiwitini, Lychee Rose, Mata D'or, Selangor Sling 145
Shanghai Royale, Shanghai Cosmo, Shanghai Sunset 181

picture credits + acknowledgements 188
index 189

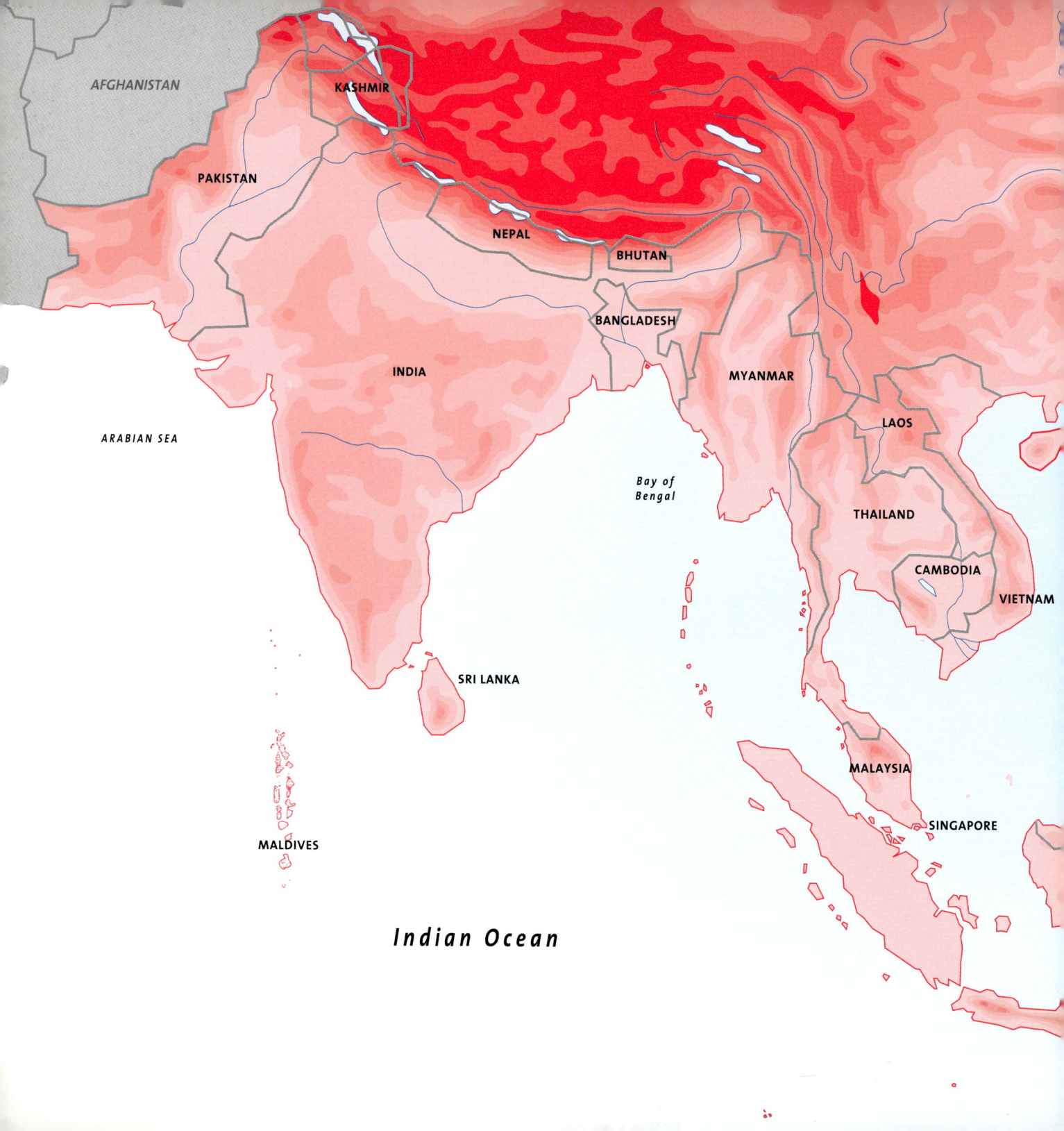

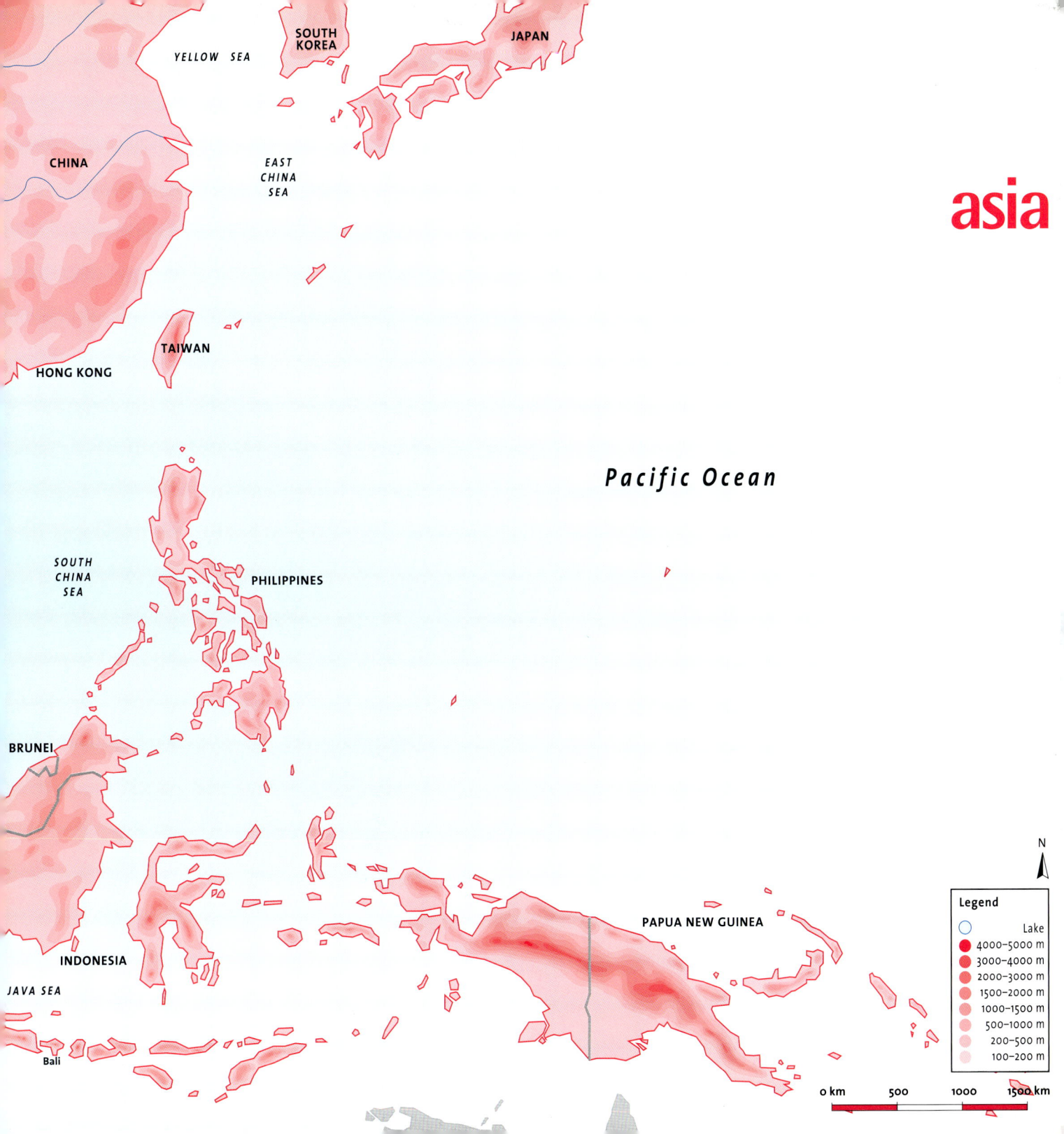

gourmet style

Asia's exciting food scene encompasses an array of cuisines from Singapore to Shanghai and Bali to Bangkok. What used to be rough-and-tumble street fare has been elevated to *haute*-cuisine, and Chinese chefs are awarded much-coveted Michelin stars. While some chefs seek out purely organic produce, others entice with their brand of molecular gastronomy. This section explores everything culinary—Asian, Western and variations in between—for epicureans looking to indulge the palate as well as the senses.

introduction: the art of eating in asia

Nothing has evolved so quickly and completely as the process of putting food in the mouth. The art of good food has been elevated to heights our hunter-gatherer ancestors would not have imagined even in their wildest dreams. Dining out is a lifestyle luxury and eating has become a science involving the knowledge of nutrition, environmental and ethical issues in production and marketing as well as the more classic concerns of taste, texture and presentation.

epicurean adventures

The modern gourmand is a sophisticated consumer out to capture the latest and best experience and stimulus. No longer satisfied by the corner bistro, good-food lovers hunt down the rare and exotic, as well as the just-plain-delicious with great determination, often willing to travel far and wide to taste the best. The indulgences range from exotic seafood in a restaurant under the sea in the Maldives, fusion cuisine while reclining on outsized pillows and pillowy white mattresses in Bangkok, to an intimate candlelight dinner for two on a beach with your toes digging into the sand and gentle waves lapping at your ankles in Bali.

It's no longer just the food, ambience and location that set the stage for the globe-trekking gourmet. Thrill-seekers seeking altitude dine at the world's highest restaurant, 100 Century Avenue, currently in the towering Shanghai World Financial Centre in Pudong, until such time a more highly placed competitor knocks it off its perch. Asia seems to enjoy dining with a view and notable restaurants with altitude include Shinyeh on the 85th floor of the Taipei 101; Bangkok's Sirocco on the 63rd floor of The Dome at Lebua overlooking the city and the Chao Praya river; China Grill on level 66 of Park Hyatt Beijing and the Equinox Restaurant on the 70th floor of Swissotel The Stamford Singapore, to name a few.

Television, mainly, and other media are major influences on how, where and what we choose to eat. Through reality shows, we join would-be master chefs in cooking up a storm. Through the celebrity chefs who desert hob and home to go travelling the world, we learn about lesser-known cuisines that are slowly coming to the fore. Apart from the vicarious epicurean pleasures on screen, reading the restaurant menus of the more avant-garde chefs in our cities can be an education in culinary arts, kitchen science, ingredient sustainability and conservation issues.

Wine and food pairing has reached new heights, and it's no longer vintages from the Old World or New World that dominate the wine lists. There are also the emerging New Latitude wines from China, India, Thailand and Bali. With more sophisticated viticulture, even an island sitting on the equator like Bali can producing quaffable wines suited to spicy cuisine. For these wine-makers-come-lately, it is the local flavours and tastes that are uppermost in their minds when they craft and mature their wines.

THIS PAGE (FROM TOP): *The modern gourmet is culturally and ecologically aware, with a return to fresh and organic food; cocktails are concocted to complement specific cuisine.*

OPPOSITE: *Contemporary Chinese cuisine coupled with artistic modern décor provides an exceptional dining experience at My Humble House, Singapore.*

cross-culture melting pot

Globalisation has spread to the top kitchens of the world, and the commercial pantry is stocked with meat, vegetables, herbs and spices that come from all corners of the earth. Mediterranean olive oil has become the oil of choice. Asian cinnamon, star anise and especially cumin have revived the ancient spice trade. Southeast Asian basil, coriander and lemongrass have gone into Western kitchens, while chefs and cooks east of the Suez now use rosemary, oregano and thyme.

These new flavour trends are best seen when international chefs and travelling gourmets gather at the region's culinary summits and epicurean festivals, of which there are many. Some are organised by the tourism boards, others mooted by passionate chef-entrepreneurs dedicated to promoting their unique industry and culture, such as the annual World Gourmet Summit in Singapore, the World Gourmet Festival in Bangkok and the Hong Kong Food Festival. Whatever the scope and duration of the very many epicurean gatherings in Asia, they are all well patronised—another indication that food is no longer a mere necessity to keep the hunger pangs away, but has morphed into a culture and lifestyle that is evolving constantly.

food fads and lifestyle options

The way we eat evolves, and what we eat is also evolving. Organic is the new gourmet buzzword as foodies learn valuable lessons on sustainable farming and the evils of excessive use of pesticides and insecticides. Micro-greens, heirloom vegetables and free-range animals are attractions in themselves. Sustainability is right up there, too, and food-lovers are learning to curb their appetites enough to allow Mother Earth time to recover from over-fishing in the seas and over-farming on land.

An increasing social consciousness to eating more healthily is manifested in the mushrooming of resorts offering organic and spa cuisines. Recent research may question its perceived benefits, but the belief that organic food is better for health is not going to go away. Consumers are more concerned about health and wellness, and many are willing to pay a premium for brown rice, healthier oils and leaner meats.

THIS PAGE: In Bali, free-range duck and geese are enjoying a new popularity, paired with the organic vegetables now coming out of its hill-top farms.

OPPOSITE (FROM TOP): Chefs are experimenting with micro-greens, lentils and seafood in innovative combinations of ingredients and cooking styles; cookery classes are attracting a growing following of hands-on foodies.

Cities all over Asia have responded to the trend. In Singapore, major supermarkets have organic sections devoted to fruit, vegetables and even meat, while independent organic stores are cropping up all over the island. Even hotels such as the Four Seasons Singapore have started eco-vegetable patches to supply ingredients for their tables. At The Farm in Batangas, the Philippines, soups, cookies and ice-cream subscribe to the raw-food philosophy and the restaurant is part of what has been described as a "life-changing retreat". All dishes are composed of almost entirely uncooked (or gently heated) fruits, vegetable, grains and nuts.

Spa cuisine at its best can be found at Bali's award-winning Maya Ubud Resort & Spa, which offers exotic and invigorating treatments complemented by microbiotic cooking. The menu focuses on a selection of low-calorie and vitamin-rich food such as tofu, asparagus, salmon, scallop and seaweed. The vegetables are harvested from selected organic farms in Bali and used together with unrefined sugars, fresh fruit nectars, natural Bali sea salt and extra virgin olive oil in its dishes. Bali is also home to the COMO Shambhala Estate at Begawan Giri which serves organic, locally sourced ingredients, and delivered from field to table with minimum delay.

And then, there is method in madness. While past chefs have shown that plating and styling food on a plate can create trends, like minuscule portions of nouvelle cuisine on oversized white plates, some have now swopped toques for laboratory coats and spatulas for calipers to create molecular gastronomy—turning solids into liquids, liquids into gels and gels into vapour. The serious diner has tried the test-tube portions of nitrogen-frozen mango caviar and steak-flavoured meringues, but decided that molecular gastronomy can be an interesting, but occasional, option.

the travelling gourmet

Not content with mere eating, many gourmets these days are interested in hands-on experiences. From Chile to China, from Tuscany to Thailand, cookery courses are all the rage, especially when combined with travel. While many are learning to cook at home through celebrity cooks and FoodTV, it has never been more exciting to sign up for cookery lessons in some exotic locale.

Food tourism is one of the fastest growing sectors in many countries, including Thailand, Bali, Singapore, Hong Kong and China. There are specialist tour packages that include intensive cookery classes which start with visits to produce markets and plantations. Heritage recipes are introduced and taught in one-day sessions.

Tourists tired of sun, sea and surf in Bali can head for the hills to organic vegetable and herb farms to see what the ingredients look like growing in the ground. They are then introduced to age-old cooking methods, given a hands-on cooking lesson and then proceed to eat their handiwork for lunch. Thailand offers similar lessons in the verdant and fragrant backyards of

introduction 15

THIS PAGE (FROM TOP): *Andre Chiang's very precise presentation and molecular gastronomy methods have turned food into art; some diners are showing a preference for the rustic, and return to comfort food.*

OPPOSITE: *Food tourism is a growing segment of the industry and hotels are cashing in on the trend. Here, staff at the Ginga Cooking School of the JW Marriot Phuket preps for the next arrivals.*

country homes—with students learning Northern Thai cuisine redolent of fresh herbs and honey. More sophisticated cookery lessons are offered in major cities such as Hong Kong, Singapore and Kuala Lumpur, with French-trained master chefs parting their skills for a price and a dedicated afternoon.

the cult of the celebrity chef

The eating adventurer's best friend is the man who rules in the kitchen, and Asia has more than its share of culinary heavyweights who influence, and even dictate, how the gourmand dines and wines. Hong Kong, recently awarded its own Michelin Restaurant guide, was quick to pin the ribbons on Siu Hin Chi, the Chinese Executive Chef of The Langham Hong Kong. His seafood creations are recognised as classics of Cantonese cooking (especially the flawlessly executed sautéed prawns and crab roe with golden fried pork and crab meat puffs) and the chef was duly awarded two Michelin stars in 2009. He humbly credited the success to his whole team. Another Chinese chef who has transcended traditional boundaries and updated food to better suit today's modern gourmet is Alvin Leung, Chef-owner of Bo Innovation in Hong Kong. Edgy, on-the-ball and always aware of the latest cutting edge news and views, Leung is best known for his so-called X-treme Chinese cuisine. The self-taught chef has deconstructed traditional Chinese food and added his own take on molecular gastronomy.

Taking a more conservative but no less innovative route is Sam Leong, Corporate Chef/Director of Kitchens of Tung Lok Group in Singapore. He is the main motivator behind the creative modern Chinese dishes at My Humble House, Space@My Humble House and the Tung Lok Group's string of restaurants overseas. His signature dishes show off both his cultural and culinary background. Chef Leong says this demonstrates that you can create an outstanding dish with "even simple ingredients as long as the ingredients are fresh."

There are other great chefs making their names in Asia, some of them willing migrants from Western countries attracted by the region's vibrant dining scene and appreciative audience, and the cornucopia of exotic spices, herbs and other ingredients at their fingertips. Great chefs, good food, a pleasant locale, soothing ambience and most of all, appreciative diners—these are the crucial elements towards making the epicurean experience. Eating is indeed one of life's main pleasures and there is no better time or place than the now and here to enjoy it all. ~ PDL

evolving food trends

There are countless appetites to satisfy and satiate—and both plate and the pantry have come to mirror our needs and wants. Eating in or dining out, the decisions we make about food are reflective of our lifestyles. Gone are the days when food on the plate was simply to satisfy mere hunger pangs.

The media has become one of the greatest influences on our epicurean indulgences. Television chefs, food bloggers on the Internet, online food reviews and recipe banks are constantly influencing decisions on where we eat, what we eat and how we eat.

Globalisation and fast efficient freighting of produce supply chains, the proliferation of international fast food franchises, the cross-continental exchange of ethnic food knowledge have all helped to make eating in the 21st century a truly whole-earth experience.

asian spices

Bibimbap and *pho bo* are as common in New York as in their native Seoul and Hanoi. Asian herbs and condiments like Thai lemongrass and Sichuan peppercorns are used in Michelin-starred establishment across on the other side of the world.

In exchange, French bistros and Italian pizzerias are known and loved from Singapore to Shanghai. Brazilian charcuterie and Turkish kebab shops proliferate in Beijing, a long way from Buenos Aires or Ankara.

Chefs in Australia have successfully married local produce, European cooking methods and later immigrant influences from Vietnam, Malaysia and the Middle East to create New Australian cuisine.

Australian chef Neil Perry claims salt and pepper squid as a signature dish of his restaurant Rockpool, much to the amusement of Chinese chefs who have been tossing this up for longer than they can remember. Other chefs regularly serve up star-anise braised pork belly which, again, bears startling resemblance to *dongbo rou*, the classic Hangzhou dish credited to Song Dynasty poet and civil servant Su Dongbo.

the organic drive

New Australian cuisine is a sister development that has grown in tandem with the Californian food revolution of micro-greens and the rise of "localvore"', people dedicated to consuming food grown locally — a conscious protest against imported food and the carbon created in flying them in.

Californian chefs catering to the state's fitness- and health-conscious have long been finicky about the quality of their fresh produce, artfully crafting and pairing flavours to create wholesome and healthful menus. They were the first to commission market gardeners to ensure a steady supply of organic and boutique vegetables, free range eggs and chickens, and organically bred lamb and pork.

slow food

The world has indeed shrunk in the culinary sense, but paradoxically, there has been a return to locally grown and bred produce and a new awareness and appreciation for artisan food, harking back to the Slow Food movement out of Italy.

The Slow Food movement, founded by Carlo Petrini in Italy in 1986 to combat fast food, encapsulates preservation of culinary heritage with its broad aims—to sustain seed banks to preserve heirloom fruits and vegetables, to preserve and promote local and traditional food products, to educate

consumers on ethical buying and to lobby for organic farming and against the use of pesticides. There are now 100,000 members in 132 countries, with strong support in the US, New Zealand and Australia.

While there has been criticism against Slow Food for its monocultural emphasis and leftist policies, the movement has done its part in kick-starting renewed interest and awareness in culinary heritage and heirloom recipes—a trend that continues to gather momentum in many parts of Asia and across most of the West.

It has introduced many new words to the culinary vocabulary, such as "sustainable farming", "ethical market practices" and more recently, "localvores" and "minimum food miles". Just as green lobbyists argue about reducing carbon footprints, food campaigners are talking about reducing food miles. Unfortunately, the debate can only apply to agricultural countries with a large farming hinterland. In many of Asia's major cities, almost all food is imported and the crowded urban centres have to depend on a large logistic network to supply plate and pantry.

THIS PAGE (FROM LEFT): *Organic vegetables and heirloom species are making a comeback as consumers demand greater accountability on the dining table; The Slow Food movement has stimulated a return to local produce and traditional cooking methods.*
OPPOSITE: *Asian spices and herbs are now very much part of the international mise en place.*

evolving food trends 19

evolving food trends

eating for health

If the "Slow Food" buzzwords have limited impact, there are still other factors affecting diet and dining habits. Health and wellness are two major concerns. A fluctuating economy is another.

As the multitudes of post-war baby boomers trot towards old age in their designer trainers, the newly-old cling on to vitality with a careful regimen of "functional foods" that help them manage health and wellness, or a diet designed to control middle-age spread, high cholesterol, escalating blood sugar, hypertension and diabetes, among countless other urban lifestyle's health issues.

Proactive diets aside, super foods and tonic boosters from both hemispheres have come together in organic and health food stores. The perennial buzz word is "anti-oxidant", and foods like Amazonian rainforest acai berries and Native American blueberries are believed to help the body fight oxidisation, which in turn is thought to produce free radicals that damage cells. These are expensive products and none more so than the rare and costly Moroccan argan nut butter and oils, used in organic spas serving micro-biotic diets.

Out of Asia, "miracle" foods such as gingko biloba (brain-friendly), ginseng (energy-boosting) and goji berries (vitamin-rich) are being promoted by health gurus, and often enthusiastically embraced without too many questions. Goji berry, which some folk swear by as a cure-all for a range of ailments, is often marketed as Tibetan Gojiberry when it's not grown anywhere near Tibet! It is also known as wolfberry or boxthorn, and is almost exclusively grown in the Ningxia region on the upper reaches of China's Yellow River, some 10,000 km (6,214 miles) away from Tibet.

herbs + natural sweeteners

Commercial myths aside, traditional Chinese herbs continue to be sought after as organic preventive tonics, often used together with Western medicine. Panax ginseng, cordyceps, dioscorea, Chinese angelica root are sold as capsules, pills and drinks as part of the lucrative global wellness industry.

Even previously pedestrian products such as Mediterranean blood oranges, Middle-Eastern pomegranates and tropical mangosteens have found new demand as studies discover hidden benefits which may range from being a panacea for anti-ageing to reducing risk of heart disease to being anti-carcinoma.

There has also emerged a sub-food trend in the discovery of new sugar substitutes. While consumers had to depend on chemical or artificial sweeteners in the past, there is now a growing movement to use natural sweeteners such as plant-based stevia and agave syrup—which have lower glycemic indexes— or honey or raw cane sugar.

meats

Another trend is a backlash response to recent contamination scandals that have tainted everything from beef to chicken and pork, and fish to vegetables and dairy products. Consumers now want more accountability and are prepared to pay a premium—double or triple the rate in many instances— to know that the meat and greens they are eating are bred and grown without pesticides, insecticides or chemical additives. Organic food producers are flocking to cater to these consumers. Increasingly, at Asia's cosmopolitan cities, dedicated organic shops and markets are setting up shop.

vegetarian diets

An increasing vegetarian and vegan segment has also motivated the growth of specialist greengrocers and restaurants that do not serve meat. This group is augmented by the stylishly skinny—both male and female who want to preserve their svelte figures—but most are genuinely concerned about their health and the side effects of carelessly mass-produced food.

Traditionally, being vegetarian in Asia was motivated more by religion—being Buddhist or Hindu. The new vegetarians, though, are taking this option for health and for ethical reasons —because they do not believe in killing for food. This has given rise to a new breed of smart and trendy, if slightly off main stream, vegetarian restaurants. Most restaurants also recognise the need to cater to this growing group with vegetarian alternatives on the menu.

a return to homestyle food

For the meat-loving gourmets among us, however, food is still very much a matter of taste and a continuing adventure to explore the strange and re-discover the familiar.

Molecular gastronomy captured our imaginations for a while, intrigued our palates and sapped our wallets. While the trend continues to infiltrate kitchens today, it seems to have been finally relegated to fancy garnishes such as Asian pear vapour, mango roe and nitrogen-frozen meringues.

Fruit caviar aside, the food trends are definitely swinging from kitchen laboratories to Mama's kitchen. In New York, epicurean veteran Thomas Keller's latest recipes at his celebrated Per Se restaurant eschew complicated concoctions in favour of home-style fried chicken, while new meteorite David Chang of Momofuku Noodle Bar has also succumbed—but he offers diners a choice of fried chicken, high or low style in his two-tiered restaurant.

Chang is a Korean-American who makes no apology for taking inspiration from his native cuisine and serves up pork belly ramen, but his second restaurant in the chain is a burrito bar called Ssäm, which means "anything wrapped" in Korean.

> ### Miracle foods or fads?
>
> While most are driven by the desire to eat healthy, others consume the so-called "miracle foods" because of a little science and lots of fiction. It is believed that Vodka-soaked raisins reduce blood-pressure; fruit vinegars melt the fat around the waist; crushed coal added to unpolished rice clears the system of toxins; and gingko biloba fruits improve memory. While some truth may be hidden among these culinary myths, a balanced diet is still key to health.

THIS PAGE (FROM TOP): *The vegetarian movement is given impetus by a growing segment against the taking of life for food, and believes that dining choices can be a political statement; On the other hand, dedicated meat-eaters are returning to comfort food, such as fried chicken.*

OPPOSITE: *Traditional herbs used in Chinese homeopathy is now incorporated into products sold internationally as part of the global wellness movement.*

evolving food trends 21

evolving food trends

Chang's cuisine is definitely characteristic of the new American flavours, Asian-inspired but driven by the bold brash approach of his adopted country. But while his fusion fast food attracts the edgy gourmands, there are those who have gone back to childhood comfort food such as macaroni and cheese. At least two restaurants in New York specialise in this down-home classic.

What it does show is the culinary curve beyond Jeffrey Steingarten's tongue-in-cheek Calamari Index. The modern gourmet knows his halloumi from his harissa but he is tiring of the exotic and wants something nearer home, closer to heart. That is probably why regional food is making a comeback, with desserts like the Pennsylvanian Amish favourite whoopie pie creeping into the best dining establishments. A whoopie pie is not a pie but a chocolate biscuit sandwich with a marshmallow filling. Pundits are saying it has kicked the cupcake off the must-eat list of luminaries like Madonna and Kate Moss.

In Asia, too, the experimenting is slowing down as the novelty of foreign cuisines wears thin. A return to roots can be seen in the rash of new home-style restaurants cropping up. In Jakarta, Bangkok, Hong Kong, Taipei and Shanghai, the trendy selling point is a call to comfort food.

China is discovering its major cuisines anew—and speciality restaurants featuring the main schools are in demand. Cantonese, Sichuan, Shanghainese and Taiwanese all compete for the dining crowd, while Xinjiang-themed restaurants complete with zither strumming minstrels and belly dancers provide entertainment.

But the one overwhelmingly apparent trend in the culinary world is an awareness of food—in both ingredients and cooking methods. Eating for better health and paying more attention to the value of food will continue to dominate dining decisions as the world economy struggles to find a balance.

the rise of television chefs

In the home kitchens, the most telling influences in recent years are the television chefs who hog prime time slots from the BBC Lifestyle channel and Food TV in the Americas to cable television throughout Asia. It looks like they will still be pointing the way to future food directions for a while yet.

No one has done more to salvage the reputation of British home-cooking than Essex-accented poster-boy chef Jamie Oliver, the purposely unkempt Oxford-educated farmer-chef Hugh Fearnley-Whittingstall and the blue-blooded domestic goddess Nigella Lawson. Their influences have stretched far beyond the Fair Isles to the rest of the English-speaking world… or at least to those countries connected to cable.

Baby-faced Jamie Oliver has persuaded a whole generation of young Britons to cook by stripping off the mystery of their favourite recipes. Roasting a chicken has never seemed so easy and puddings like a cherry clafouti are literally a piece of cake. He has also influenced how British

school children eat, by persuading those who cook school dinners to leave greasy fries behind in favour of more nutritious fresh food.

Nigella Lawson, pashmina draped elegantly over one shoulder while she wields a pair of barbecue tongs, has made cooking for family and children an acceptable and almost elegant mission. She has also casually introduced exotic ingredients to the British public, and popularised such previously unheard of luxuries such as pomegranate molasses, Greek halloumi cheese, Indonesian *sambal oelek* and Lebanese flatbread. She also contributed much to the cupcake craze that is currently taking the world by storm, Asia included, showing the way with lavender-coloured icing topped with a single gold chocolate button.

The River Cottage television series is Hugh Fearnley-Whittingstall's campaign platform for a return to the land. By farming and foraging in Dorset, Whittingstall has led the way back to organically raised lamb, pork and chicken and persuaded many of his countrymen to give up buying battery-fed chicken with his food reality show, *Hugh's Chicken Run*.

Other popular reality shows also changed the way we look at professional cooking and the restaurant kitchens, the foremost being bad-boy, bad-mouthed Gordon Ramsay's *Kitchen Nightmares*.

Over the other side of the pond, Les Halles lost its executive chef and television won a happy wanderer in Anthony Bourdain, who broadened the viewers' perspectives of food in exotic places in his TV series, *No Reservations*. His enjoyment of the Asian exotics is matched only by fellow American Andrew Zimmern who takes delight in chomping on insects and grubs, but cowardly stops short of the pungent durian.

Food television has made exotic eating an acceptable pastime, and given the eating of strange things a smidgen of respectability that was never endorsed before. Media also taught more people to cook, and as part of pop culture, persuaded more young people to actually cook in the kitchen instead of assembling and wolfing down fast food. There is no longer an excuse not to cook, for the knowledge to cook, like so much more, is now as readily accessible at the click of a button.

Food, and its eating and cooking, will continue to evolve with our lifestyles. But now, more than at any other time, we know more about our food—its sources, its history, its methods and its ethical issues. All that remains for us to do is to taste. Bon appetit!   ~ PDL

THIS PAGE (FROM LEFT): Television celebrity chefs such as Jamie Oliver, Nigella Lawson, Anthony Bourdain and Gordon Ramsay have all done their part in reviving the interest in kitchen arts.

OPPOSITE (CLOCKWISE FROM TOP LEFT): Mapo doufu is a Jiangsu provincial favourite that now enjoys worldwide popularity; In America, the appeal of molecular gastronomy is fading as diners return to comfort foods such as macaroni and cheese; The cupcake craze was one of the fads that captivated consumers.

leading chefs

Asia is home to a host of culinary heavyweights, trained in Western and Asian kitchens. Helming top-notch restaurants, these chefs have made a name for themselves in the region as well as internationally for their artistry and flair.

singapore

Emmanuel Stroobant established **Saint Pierre** (3 Magazine Road, #01-01, Central Mall; +65.6438 0887; www.saintpierre.com.sg), a fine-dining modern French restaurant in Singapore, in 2000 after gaining much experience in Michelin-starred restaurants back home as well as abroad. The Belgian chef's signature style, which features subtle hints of Japanese influence, has won him rave reviews and established Saint Pierre as one of the top restaurants in Singapore. Over the years, the charming and telegenic cookbook author and TV personality has also managed to clinch several awards for the restaurant and himself.

He attributes his success to the competitive fine-dining scene in Singapore: "The city has nurtured me to be a chef with integrity. Most Singaporeans are well-travelled and discerning diners, and I can't bluff my way through. It keeps me on my toes and pushes the boundaries of my creativity. And if this has contributed to the F&B scene in Singapore, it is only because the country demands it so."

To set himself apart from the rest, Stroobant strives to be true to what he delivers. "I don't believe in serving a dish that I myself will not enjoy. I also try to infuse the dishes with some creativity to keep it exciting." Among his scores of inventive seasonal items is St Pierre's signature dish, the classic pan-fried foie gras with caramelised green apple and old port sauce. "I like my dishes to be original. I need to be aware and to keep a balance between the purity of the ingredients and creativity," added the chef who gets his inspiration from travelling and visiting established restaurants overseas.

Corporate Chef and Director of Kitchens, **Sam Leong**, joined Tung Lok Group in 2000 and was instrumental in establishing Jade at the Fullerton Hotel as one of Singapore's finest restaurants. The maestro is today the brains behind the creative modern Chinese dishes at **My Humble House** (#02-27/9, Esplanade Mall, 8 Raffles Avenue; +65.6423 1881; www.myhumblehouse.com.sg), the adjoining **Space@My Humble House** (#02-25) as well as the group's other restaurants in Singapore and overseas.

Leong's first experience in the culinary world began when he worked for his famous father—the "King of Shark's Fin" in Malaysia. "I looked up to my dad. He was the one who started me on this career. I admired him greatly." Over the decade, Leong won numerous accolades, including in 2008, the prestigious International Star Diamond Chef Award presented by the New York-based American Academy of Hospitality Sciences. True to form he adds: "After being in the F&B industry for the past 25 years, I'm very honoured and humbled to have received these awards. These internationally-acclaimed platforms have help me in my career tremendously. Ten years ago, Chinese chefs did not get much recognition. This award is a sign of how much we have evolved and improved through the years."

Leong said if he has to pick one signature dish, it would be his coffee pork ribs, which he created in 1996. "One day, while I was enjoying my coffee, I was inspired to create a dish using coffee and pork ribs. After numerous attempts and experimenting, I finally got the recipe right. Coincidentally, the same year, I was invited by Wolfgang Puck as guest chef at a Universal Studios event in the US. I recommended serving cocoa pork ribs. The dish was initially rejected, but after my persistence, it was accepted and extremely well-received."

Besides innovation, Leong is also a firm believer in using fresh ingredients. "You can create a wonderful dish that is cooked simply as long as the ingredients are fresh." The cookbook author and celebrity chef adds: "I also like to constantly update myself with recent culinary trends. I learn and absorb during my travels, which have helped my creative process."

Taiwan-born **Andre Chiang**, Chef de Cuisine at **Jaan par André** (2 Stamford Road, Swissôtel the Stamford; +65 6338 8585; www.swissotel.com) has captivated diners since he arrived in Singapore in 2008. The former Executive Chef of Seychelle's Maia Luxury Resort & Spa crafts his own style by boldly re-defining French nouvelle cuisine with his ingenious blend of unique ingredients and pure flavours. "Jaan par André is the only French Nouvelle Cuisine establishment in Singapore. I see myself as a fourth generation nouvelle cuisine chef; I've trained under the godfathers of

THIS PAGE (CLOCKWISE FROM TOP LEFT): *My Humble House's seafood coconut soup; Sam Leong is the brains behind My Humble House's modern Chinese cuisine; Chiang's ever-evolving Snickers dessert; Andre Chiang re-defines French Nouvelle Cuisine at Jaan par Andre.*

OPPOSITE (FROM TOP): *Emmanuel Stroobant creates modern French cuisine injected with Japanese ingredients; Stroobant's miso cod signature dish.*

leading chefs

Cult of Celebrity Chefs

A huge band of celebrity chefs with signature dishes and styles has emerged over the past decade or so. These famous personalities front their restaurants (or culinary empire), write books, and appear on cooking and reality shows on TV. The trend is having the chef's high-profile name as the tagline as opposed to just a restaurant's name. This move has in effect created a branding that appears to be a successful recipe in today's dining scene.

nouvelle cuisine—Joel Robuchon and Pierre Gagnaire—as well as the modern masters—the Pourcel Brothers and Pascal Barbot," he says.

As Chiang's menu changes every season, he presents more of a "signature style" rather than a "signature dish". For instance, his ever-evolving and cheeky Snickers dessert and "forgotten vegetables", the latter featuring 21 heirloom vegetables, are examples of dishes where the ingredients and presentations are transformed seasonally. "My signature style of cooking changes to suit the quality of each season's produce. The changing conditions of natural produce give me different inspirations. This is true to the philosophy of nouvelle cuisine, which guides my own philosophy of 'pure flavours, unique ingredients and creative harmonies'."

The chef explains his plating style: "If people describe molecular cuisine as 'Pop Art', perhaps I can be classified as an 'Impressionist'. I plate my dishes very much by instinct—often, I decide how to dress each plate as I am assembling the dish. This freedom allows me to plate up to 400 dishes during a dinner service, while still presenting to diners a sense that the dish is 'a creation of the moment'."

Chiang believes that each chef and each restaurant should have a distinctive style. "I am providing another option for Singapore to experience the allure of natural produce, and the sensation of experiencing pure satisfaction… instead of showing off some fancy new technique or equipment."

bangkok, thailand

Chef **Norbert Kostner**, a native of Southern Tyrol in Italy, arrived in Thailand in 1970, fell in love with the country and made it his second home. As Executive Chef of the legendary **Mandarin Oriental, Bangkok** (48 Oriental Avenue; +66.2.659 9000; www.mandarinoriental.com/bangkok), his culinary career has been focused on developing a comprehensive knowledge of various international cuisines served at the hotel's restaurants. His role is also to source for the best ingredients locally and from overseas.

The chef's philosophy is to "cook what people like to eat and not force them to eat what I like to cook. Keep the food simple and respect the produce. Use herbs, spices and other aromatic agents to enhance the flavour of the food and not to mask the natural flavours. Food should be nourishing and energising."

Beyond managing the hotel's kitchens, Kostner has also been an ongoing advisor to the Royal Project implemented by His Majesty King Bhumibol Adulyadej of Thailand to transform opium fields in the mountains of northern Thailand into organic farms that cultivate temperate-zone fruit, vegetables, herbs and spices previously not found in Thailand. This programme also pioneered the rearing of the much sought after Bresse chicken outside of France. One of Kostner's significant achievements in 2006 was the planning and preparation of the gala dinner marking the occasion of King Bhumibol's 60th year on the throne.

hong kong

Chef **Lau Yiu Fai**, Executive Chinese Chef, joined **InterContinental Hong Kong** (18 Salisbury Road, Kowloon; +852.2313 2323; www.ichotelsgroup.com/intercontinental) when the hotel first opened in 1980 and was part of the pioneering team of **Yan Toh Heen** (previously called Lai Ching Heen) when the restaurant was launched in 1984. He trained under Chef Cheung Kam Cheun, who was the hotel's Executive Chinese Chef at that time and one of Hong Kong's greatest Chinese chefs.

At 14, Lau apprenticed at some of Hong Kong's top Chinese restaurants including Tai Sam Yuen and Fook Lam Mun. After working in Canada and Tin Shan Palace in Hong Kong in the 1990s, he re-joined the hotel in 2000 to helm Yan Toh Heen's kitchen. Under his direction, the restaurant was awarded its first Michelin star in 2010.

To ensure that his innovative Cantonese-style cuisine remains distinctive, the chef uses refined traditional Chinese cooking methods, and the best seasonal ingredients, along with modern presentation. Apart from his speciality dishes prepared with shark's fin, abalone, lobster and bird's nest, Lau's signature dishes include crispy Lung Kong chicken, which received the Gold Medal from the Hong Kong Tourism Board's Best of the Best Culinary Awards, and wok-fried lobster with crab roe and fresh milk.

Lau says that he is privileged to use some of the rarest and most prized ingredients in the world and to have the opportunity to be the first to try the ingredients and

THIS PAGE (FROM TOP): Chef Lau Yiu Fai creates innovative Cantonese-style cuisine; Lau's sautéed diced wagyu beef with shishito pepper.

OPPOSITE (FROM TOP): Mandarin Oriental Bangkok's Chef Norbert Kostner likes to keep the food simple and respect the flavours of the produce; Kostner's crispy belly of porchetta pork with colonnata flavours, salt turnips, chick pea puree and reduced broth.

leading chefs 27

leading chefs

prepare them. "I also have a great sense of achievement when a newly created menu or dish is well received by our customers."

Kicking off his career at **T'ang Court** (see pages 110–111) at **The Langham Hong Kong**, in 1991 as junior line chef, **Siu Hin Chi** assiduously worked his way up the ranks to become Executive Sous Chef six years later. In the early days, he worked under Chef Kwong Wai Keung (currently Group Chinese Executive Chef of Langham Hotels International), who was The Langham Hong Kong's Executive Chinese Chef from 1994 to 2005. Siu is a great admirer of Kwong and was very impressed with his mentor's drive, enthusiasm and passion for cooking.

Siu subsequently garnered numerous accolades, including two Gold with Distinction Awards in Hong Kong's Best of the Best Culinary Awards organised by the Hong Kong Tourism Board in 2001 and 2002. A deft hand with seafood, his winning dishes were the mouthwatering and flawlessly executed sautéed prawns and crab roe with golden fried pork and crab meat puffs, and stir-fried fresh lobster with spring onions, red onions and shallots.

In 2009, T'ang Court was awarded two Michelin stars, an occasion of great pride for Chef Siu and a major milestone in his career. However, Siu humbly considers this a success for the whole team of T'ang Court. He commented: "The award is mainly due to the excellent service, work attitude, good cooperation and communications of the team." He considers the respect and friendship he has gained from the strong team his greatest achievement of all.

The award-winning **Gray Kunz** recently returned to Hong Kong to launch **Café Gray Deluxe** (Level 49, The Upper House, Pacific Place, 88 Queensway; +852.3968 1106; www.cafegrayhk.com). Born in Singapore and raised in Switzerland, he previously served as Executive Chef at the famed Plume restaurant in Hong Kong's Regent Hotel. He is best known for fusing complex flavours and ingredients with the classic elegance of Asian and European culinary traditions.

During his career, Kunz has earned numerous accolades, including a four-star rating from *The New York Times* while at New York's now defunct Lespinasse restaurant. In 2002, he was recognised by The Culinary Institute of America as a Master of Aesthetics. He was nominated Best American Chef in 1995 by the James Beard Foundation, and inducted into the Restaurant Hall of Fame three years later. Launched in New York City in 2004, the original Café Gray received a Michelin star in its first year.

"As far as being inspired by cooking, I know what I don't like, and that is, by far, the copycats of molecular cuisine. Cooking is soulful—make it taste good, put your heart into it, demand the best products you can get and treat them appropriately. If anyone can inspire me, it would be the young chefs full of desire to do well with 'can do' attitudes under all circumstances… I know a few of them!"

Chef **Thomas Mayr** joined the acclaimed Les Amis Singapore as Resident Chef in 2007, and was transferred to Hong Kong in 2009 to set up **Cépage** (23 Wing Fung Street; +852.2861 3130; cepage.com.hk), also by the Les Amis group. The restaurant, which serves contemporary European cuisine, has received favourable reviews and won its first Michelin star in its first year of operation.

Mayr worked in several Michelin-starred restaurants in Italy before training under Chef Hans Haas of the two-star Michelin restaurant Tantris in Munich. "Chef Haas strongly influenced me and quickly became my mentor when I started working for him in 1997. It was from him that I learned the importance of using only the highest quality ingredients and produce in season."

"My cooking style is French-Mediterranean, a lighter take on French cuisine. My philosophy is rather simple: to bring the freshest, highest quality ingredients to the guest, letting quality speak for itself. I use modern techniques and preparations to provide a unique dining experience that combines quality and creativity."

Some of Mayr's notable signature dishes at Cépage include chilled Alaskan crab with avocado ball and green apple gelee; and Taiyouran organic egg confit in truffled chilled oxtail consommé with Lomo Iberico and croutons.

Alvin Leung, Chef-owner, is known for the so-called "X-treme Chinese" cuisine served at his privately-owned one-Michelin-starred **Bo Innovation** (Shop 13, 2/F,

THIS PAGE (CLOCKWISE FROM TOP LEFT): Gray Kunz places much emphasis on wholesome and locally sourced ingredients; Gray's steak tartar gaufrette, Kunz ketjap; Thomas Mayr introduces a lighter take on French cuisine at Cépage; Mayr's Japanese egg confit creation.
OPPOSITE (FROM TOP): Chef Siu Hin Chi has worked at T'ang Court for almost two decades; T'ang Court's succulent baked oysters with port wine.

leadingchefs 29

leading chefs

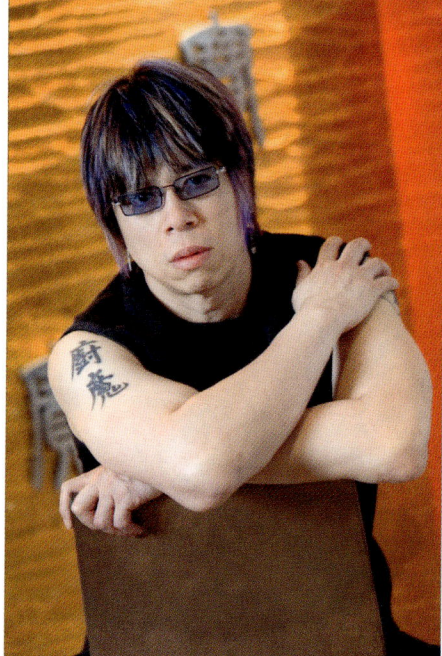

J Residence, 60 Johnston Road; +852.2850 8371; www.boinnovation.com). Born in London in 1961 and raised in Toronto, Alvin has travelled extensively and visited many celebrated restaurants for inspiration. Trained as an engineer, he later decided to join the culinary world when he became a shareholder of a private kitchen and realised he could cook better than the chefs there.

The self-taught Leung has revolutionised Chinese cuisine with his inventive cooking techniques using a mix of traditional Chinese as well as non-Chinese ingredients in centuries-old Chinese recipes. Hailing this as "X-treme Chinese" cuisine, Leung has essentially broken down traditional pre-conceptions of Chinese food and brought the cuisine to a whole new dimension. In a nutshell, it's his own imaginative take on molecular gastronomy and traditional Chinese cuisine. Some of his novel dishes include thousand-year-old egg in ginger cone oyster; green onion lime sauce with ginger snow; and caviar abalone congee.

bali

Chef **Chris Salans** of **Mozaic** (Jln Raya Sanggingan, Ubud; +62.361.975 768; www.mozaic-bali.com) in Bali was born in Washington DC to a French mother and an American father. He moved to Paris as a toddler. After his training at Le Cordon Bleu Paris, Salans interned at various three Michelin-starred restaurants. Over the years he has worked as Sous Chef for Bouley, New York City, as well as Head Chef for Thomas Keller's (of The French Laundry fame)

Bouchon in Napa Valley, California. "My greatest mentor is David Bouley who taught me to be spontaneous in my cuisine. This has turned out to be both an asset and a drawback. Spontaneity brings freshness and creativity but it also brings chaos and constant change which can be difficult on the team."

Salans later moved to Bali and became Head Chef at Ary's Warung, where he melded the flavours of Indonesian cuisines with the techniques of modern cooking and presentation. He eventually developed his own style of Modern International Balinese cuisine and launched his new endeavour, Mozaic restaurant, which became an instant success. Within three years the restaurant was recognised by the prestigious European association, Tradition et Qualité, as a member of Les Grande Tables Du Monde (The Grand Tables of the World).

According to Salans, Mozaic's cuisine is best defined as *cuisine du marché* (market cuisine). "It's based on the ingredients in season in my environment; I apply the cooking techniques that I know and flavours I like. Using mostly modern techniques of preparation and presentation, I would further describe the food as Modern French cuisine. So I guess Mozaic's cuisine is modern French cuisine using the Balinese terroir!"

Chris Miller, Executive Chef of **COMO Shambhala Estate** (see pages 120–121), contributed to Bali's F&B scene by "bringing a fresh healthy slant to both the dining scene and to local eating habits." His food presentation is "free flowing and unpretentious, letting vibrant colours and shapes speak organically for themselves."

Before Bali, the chef worked at Rockpool and Wockpool (by Neil Perry) in Sydney. Currently, he runs COMO Shambhala Estate's two restaurants: **Kudus House** which showcases the diverse influences, flavours and spices of Indonesia's regions and **glow**, an all-day dining place, featuring healthy menus. Simultaneously, he is also the Executive Chef of **Uma Ubud** where he manages **Kemiri**, a restaurant that presents Southeast Asian cooking techniques using Indonesian spices.

shanghai, china

Chef **Paul Pairet** gained a reputation for his highly daring, sophisticated and original cuisine at Pudong Shangri-La's Jade on 36. In 2009, the culinary wizard opened **Mr & Mrs Bund** (Bund 18, 6F, Zhongshan Dong Yi Lu; +86.21.6323 9898; www.mmbund.com), a French restaurant for everyday dining with a novel Chinese communal-style concept.

Pairet shared his inspiration: "My early influences were iconic chefs like Jacques Maximin, Michel Trama, Alain Senderens and Joel Robuchon, and later Alain Ducasse and Ferran Adria. But if I had only one chef to name, it would be Paul Bocuse. He was the reason why I chose to become a chef."

Although Pairet has received various accolades for both restaurants in Shanghai, he said that his greatest achievement is yet to come. In mid 2010, he opened **ULTRAVIOLET**, (www.uvbypp.cc), an exciting new concept restaurant that he has been working on for over 10 years.

THIS PAGE (FROM TOP): *Chris Miller of COMO Shambhala Estate in Bali; Miller's spa creation is a vibrant mix of colours and textures.*

OPPOSITE (CLOCKWISE FROM TOP LEFT): *Chris Salans introduces his own style of international Balinese cuisine at Mozaic; Salan's New Zealand squab with bitter chocolate and horseradish; Alvin Leung revolutionises Chinese cuisine at Bo Innovation; Thousand-year-old eggs in ginger cones; Leung's uni dan dan noodles and grilled salmon roe.*

leading chefs

THIS PAGE (CLOCKWISE FROM TOP LEFT):
Jade on 36's Le Canard creation
by Fabrice Giraud;
Giraud presently helms Jade on 36;
Mr & Mrs Bund's short ribs dish;
Paul Pairet is the culinary maestro
behind Mr & Mrs Bund.

OPPOSITE (FROM TOP): Shuzo Kishida is
the only Japanese chef of French
cuisine to be awarded three
Michelin stars for Quintessence,
his restaurant in Tokyo;
Kishida's exquisite sable champignons.

Chef **Fabrice Giraud** joined **Jade on 36** (33 Fu Cheng Road, Level 36, Grand Tower, +86.21.6882 3636; www.jadeon36.com) at **Pudong Shangri-La, Shanghai** in 2009, taking over the role of Chef de Cuisine from his predecessor, Paul Pairet. With 18 years of experience in French gastronomy under his belt, he has chalked up stints at well-known establishments, including the one-Michelin-starred Restaurant le Pain et le Vin in Brussels, where he was Head Chef from 1999 to 2001. According to Giraud, it was one of his greatest achievements when the restaurant was awarded the Michelin star.

The chef says that he places much emphasis on modern cooking. "But do not mistake this for molecular gastronomy or avant garde cuisine. I do not want to go so far, but I am always open to techniques which will help us on a daily basis." He adds: "I feel that Chinese guests like to understand what they are eating and this suits my style of cooking really well."

Since his days in Europe, Giraud's cooking has "evolved a lot". "For me, creating, sharing, teaching and leading my team are important factors that keep me going. We have to always be moving forward and keeping up with the times... Creating a signature dish can be compared to an artist creating a beautiful painting, except that with a dish, the palate is also teased and tantalised. More importantly, you know that whatever you do, you can't do better with the dish. I like to think that with a white plate (which will be a frame) I am the artist creating a masterpiece."

tokyo, japan

Shuzo Kishida at **Restaurant Quintessence** (1F "Barbizon 25" building, 5-4-7 Shirokanedai, Minato-ku; +81.3.5791 3715; www.quintessence.jp) in Tokyo started learning the culinary ropes in French restaurants in Japan at the age of 19. He moved to France in 2000 in search of ways to perfect his skills. From 2003 to 2005, he trained at a three-Michelin star restaurant L'Astrance, Paris, under the wings of Chef Pascal Barbot.

After returning home, the young chef opened Restaurant Quintessence in 2006 at the age of 32. Just a year later he became the only Japanese chef of French cuisine awarded three stars in the *Michelin Guide Tokyo*. His food follows the "culinary flow" of L'Astrance, that is, respecting the quality and potential of the produce, understanding the cooking process, and giving attention to detail in the seasoning process. He adds his own personality to his food, including "a touch of humour and poetic accent" for the enjoyment of his guests.

Eschewing fixed menus, Kishida surprises his guests with a *menu carte blanche* (chef's selected menu) using only fresh seasonal products and premium ingredients from around the globe.

Yoshihiro Murata is Chef-owner of the famous two Michelin-starred **Kikunoi** restaurant (6-13-8 Akasaka, Minato-ku; +81.3.3568 6055; kikunoi.jp) in Tokyo and in Kyoto (459 Shimokawara-cho, Yasakatoriimae-sagaru, Shimokawara-dori, Higashiyama-ku; +81.75.561 0015 and 118 Saito-cho, Shijo-sagaru, Kiyamachi-dori, Shimogyo-ku; +81.7.5361 5580). Murata is most celebrated for injecting the centuries-old art of *kaiseki*, a traditional multi-course dinner, with his own flair. He is a third generation *kaiseki* chef who has proudly carried on his family's culinary heritage. Murata has appeared on many Japanese TV shows and penned 15 cookbooks including the award-winning *Kaiseki: The Exquisite Cuisine of Kyoto's Kikunoi Restaurant*.

The chef's philosophy is to unveil what genuine *kaiseki* culture is, and to maintain the restaurant's high standards. To complement tradition, Murata continues to invent new dishes regularly.

Jino Ono is the Master Chef behind the most venerable sushi restaurant, **Sukiyabashi Jiro** in Tokyo (4-2-15 Ginza Chuo-ku; +81.3.3535 3600). The restaurant, established for over 40 years, has become renowned internationally after being awarded three Michelin stars. Tucked away in a small basement area in Tokyo's Ginza district is a 23-seater space run by Jino and his son. In their kitchen, the environment in which the sushi is prepared is precisely controlled, with the seafood and rice maintained at different temperatures.

In his 80s, Ono was hailed as a "modern master" by Japan's Ministry of Health, Labour and Welfare in 2005 for his contributions to Japanese cuisine. The Japanese government also recognises Ono as a living national treasure. The icon of Japanese cuisine says that he is motivated by his love for work and strives constantly to improve and acquire new skills and ideas. ~ AV

signature dishes

Chefs in both Western and Asian kitchens create pure alchemy when they conjure up new and unique creations that represent their artistry and skill. The best signature dishes—Asian, Western or fusion—are hauntingly evocative, leaving an aftertaste that stays in the memory like a guilty pleasure long after the meal has been consumed and the bill paid.

singapore
Chef-owner **Emmanuel Stroobant** of modern French restaurant, **Saint Pierre** (1 Magazine Road, #01-01 Central Mall; +65.6438 0887; www.saintpierre.com.sg), has made a name for himself with his faultlessly executed foie gras dishes. One of his signatures is the classic pan-fried foie gras with caramelised apple and old port sauce. The chef explains: "It is a dish that I have been doing for 20 years. Until last year it was done and presented the same way, and only recently my Chef de Cuisine asked to change the presentation. It is a very traditional dish—the acidity of the green apple is toned down with the caramel and it gives a sweet and sour combination that you can find in a lot of fatty dishes such as Peking duck (where the accompanying plum sauce is sweet and sour) or the obvious sweet and sour pork."

He added that the port sauce is actually a secondary "actor" meant to match the wine. A sweet wine such as Sauternes (a classic combination with foie gras) will marry perfectly with the sweetness of the port, but a red wine will pair just as well because the port actually enhances the flavours, resulting in a flawless combination. "It is very unique to create a sauce that can equally match such different wines," says Stroobant.

Another one of his famous recipes is cod with *miso*, eggplant and red wine sauce. "I work on a similar pattern (with the wine matching) as I had a lot of guests who want to order fish yet choose to drink big Australian Shiraz or Côtes du Rhône wines. In this case, the red wine-based sauce is a match. And the *miso* is a "natural" taste enhancer that partners the natural (good) fat from the deep water cod." Over the years Stroobant has experimented with different presentations and devised many variations of cooking the same ingredients. For instance, for this cod speciality, he uses the Japanese eggplant or *nasu* in various ways, such as eggplant chips, eggplant caviar, or char-grilled, pureed, smoked, braised and marinated eggplant.

An expert in exquisite *kaiseki* fare, Executive Chef **Shinji Morihara** at **Inagiku** (see pages 170–171) crafts masterpieces using the best ingredients each season has to offer. One of his specialities is an elegant winter appetiser *kaiseki* set-piece of winter turnip and braised angler liver, with egg cake, ginkgo nuts and soft simmered abalone. The chef uses the fatty liver of angler fish as it is well-fattened to weather the cold. Evoking the season's call for heart-warming fare, Morihara ensures that the baby abalone is simmered in flavoursome *dashi* stock and served warm; the ginkgo nuts are deep-fried and dusted with salt just before serving. Egg is fused with fish and honey, then baked into a hearty sweet cake to balance the fatty and salty flavours from other ingredients.

Housed in a beautiful 1920s colonial residence, **Au Jardin** (1 Cluny Road; +65.6466 8812; www.lesamis.com.sg) is one of Singapore's most prominent fine-dining French restaurants. The kitchen is helmed by Resident Chef **Galvin Lim** whose culinary style zeroes in on the

THIS PAGE (FROM TOP): *Emmanuel Stroobant's pan-fried foie gras is livened up with a sweet and sour combination of caramelised apple and old port sauce; Spoon's speciality, steamed duck foie gras 'Landes', is encircled by a combination of sweet raisins, apricots and figs, and served with Parisian brioche.*

OPPOSITE: *Inagiku's exquisite kaiseki creation comprises winter turnip and braised angler liver, with egg cake, ginkgo nuts and soft simmered abalone.*

signature dishes 35

signature dishes

balance and contrasts of flavours and textures while using a combination of various produce.

One of his signature items is carpaccio of seafood, a dish that is consistently on his menu, albeit in various permutations. What he cooks depends on the freshest seafood he can source or ingredients that are in season. The chef always dresses the dish with herbs that he grows in the garden next to his kitchen, as well as with some edible flowers, in keeping with the botanical theme of the restaurant. Au Jardin is located in the lush Singapore Botanic Gardens.

The carpaccio of seafood is appealing for various reasons: it's very healthy, and the dressing and the raw seafood is very light, perfect for warm climates. The dressing is subtle so as not to overwhelm the freshness of the seafood, and the caviar gives it a touch of saltiness.

My Humble House at The Esplanade, Theatres on the Bay (8 Raffles Avenue, #02-27/29 Esplanade Mall; +65.6423 1881; www.tunglok.com) is celebrated for its contemporary Chinese cuisine. The menu combines the private recipes of Tung Lok's creative team of chefs led by Corporate Chef/Director of Kitchens, **Sam Leong**, complemented by remarkably artistic presentations. One of the restaurant's notable favourites is "The Passion that Lasts, Knows No Bounds", a hot-and-sour broth with freshly-peeled crab meat and ginger flower. Although the broth looks rather light, its taste is intense. Sarawak white pepper and *kampung* (village) chicken are simmered together as a base for the stock, and ginger flower is added for a unique fragrance. The dish is then topped with freshly peeled crabmeat, infusing a welcome sweetness to the broth.

hong kong

The two Michelin-starred **T'ang Court** (see pages 108–109) boasts dishes that are well-thought-out and expertly executed by Executive Chinese Chef **Siu Hin Chi** and his team. The superb crispy salty chicken is one of T'ang Court's most guarded recipes. It takes time, care and passion to prepare the chicken whose skin is crispy and its meat incredibly tender and juicy. The chicken is first stewed for 35 minutes in a broth made of dried scallops, Chinese ham and dried shrimp that has been simmered for an hour. After it is completely drained, the chicken is then deep-fried until golden brown.

Another one of T'ang Court's winning combinations is a fresh prawn dish done two ways—sauteed prawns with baby asparagus and mustard sauce, and crispy-fried shrimp with goose liver terrine. For the crispy version, the prawn is butterflied, a slice of goose liver inserted (for a distinctive aroma), then wrapped with flour noodles and deep-fried until golden brown. In the other presentation, a piece of mini asparagus is inserted into the sauteed prawn, blanched and quickly sautéed, then topped with mustard sauce. The aim of this crowd-pleaser is to delight diners with different tastes and textures.

One of only two restaurants in Hong Kong to receive three Michelin stars, **Caprice** at the **Four Seasons Hong Kong** (8 Finance Street; +852.3196 8888; www.fourseasons.com) is a contemporary French restaurant led by Chef de Cuisine **Vincent Thierry**. Working with a team of 25 chefs, he devises innovative dishes that are light and refreshing, yet rich in taste and flavour.

Among the many noteworthy dishes, the spotlight shines on the Challans duck fillet *cuit au plat*, with buttered savoy cabbage and parmentier in natural jus. Roasted duck breast is partnered with duck leg confit parmentier—the duck leg meat is deboned, covered with celeriac and mashed potato, and gratinated under the grill. This is complemented with buttered Savoy cabbage (infused with duck foie gras for an incredibly rich flavour) and a small fresh green salad on the side to provide contrast to the robust flavours of the duck. The quality of the Challans duck (once served to French kings and enjoyed by royalty), the contrasting tastes and textures, and the richness of the cabbage make this main a standout.

Since **Spoon** (18 Salisbury Road, Kowloon; +852.2721 1211; www.hongkong-ic.dining.intercontinental.com), the only Alain Ducasse restaurant in Asia outside of Japan opened at the **InterContinental Hong Kong** in 2003, the steamed duck foie gras from "Landes" with dried fruit condiment and Parisian brioche has been one of its mainstays. This item is different from the usual terrine of foie gras or pan-fried foie gras. Inspired by Hong Kong's popular steamed *dim sum*, the restaurant's pioneer chef decided to invent a steamed foie gras dish. After steaming, the goose liver is coated with a ginger glaze and served with a mix of raisins, apricots and figs that have been pan-fried, deglazed with

THIS PAGE (FROM LEFT): *Au Jardin's light and delicate carpaccio of seafood embellished with edible flowers and herbs plucked from the kitchen's garden; Caprice's fine quality Challans duck fillet from France is served with buttered savoy cabbage and parmentier in natural jus.*
OPPOSITE: *My Humble House's "The Passion that Lasts, Knows No Bounds" is a hot and sour speciality brimming with fresh crabmeat and perfumed with ginger flower.*

signature dishes

vinegar, and enlivened with orange skin. Working closely with Alain Ducasse, Executive Chef **Philippe Duc** has been instrumental in the evolution of the Spoon concept and the development of the restaurant's new menu. He and Ducasse have since given this foie gras creation a new spin, although the main concept remains true to its original inspiration.

Resident Chef **Thomas Mayr** started serving his delicate Japanese egg confit, truffled oxtail gelee, Lomo Iberico, and croutons at **Cépage** (23 Wing Fung St; +852.2861 3130; www.lesamis.com.sg) when it opened in Hong Kong in early 2009. The modern European restaurant has since received one Michelin star for its notable contemporary cuisine. This particular star dish comprises a "Taiyouran" egg that has been cooked for 20 minutes at very low temperature, rendering a perfectly silky smooth texture. The organic, free-range eggs are sourced from Japan. According to the chef, they are pure in taste with high fat-content in the yolk. Mayr also serves the egg confit alongside other seasonal ingredients such as girolle mushrooms, sweet corn and pork belly sous-vide as well as with truffle carpaccio and Joselito ham "Gran Reserva".

Lung King Heen (8 Finance Street, Central; +852.3196 888; www.fourseasons.com) at the **Four Seasons Hotel Hong Kong** is the only Chinese restaurant in the world to receive three Michelin stars. Executive Chinese Chef **Chan Yan Tak** is the maestro behind the contemporary Cantonese menu which places emphasis on seafood and *dim sum*. One of the restaurant's pièce de résistance is the crispy scallop with fresh pear. A slice of pear is topped with minced shrimp meat, then a plump scallop, salty Yunnan ham and parsley. It is then coated with corn flour and deep-fried until golden brown, and served simply with a drizzling of lemon juice and sea salt on the side.

Lau Yiu Fai, Executive Chinese Chef calls the shots at the one-Michelin-starred **Yan Toh Heen** (18 Salisbury Road; +852.2313 2323; hongkong-ic.dining.intercontinental.com) at the **InterContinental Hong Kong**. Among his many impressive specialities is the lobster with crab roe and fresh milk. The lobster is wok-fried until about 60 percent cooked and then tossed together with stir-fried fresh milk and egg whites. The chef expertly fuses the milk and lobster meat to create a moreish tenderness.

Besides the fine Cantonese menu, Lau also rustles up unique nutritionist-endorsed "ihealth" dishes for the health-conscious diner. One of the signature ihealth items is simmered star garoupa with fresh lily bulbs and green apple. The unique dish uses ingredients and cooking methods which are ideal for the prevention of major health problems such as heart disease, diabetes and hypertension, and the need for anti-oxidants. According to him, the skill in using the right cooking method is important to preserving the natural form and flavour of the ingredient.

shanghai, china

Dane Clouston, Executive Chef of the new **Jing'An** restaurant at **The**

PuLi Hotel & Spa (1 Chang De Road, Jingan District; +86.21.2216 6988; www.jinganrestaurant.com) has been highly commended for his inventive menu, in particular his signature pastrami of salmon with rye wafers. Clouston said: "I love this dish because it's a fun take on the classic cured salmon. It's a real balance of sweet, spicy, salty and textures." He added, "Basically the hard part is to find some great salmon and then lightly cure it in brown sugar and sea salt. The beetroots for the sorbet are roasted, pureed and then combined with sherry vinegar and churned."

The spices (smoked paprika, cumin, coriander and yellow mustard seeds) for the pastrami are all lightly toasted and then hand-ground. The spice mix as well as lemon oil are rubbed onto the salmon, which is then sliced. For the dressing, sesame, garlic and star anise are heated and taken off the heat to infuse. The mixture is then strained and mixed with soy. Finally the salmon is garnished with Osetra caviar, baby celery cress, shaved beetroot, crisp rye wafer and voila flower.

mumbai, india

Fratelli Fresh at the **Renaissance Mumbai Conference Centre Hotel's** (#2 & 3B, Near Chinmayanand Ashram; +912.2.6692 7777; www.marriott.com) features an authentic Italian menu that places emphasis on seasonal ingredients such as imported porcini, cured meats and cheese, as well as home grown herbs and vegetables fresh from the kitchen gardens. The cooking style of Enrico Luise, Italian Chef de Cuisine (a native of Verona, Veneto), is simple, uncomplicated and yet doesn't compromise on taste.

One of his signature dishes is the ravioli al porcini—handmade stuffed pasta with ricotta cheese, porcini mushroom sourced from Borgotaro, Italy, served with freshly made tomato sauce. "Made from scratch, the freshness of the raw ingredients like the flour and eggs, as well as the ricotta cheese and porcini balance each other perfectly. My keen pasta team who has been with me since the opening of Fratelli Fresh, still maintain their enthusiasm for making fresh pasta every day. The tomato sauce enhances the flavour of the ravioli without ruining the delicate fragrance of the mushrooms."

The Ossobuco Milanese has always been a part of the chef's portfolio of dishes. "Not only is it one of my personal favourites to eat, it has proven time after time to be a well balanced and satisfying dish for everyone who chooses it. When I cook the shank, I usually braise the meat in red wine, herbs, tomatoes, carrots, celery and onion, which I flavour with a bouquet garni. I serve the shank with 'risotto alla milanese'. The risotto is enhanced with saffron threads and is one of the few dishes where a grain and meat dish are served together. It is a modern take on a traditional dish that I like," Luise shared. His secret in this recipe is "to give love and care to the lamb whilst cooking" and also braising the meat until it is fork-tender but not mushy.

~ AV

THIS PAGE (FROM TOP): Lung King Heen's crispy scallop with fresh pear is served with lemon juice and sea salt; Jing'An's pastrami of salmon with rye wafers is a perfect balance of taste, texture and temperature.

OPPOSITE: One of Yan Toh Heen's outstanding creations by Chef Lau Yiu Fai—wok-fried lobster expertly cooked with fresh milk and egg whites.

chefs' tips + secrets

Chefs from Asia's top restaurants share their cooking tips and techniques, acquired through years of slaving away in hot kitchens. Equal parts common sense and hard-won experience, these practical know-hows will help turn amateur home chefs into culinary wizards.

salt, herbs + spices
Ebony Huebner, Sous and Pastry Chef, Kathleen's 5 Rooftop Restaurant, Shanghai

An easy way to enhance your cooking is through the use of flavoured salts—also called "finishing salts". Although you can buy many types of flavoured finishing salts from gourmet shops, it is easy (and cheaper) to make your own using sea salt and various herbs and spices. It is useful and fun to keep a fresh supply of these flavoured salts within easy reach. Add unusual flavour and visual interest by sprinkling coloured salts over dishes just before serving.

Place 1/4 cup of sea salt in a bowl, add 1 tsp of flavouring and rub together with your fingertips. If using wet ingredients such as lime zest, spread the salt mixture on a tray and bake on low heat (100°C/212°F) to dry it out completely. When cool, rub again between your fingers and store in a container. Keep this flavoured salt near your stove for easy access.

Below are some recommended pairings for flavoured salts:
• Matcha (green tea) salt with steamed egg custard or even chocolate;
• Citrus salt with beetroot, prawns or to rim a margarita glass;
• Saffron salt with rice dishes or scallops; and
• Szechuan pepper salt on fried tofu or chips.

Zulkifli Razali, Chef de Cuisine, Bijan Bar & Restaurant, Kuala Lumpur
When preparing chilli paste the traditional way, the blended paste of dried and fresh chillies should be cooked slowly over low heat. Never

add any sour liquid like lime or vinegar while the paste is cooking as this will hinder the cooking process and leave the chilli paste with a raw taste, besides making it very spicy and hot. Always add the sour ingredient only after the chilli paste is cooked. You know it's ready when the oil separates from the chilli paste.

When using dried spices like cloves, cardamom, cinnamon sticks, and star anise, first soak them in water for about a minute to enhance their flavour. To extract a deeper flavour, stir-fry the spices in a dry pan.

Philip Mimbimi, Executive Chef, nutmegs restaurant – dining at hu'u
Freshly ground pepper from a pepper mill should never be substituted with pre-ground or cracked pepper. The aroma and taste of freshly ground pepper is irreplaceable, no matter what the recipe book says.

Darren Lauder, Executive Chef, Nusa Dua Beach Hotel & Spa
Forget about using a blender or food processor in Balinese cuisine. Your best tip is to prepare the ingredients using traditional tools such as a mortar and pestle. This will bring out the oils from the herbs and spices and impart a wonderful aroma when you cook the dish.

rice + pasta
Shinji Morihara, Executive Chef, Inagiku, Fairmont Singapore
A staple such as rice is very carefully handled at Inagiku. Only two scoops of rice are placed into each bowl, and each scoop must be lifted out of the pot, not scraped out. This prevents

THIS PAGE: *Use a mortar and pestle to bring out aromatic oils from herbs and spices instead of grinding them in an electric blender.*
OPPOSITE: *Enhance your dishes with a variety of flavoured salts that you can create at home.*

chefs' tips + secrets

the rice grains from breaking, and retains the grain's fluffiness and soft, gentle feel on one's tongue.

Wicus Prinsloo, Director of Culinary & Restaurants, W Retreat & Spa Maldives

To make sushi rice, use 500 g (17.6 ounces) of sushi rice and 1/2 cup of sushi vinegar sweetened with 80 g (2.8 ounces) of white sugar.

Wash good quality Japanese short-grain sushi rice carefully two or three times. Discard the starchy water and repeat till water runs clean. Cover the washed rice with fresh cold water. Allow the rice to soak and absorb the water for approximately 30 minutes, then drain the remaining water completely. In a rice cooker, add the washed rice and fresh cold water to cover the rice by 1 cm (0.4 inches). Cook for 20 minutes, then allow to rest, covered for 20 minutes.

Place cooked rice into a basin-like container, preferably a wooden bowl, and add sweetened sushi vinegar to the rice. Mix the rice well by using a moistened wooden flat spoon in a gentle slicing motion. Do not press the rice or crush it. Allow it to cool for five to seven minutes in a well-ventilated area, before turning over the rice using the same method. Allow for another five minutes of cooling, while monitoring the rice's temperature. At about 37°C (98.6°F), the rice has reached the desired temperature and texture. If it is still warm, repeat the turning process. After cooling, place the rice in a clean container, and cover it with a clean moist cloth to keep the rice from drying out. The rice is now ready for serving.

Note: If refrigerated, the starch of the rice will change, so this is not advisable. Leftover rice should be discarded if not consumed within two hours.

Fabrizio Bigi, Italian Chef, Prego, The Westin Beijing Financial Street
There are only a few important tricks to making fresh pasta as the recipe is very simple. However, even a simple recipe can easily be mishandled. The most important aspect of making good fresh pasta is in the "handling"— this must be kept to the bare minimum. If you over-knead pasta in the machine, it becomes "plastic-like", resulting in a texture similar to the dried ones sold in supermarkets.

Philip Mimbimi, Executive Chef, nutmegs restaurant – dining at hu'u
I like to add some risotto rice into my lobster or prawn bisque during the stage of cooking where I add my "aromatics". This helps to gradually and naturally thicken the base.

To prepare a flavourful bisque, I first sauté the mirepoix (diced onion, carrot and celery), add tomato paste, then deglaze with brandy or wine. Then, I add the aromatics such as prawn or lobster shells, fish stock, herbs, peppercorn, garlic, bay leaves, lemon zest along with some risotto rice (either arborio or carnaroli). The bisque is brought to a full boil and then simmered for a prolonged period of time to extract all the flavours slowly.

meat + poultry
Chris Salans, Chef-owner, Mozaic, Bali
There are several ways to make duck skin crispy. The technique that I use is to score the fat of the duck as deeply as possible (without cutting into the meat) and to pan sear the duck skin side down in a dry pan until it is about three-quarters cooked. By doing this, the fat will melt away immediately. I then remove the liquid fat, forcing the duck to render more fat in the pan. This is done continuously until all the fat is dully removed and the skin becomes crisp.

There are different techniques in handling foie gras. In Southeast Asia, the climate is rather hot so I tend to put the foie gras in the freezer for 15 to 30 minutes before cooking, to ensure that it is nice and firm when seared. This method gives me more time to sear the foie gras properly. I also coat a thin layer of flour on both sides of the foie gras before searing it in the pan, so that a nice crust forms on the outside within the first few seconds.

Shigeru Akashi, Executive Chef, Meritus Mandarin Singapore
The best way to prepare *teppanyaki* is to make sure the hotplate is sufficiently hot. If not, the juice or fluid from the meat, seafood or vegetable will ooze out onto the pan and make the dish soggy and unappetising.

Nabil Taufiq Tan, Group Head Chef, Bedrock Bar & Grill, Singapore
I go for the best and freshest ingredients whenever possible. I prefer to let chilled raw food reach room temperature before grilling. Also, always use high temperatures to grill meats to seal in their natural juices, and then finish off at a moderate heat.

THIS PAGE (FROM TOP): Place foie gras in the freezer before cooking so that it is firm when seared; Use high temperatures to seal in juices in meats.

OPPOSITE (CLOCKWISE FROM TOP LEFT): Freshly cooked rice should be used for preparing sushi; The steps in creating dough is as important as in the kneading; When making pasta from scratch, do not over-knead the dough or it will have an unpleasant texture; A variety of freshly made pasta and noodles.

chef tips + secrets   43

chefs' tips + secrets

Junious Dickerson, Executive Chef, Hotel Equatorial Penang
An increasingly popular way to slow-cook red meats is a technique called *sous vide*, a process whereby meat cuts such as rumps, racks, cheeks and shoulders are first vacuum-packed, and then cooked by braising, poaching or steaming the packets. This style of cooking will result in meat that is more tender and juicier. It also retains more of its natural flavours with less shrinkage.

Fabrice Giraud, Chef de Cuisine, Jade on 36, Pudong Shangri-La, Shanghai
Recommended cooking meat temperatures using a thermometer:
• For rare meat, the temperature must be 50–55°C (122–131°F).
• For medium rare meat, the temperature must be 55–60°C (131–140°F).
• For medium, the temperature must be 60–65°C (140–149°F).
• For well done, the temperature must be 65–70°C (149–158°F).

To ensure meat is tender, always allow it to rest (about five to eight minutes) before carving. During the resting time, the meat will continue to cook as the temperature will increase about 5°C after it has been removed from the heat source.

For example, if you want the meat to be cooked medium, you should remove it from the skillet, oven or grill at 60°C (140°F). Let it rest on a plate or chopping board and lightly tent it with foil. Because of the surrounding heat, the meat will continue to cook until the temperature reaches about 64°C (174°F). In my opinion, any meat cooked beyond 65°C (149°F) will be overcooked and leathery. The amount of time required for resting also varies depending on the size and type of the cut of meat.

Lau Yiu Fai, Executive Chinese Chef, Yan Toh Heen, InterContinental Hong Kong
My signature Lung Kong chicken is the most moist and flavourful poultry I have ever eaten. At Yan Toh Heen, we get our chicken straight from the farm in Lung Kong. The secret is to select a big chicken that weighs about 2.5 kg (5.5 pounds). Blanch the chicken until the bird begins to turn pale, and then air-dry it for at least two hours. The skin has to be completely dry, the wok has to be deep enough and the oil hot enough to give the chicken a nice crispy skin. The secret Chinese spice marinade I use also gives this dish a unique flavour.

If you buy roast goose from a restaurant to be enjoyed at home, you can use hot oil to deep fry the goose again or re-heat the goose in a hot oven. This will ensure that the skin turns crispy again.

vegetables + salads
Chris Salans, Chef-owner, Mozaic, Bali
The key to a good vegetarian dish is to have a variety (not only vegetables but also starches, legumes, items like *tempe* or tofu, different kinds of carbohydrate and dairy products) and to have really good quality ingredients. Then add a little bit of aromatic herbs or spices and you should be on the way to making a great dish for vegetarians.

THIS PAGE (FROM TOP): *When roasting beef, rest it for five to eight minutes before cutting; Blanching a whole chicken and air-drying it for about two hours before deep-frying results in a crispy skin.*

OPPOSITE (CLOCKWISE FROM TOP LEFT): *Use icy cold batter to yield crispy tempura; Fry tempura in oil heated to 170°C; Lemon helps to prevent oxidation in avocados; Use colourful ingredients to enhance the salad presentation.*

Personally I am not a vegetarian so cooking for vegetarians is very intimidating. However, over the last few years at Mozaic, I have learnt to cook good vegetarian food. My secret, as with all of our other menus, is to serve a menu of six different dishes. This gives the diner the opportunity to taste a variety of ingredients and flavours within a single meal. Our menus are usually composed of a soup, a salad, a carbohydrate dish (pasta, gnocchi, risotto, phyllo pastry, etc) a dairy dish, a fruit dish and ending with dessert.

Richard Millar, Chef de Cuisine, Conrad Bali
To make tempura's light and crispy batter, make sure the batter is icy cold. Another tip is to use soda water to add air to lighten the mixture. Do not mix the ingredients too much; the more the flour is handled the heavier the batter will be. Don't worry about lumps. In tempura-type batters, lumps are good. Do use chopsticks to evenly coat your vegetables, again avoid too much mixing. Ensure that the oil is not too hot; a temperature of 170°C (338°F) is perfect for frying tempura. Using a deep fat or hot oil thermometer is one way of achieving fault-free results.

Michael Muller, Executive Sous Chef, Fairmont Singapore
For an out-of-the-ordinary surprise in salads, soak a hard-boiled egg (shelled) in tinned beetroot puree overnight. The next day, you'll find a beautifully coloured purple egg that will make any dish presentation stand out.

chef tips+secrets 45

chefs' tips + secrets

Abraham Tan, Culinary Executive Chef, Royal Plaza on Scotts, Singapore
Fruits and vegetables that are high in oxidants require a touch of acidity to prevent oxidisation. For instance, avocado is usually paired with lemon vinaigrette to prevent oxidisation.

Fabrice Giraud, Chef de Cuisine, Jade on 36, Pudong Shangri-La, Shanghai
To keep vegetables really crispy and green, bring a large pot of water and some salt (30 g of salt per litre of water) to a rolling boil. Keep a bucket of iced water on the side. Cook the vegetables in the hot water until al dente (about 2–3 minutes) and then quickly dunk them in iced water before draining. Dry the vegetables on paper towels until ready to use.

seafood
Siu Hin Chi, Executive Chinese Chef, T'ang Court, The Langham Hong Kong
The most essential tip is to cook sincerely. If you truly understand the theory of each cooking method and the characteristic of each ingredient, then you can whip up good food.

One example is my award-winning dish—stir-fried fresh lobster with spring onion, red onion and shallots. I use lobster from South China Sea instead of those from Boston or Australia (even though they have been widely used by both Western and Chinese restaurants). Lobsters from Boston or Australia are meaty and good when poached or grilled but not when stir-fried the Cantonese way. South China Sea lobster has a crispier texture, which is perfect for stir-fries.

Shigeru Akashi, Executive Chef, Meritus Mandarin, Singapore
When choosing fresh tuna for sashimi, use your five senses. The tuna should not smell fishy or feel wet and sticky. The colour of the fish should not be dull. Always buy tuna from a reputable shop. Head to where the Japanese buy theirs. You cannot go wrong at these shops!

Nabil Taufiq Tan, Group Head Chef, Bedrock Bar & Grill, Singapore
Be careful not to overcook seafood, especially crustaceans and squid, as they become rubbery when they are cooked for too long.

stocks and soups
Sam Leong, Corporate Chef/Director of Kitchens for Tung Lok Group
To make a good stock or broth in Chinese cuisine, four key ingredients are imperative: ham for flavour and taste; an old hen to ensure richness; lean meat to give a natural sweetness; and chicken feet to thicken the broth. It is important to use fresh and good quality ingredients. Sufficient time is also required to slowly boil and extract the flavours from the ingredients. Lastly, always make sure the broth is made on the day of use. Do not keep stock overnight as the taste and nutrition level will be compromised.

pastries and biscuits
Kenny Kong, Executive Pastry Chef, Fairmont Singapore and Swissotel The Stamford, Singapore
The secret to baking a perfect gingerbread man—with a smooth underside and even topside—is to

place the prepared dough directly onto a baking tray. Do not grease the baking tray or place a piece of silicone paper on the baking tray as this will cause the gingerbread to bubble up and bake unevenly.

Cassian Tan, Executive Pastry Chef, Equinox Complex, Swissotel The Stamford, Singapore
Pastry work is all about precision. From selecting raw materials to measuring ingredients accurately and processing them according to the recipe, precision in your work will yield success. It's also important to work with chilled ingredients, including your mixing bowl.

Daniel Tay, CEO, Bakerzin, Singapore
It is a myth that one is not supposed to open the oven door when baking because it will cause the cake to collapse. It's more important that you preheat the oven before you start baking, but opening the oven to check on your cake is not a problem, even when baking soufflés.

When serving crème brulee, it is best to enjoy the dessert at room temperature. Crème brulee is meant to be a light dessert and is perfect when eaten at room temperature. Placing it in the fridge before serving tends to make the cream heavier on the palate, and the caramelised glaze on the top will also lose its crustiness.

other tips + techniques
Dane Clouston, Executive Chef, Jing'An, The Puli Hotel and Spa, Shanghai
Look at alternative, more natural cooking methods. Often a dish is at its best if cooked longer at lower temperatures; sometimes a dish has a cleaner and more balanced flavour and texture when served at the correct temperature. There seems to be a misconception that food should always be served piping hot, like what our mothers used to do and tell us. Sometimes, in order to get the full appreciation of flavours and textures, it is best to serve a dish (like chicken for instance) at a moderate temperature to enjoy its well balanced flavours and textures.

Andre Chiang, Chef de Cuisine, Jaan par André, Equinox Complex, Swissotel The Stamford, Singapore
At Jaan par André, we use the freshest produce available—often sourced directly from the producers or growers. This way, diners can taste unusual, even rare, ingredients that are not available in the regular markets. One of my signature dishes called "forgotten" vegetables uses up to 21 heirloom vegetables, all of which impart different flavour dimensions.   ~ AV

The perfect fruit cake
When baking a light fruitcake, chop the mixed dried fruits finely before soaking them in brandy. Lightly sprinkle some flour over the fruits, cover the bowl with cling film and set aside in the refrigerator overnight. Chopping the fruits will result in a fine-textured cake that is less dense. In addition, it will also prevent the fruits from sinking to the bottom of the cake during baking. For extra flavour, drizzle a tablespoon of brandy over the cake batter before baking. Set the oven at a moderately low 160°C (325°F) so that the cake has a lovely golden brown hue when it is baked.

THIS PAGE (FROM TOP): When baking gingerbread men, avoid greasing the baking tray or using silicone paper. This will ensure that the dough bakes evenly; The ingredients for pastries and cakes must be precisely measured.

OPPOSITE (CLOCKWISE FROM TOP): Dunking freshly blanched vegetables in ice-cold water helps to retain the colour and crunchiness; Fresh tuna is not fishy or sticky, and is not dull in colour.

restaurant interiors

Not just food, but ambience is the defining feature of Asia's best restaurants. Whether it's the natural environment or designer-chic surroundings that dazzles, the settings are often as memorable as the food.

Forget the drama. The best designed restaurant is one that does not shout design, but rather one that makes the diner feel at home, comfortable and welcome. This is why Singapore-based architect and interior designer Ernesto Bedmar rates Iggy's restaurant as one of Singapore's best in terms of design. Despite being housed in a small space in the Regent Hotel Singapore, Iggy's offers three dining options: kitchen, counter or private dining room. The spaces, lined with bookcases and decorated with the owners' own paintings, do not feel overpowering. They are elegant, with a great sense of balance. And, of course, the restaurant serves wonderful food.

While many new restaurants sport clean, minimalist designs using glass and steel, reflecting current trends in restaurant interiors, Bedmar says comfort and intimacy are equally important. A director of design firm Bedmar and Shi, he designed the early Lei Garden restaurant in Singapore, which used to be sited in the unprepossessing space of a hotel basement. The latest seems to be counter or kitchen dining. He adds, "It is very common these days to see the chef organising all the food we eat." And this is hot concept used in some of Asia's leading eateries, including Hong Kong's L'Atelier by Joel Robuchon.

"Still, good food is a number one priority. You can have beautiful views, a lovely location and an ambitious structure but it will not work if the food is bad!", Bedmar adds. Beyond this, restaurants everywhere will aim to have a unique design feature to create a suitable setting for its food.

This can be a wonderful view, a beautiful sculpture or a priceless antique. Others may opt for extravagant colours and décor that give a sense of theatricality to a space.

Whichever it is—décor or colour scheme—the setting creates a sense of occasion that matches the food and makes the evening an unforgettable one. And surely that is what eating out is all about.

shanghai, china

Conveniently located on the Bund, the interior of **Whampoa Club** (3 Zhong Shan Dong Yi Road; +86.21.6323 3355; www.threeonthebund.com) boasts stunning furniture and lighting by renowned designers Frank Gehry, Philippe Starck, Bertjan Pot and the Front Design Group, to name a few. The architecture is unique too—in the day, natural light is allowed to shine through the glass ceiling of the main hall, and at night, the metal structures and accessories make it a glittering haven, adding to the visual delight of the diners. The establishment also has six private dining rooms that can be expanded to accommodate a party of 60 guests.

It is like dining in someone's home when you eat at **Vue Restaurant**, the French restaurant at **Hyatt on the Bund** (199 Huangpu Road; +86.21.6393 1234; www.shanghai.bund.hyatt.com). Designed by the world famous Japanese interior design firm, Super Potato, it feels like you have entered a sophisticated gentleman's apartment complete with kitchen, library and dining room. The chairs are large and

THIS PAGE (CLOCKWISE FROM TOP LEFT): Hong Kong-based award-winning designer Alan Chan creates a modern art deco interior that echoes Shanghai's mythical 1920s decadence, with designer artefacts such as the green chair by Marcel Wanders; The cloud-shaped paper lamps by Frank Gehry add a contemporary touch in its VIP room at Whampoa Club, Beijing; Roomy lounge chairs and sofas on the rooftop terrace of Vue Restaurant, Hyatt on the Bund.
OPPOSITE: The interior of the Black Bar at Whampoa Club, Beijing—an ideal meeting place for socialising and business.

restaurant interiors

cosy, with an option of lounges to snuggle into and Sinatra (or Elvis) is playing in the background. And as in a home, there are assorted bric-a-brac scattered around the room. There are racks stacked with culinary paraphernalia to book-lined shelves, alongside eclectic collections of model cars, pipes and vintage corkscrews. Be sure to explore the library's impressive collections of classic cameras and bottle openers.

The views from this 30th-floor restaurant are equally stunning. Indeed, the glittering panoramic views of the Bund and of the skyscrapers at Pudong might just steal the thunder from the food when dinner is served.

There are also six private dining rooms with themes ranging from Chinese to Western and Japanese on the floor above to accommodate groups of between eight and 16. Like the restaurant, each of the rooms has its own unique look and feel, with a kitchen area, separate seating areas and private washrooms, giving a distinctly residential feel.

beijing, china

It is a study of contrasts at two of **The Westin Beiijing Financial Street**'s dining outlets and each draws its own fans. **Senses** (see pages 104–105), its all-day dining outlet, is cool and minimalist, and trendy and modern in feel. The overall emphasis is on clean and uncluttered lines. On the other hand, its Chinese restaurant, **Jewel**, is warm and inviting, done up in modern Chinese design with warm earthy colours. It also has five elegant private dining-room seating for 5–24 guests.

Senses draws the crowds especially to its popular Champagne Sunday brunches, topping numerous readers' choice awards, while Jewel serves sophisticated Cantonese cuisine with occasional Sichuan dishes. It won the best Chinese restaurant award from *Beijing Tatler* in its 2008 rankings.

With a name like **Cepe** (1 Jin Cheng Fang Street East; +86.10.6601 6666; www.ritzcarlton.com), which is what the French call the Italian porcini mushroom, it is no wonder that mushrooms strongly feature in both the décor and food at this Northern Italian restaurant at the **Ritz-Carlton Beijing, Financial Street**. Unmissable are the 1,000 uniquely designed mushroom sculptures made of resin and painted in silver, suspended from the ceiling. In Chinese feng shui, mushrooms represent earth.

Designed by Hirsch Bedner Associates (San Francisco office), Cepe's interiors are sophisticated with textured walls, red leather armchairs, and white tablecloths topped with cobalt blue and clear glasses. Taking centrestage is a mushroom humidor designed for storing dried and fresh mushrooms. The humidor will nurture the rich, earthy flavours that are the backbone of many of the dishes. This 70-seat restaurant also has a private dining room for 10, two romantic dining booths and an intimate chef's table for four persons.

hong kong

A more opulent dining space you will not find in this city. Inspired by the classic beauty and luxury of the Tang Dynasty, **T'ang Court** at **The Langham Hong Kong** (see pages 108–109) is a lavishly furnished and ornate space. The ceilings are covered by plush swathes of silk, contemporary sculptures dot the space, and rich red and gold brocade curtain off sections of the restaurant for more intimacy.

In addition, a dramatic spiral staircase leads up to five exquisitely furnished private dining rooms, named after Tang Dynasty's renowned poets—Tai Bai, Le Tian, Zi Shou, Bai Yu and Zi Mei. Indeed its interior is so stunning that the restaurant is on the US *Food and Wine* magazine's list of "293 Outstanding Places to Eat" (May 2008), and was named one of the world's "Best Hotel Dining Rooms" by *Gourmet* magazine (May 2004).

Fortunately, its cuisine lives up to the luxurious interior. The restaurant won the much-coveted two Michelin stars in the 2008 *Michelin Guide Hong Kong/Macau* for its fine classical Cantonese cuisine.

bali, indonesia

You would be dining amidst Indonesian antiques at **Bale Sutra** (see pages 116–117), the magnificent restaurant of the **Hotel Tugu Bali**, a boutique hotel chain that has claimed awards for its architecture. The owner, Anhar Setjadibrata, collects fine Indonesian art and cultural antiquities, which is why you will find the *cupu manik*, a 16th-century stone bowl of three parts, from which ancient priests sprinkled healing water over villagers suffering from sickness and disease, on display in this space.

THIS PAGE (FROM TOP): Hotel Tugu Bali, a hotel chain that has claimed awards for its architecture, has interiors that reflect Indonesia's rich heritage; One dining hall, Bale Puputan, commemorates Balinese heroes in the 1906 Puputan War with memorabilia dating back to that period and to the Puputan War. *OPPOSITE:* The private dining room, Senses, at the Westin Beijing which reflects the warm but minimalist feel of the dining outlet.

restaurant interiors

While the restaurant is an opulent dining space with its brocade hangings and red lanterns, it is also a beautiful boutique museum that houses a 300-year-old Kang Xi temple that was almost demolished in the 1990s in Java. The temple was transported and reconstructed in its entirety at Tugu. Today, it is housed in a dramatic red dining room, displaying a spectacular 18th-century statue of the Goddess of Mercy, an ancient gigantic mask and various other artworks.

In keeping with the respect for heritage, here you will be able to also sample Baba Peranakan cuisine, an unusual marriage of ancient Chinese and Indonesian food cultures that is rarely found in Bali.

bangkok, thailand

Despite being located on the 59th floor of **Banyan Tree Bangkok**, you will get the feeling of being under the ocean in **Pier 59** (21/100 South Sathon Road; +66.2.679 1200; www.banyantree.com), the hotel's seafood restaurant. Here, diners are surrounded by columns of effervescent bubbles in a recreated underwater chamber.

Indeed, the entire area is coloured with shades of electric blue to create the tranquillity of the marine world. Turquoise blue glass tables, a minimalist table set-up and high-backed acrylic seats add to the surreal atmosphere. This cutting-edge design is a fitting complement to its superbly crafted seafood menu, which boasts of signature pleasers such as roasted black cod and Barron Point oysters.

The private room at the entrance boasts a wine rack and is also used as a cigar room. While the restaurant already has a capacity for 90 guests, you could also book two private rooms with long acrylic tables, each able to cater for 12 persons for more intimate parties. And if you are tired of being underwater, take a look outside—the restaurant also prides itself on having an unobstructed and spectacular bird's eye view of the Bangkok metropolis and the meandering Chao Phraya river.

the maldives

You don't need much in terms of restaurant design if you can dine on a gorgeous atoll with sumptuous lagoon views. And this is what you get at the **Atoll Market** at the **Conrad Maldives Rangali Island** (+960.6680 629; conradhotels. hilton.com). As you wriggle your toes in the powdery white sand, you will get to sample different world cuisines from its eight specialist kitchens.

For underwater drama, head below the ocean to its other outlet, the **Ithaa Undersea Restaurant**, dubbed the only undersea restaurant of its kind in the world. Sitting 4.87 m (16 ft) below sea level under an all-glass ceiling, you can enjoy 180-degree views of reef and marine life. And yes, food that is a fine balance of Western cuisine and Maldivian flavours.

kuala lumpur, malaysia

Colour defines this space, which also offers cutting-edge Vietnamese cuisine. Edgy and brash, casual and chic are adjectives often applied to **Sao Nam** (see pages 152–153), a modern Vietnamese restaurant housed in a pre-war building in the heart of Kuala Lumpur.

Minimalist in décor and boldly awash with bright primary colours—think purple and red, pink and orange combinations—and with lots of equally striking street art from Ho Chi Minh City hanging on its walls, you can expect some delectable Vietnamese cuisine here.

Award-winning chef Phan Tien Minh from Ho Chi Minh City, turns out not just *pho*, but dishes such as mangosteen salad, Vietnamese pancake and lamb in coconut sauce. ~ ST

Design vs Feng Shui

Feng shui is an ancient Chinese system that creates the best environment for living, be it a workplace, a home or even a restaurant. The idea is to create harmonious surroundings to enhance the balance of *yin* and *yang* forces in a space. It may include the arranging of furniture, the use of plants, mirrors, water fountains, wind-chimes and bright colours—to bring in more light, water and air into an area.

In the same way, a feng shui-conscious designer would create an ideal interior for a restaurant though his reasons may not be the same as those of a feng shui master's. Still, the colours, furniture, decorations and textures chosen are also meant to create a harmonious and pleasing room. The idea is for the diner to feel comfortable and at home in order to maximise the dining experience. So take a second look at that water fountain playing near you.

THIS PAGE (FROM TOP): Conrad Maldives Rangali Island boasts of its Ithaa Undersea Restaurant—the only undersea restaurant of its kind in the world; Sao Nam Restaurant in Kuala Lumpur can boast not only of its modern Vietnamese cuisine, but also of its bold Pop Art décor in its dining room, awash with bright colours.
OPPOSITE: At Pier 59 of the Banyan Tree Bangkok, one dines surrounded by effervescent bubble columns in a recreated underwater chamber.

restaurant interiors 53

high-altitude dining

Nothing beats the excitement of dining up high, especially in Asia where the skyscrapers are towering, the night vistas glittering and the skyline constantly changing.

Dining with altitude, literally. You can do this in most cities of the world, but in Asia, the experience is quite extraordinary. The settings are more dramatic, even "adventurous", with the chance to dine under the stars on the rooftop of towering skyscrapers. The views are truly heart-stopping with all those glittering city lights that seem to be brighter in Asia and constantly changing, as the cities develop or are renewed.

Many return visitors to Asian cities often notice that the skyline would have changed; a modern structure or two added; in the case of Singapore, the new Marina Bay Sands casino opened in 2010, dominating the cityscape irrevocably. It also helps that many Asian cities are built round major rivers—even tiny Singapore has the historic Singapore River snaking round the buildings—it just makes for a more interesting picture.

Superlatives abound in this category of dining. The restaurant is sited in either the city's highest space, in the world's tallest skyscraper or even in the world's highest al fresco dining space, which is the current boast of Sirocco in Bangkok.

In case you're wondering, the world's highest restaurant, 100 Century Avenue, is in the towering Shanghai World Financial Centre in Pudong, Shanghai. But for how long, no one knows, as a competitor is sure to arise soon in the region, if not the city. And no wonder, for the attraction of heights to most people is undeniable, as can be seen in the snaking queues that form outside these high-altitude restaurants.

Up high, confronted face to face with the elements, you feel almost a palpable excitement. The breeze, nay wind, is strong, and indeed most outdoor places close if it is too windy. You are at the mercy of nature and some cannot get too close to the edge, despite the views. But then sweaty palms and bated breath are all part of the sky dining package.

While the views are indeed a drawing point, unless of course you suffer from vertigo, at some restaurants, the vistas seem to be all there are to it. But the situation is changing and these days the food can be good as the views, especially in places like Hutong restaurant in Hong Kong and Shinyeh 101 in Taipei.

Being 60, 70, 90 storeys high truly represents a different way of looking at a city. The angles are unique and the vistas magnificent as compared to being at ground level. Whatever the cynics may say about falling for the hype surrounding this kind of high-drama dining, nothing can beat the experience of seeing Shanghai, Beijing, Bangkok, Tokyo, Hong Kong, Taipei and Singapore from such towering heights. Altitude truly lends enchantment to the view.

beijing, china

Every major city has one and this is Beijing's highest restaurant. Located in a glass box on Level 66 of the **Park Hyatt Beijing** is **China Grill** (2 Jianguomenwai Street, Chaoyang District; +86.10.8567 1234; beijing.park.hyatt.com), an international eatery serving prime meats, fish and seafood in both Western and Chinese styles.

Set high in a new tower at the Yintai Centre, you get no less than 360-degree views of Beijing. From its windows, you will be able to see the Great Hall of the People, The Forbidden City, the old and new CCTV Towers—all lit up and clearly visible—and from an angle seldom seen before.

And the food is good too. Its blue crab fish cakes have large chunks of white crab tumbling out of the light, crisp filling. Among the main courses, choose from lamb chops, Wagyu steaks, beef sirloin and lobster, and if you prefer Chinese, a sweet and sour black cod, large enough to be shared.

For a more intimate setting, **The Private Room**—part of the same eatery—comprises 16 dining suites serving Cantonese cuisine, each with its own butler service. Pantry and washroom facilities accompany every suite, with many featuring private balconies with stunning views.

shanghai, china

Finally we have it—the world's highest restaurant. And **100 Century Avenue Restaurant** at the **Park Hyatt Shanghai** (100 Century Avenue, Pudong New Area; +86.21.6888 1234; shanghai.park.hyatt.com) claims this title at the moment. Located on the 91st storey of the Park Hyatt Shanghai, you literally dine here above the clouds and obtain unmatched views of the Huangpu river, the Oriental Pearl Tower and the world famous Shanghai Bund.

The hotel itself occupies the 79th to 93rd floors of the Shanghai World Financial Centre, and once you reach the restaurant with its triple storey

THIS PAGE (FROM TOP): *From the windows of China Grill at the Park Hyatt Beijing, you get 360-degree views of Beijing and from an angle seldom seen before; The entrance to China Grill, currently the highest restaurant in Beijing.*
OPPOSITE: *Gorgeous views of Taipei city from Taipei 101, Taiwan.*

highaltitudedining 55

high-altitude dining

windows, you will be undeniably impressed by the vistas. But there's much to look at as well indoors. There's a dynamic show of kitchen skills at the many open kitchens that offer three kinds of cuisines: Chinese, Japanese and Western.

While the wide menu offerings are expected, the quality is high. The Australian lamb rack is a generous, juicy and extremely tender serving while the Alaskan halibut is deliciously delicate, served with a drizzle of light olive oil and a squeeze of lemon. For a feel of old Shanghai, do visit its bar at the east wing, which features a Shanghainese singer and a ballroom dance floor.

hong kong

Hutong (1 Peking Rd, 28th floor, Tsim Sha Tsui; +852.3428 8342; www.aqua.com.hk), the restaurant, is about as far as you can get from a real *hutong*. Instead of being huddled in an alley in one of Beijing's old vanishing neighbourhoods, it is located on the 28th floor of a modern high-rise building in Hong Kong.

Here you get expansive views of Hong Kong's famous harbour, if you can tear your eyes away from the dramatic décor within. Birdcages are hung everywhere—from the ceiling, over tables, and as a sculptural accent, against the windows. The cuisine served here explains its name: it is northern Chinese with fusion touches. Highlights include soft-shelled crab with dried red chilli and a whole pigeon complete with its head poached in a white pepper broth, both unexpected treatments for the ingredients.

Indeed the food is so good that this is another great reason to visit high-rise Hutong, aside from the dazzling views that is.

tokyo, japan

The views keep changing at this revolving restaurant, **The Sky**, on the 17th floor of **Hotel New Otani Tokyo** (4-1 Kioi-Cho, Chiyoda-Ku; +81.3.3265 1111; www.newotani.co.jp/en/tokyo) but you can order the food exactly as you like it. The original revolving restaurant used to be the world's largest when it opened four decades ago, and while it has been revamped, the views remain unchanged and Mount Fuji still stands majestic and impressive.

As the restaurant slowly revolves, from its vantage point, you can still see all of Tokyo by night. Here you can order your own buffet. You choose your own ingredients—meat, seafood or vegetables—and the chefs will cook them the way you like it, right before your eyes.

The restaurant calls it a stage kitchen where *teppanyaki* and sushi, along with classic Western dishes are whipped up by Chinese and Western chefs. It's like having your own, and very large, private kitchen and chef!

taipei, taiwan

Even Taipei, a gritty city by some people's standards, looks idyllic from 85 storeys high. This is the view of the city from **Shinyeh 101** (Taipei 101, 85th floor, 7 Xin Yi Road; +886.2.8101 0185; www.shinyeh.com.tw). To get to where you want to go quickly, look for the ultra-fast elevators inside Taipei 101, Asia's tallest skyscraper at 509 m (1,670 ft) high, and ride one to get to the restaurant. After the exhilaration from these high-speed lifts, you will enter a comfortable space with a distinct Asian ambience. The subtle décor of the dining room of Shinyeh 101 however does not detract from the awesome panorama that lies outside its windows. Neither does the food, which is good.

Shinyeh 101 is part of a well-known restaurant chain and while it does not serve gourmet fare, its hearty and honest traditional Taiwanese dishes such as stewed shark's fin soup and stir-fried lobster in XO sauce stand out. The restaurant, which focuses on quality ingredients and healthy food without MSG, offers six set-menu meals rotating on a seasonal basis.

bangkok, thailand

Another superlative experience awaits the diner at the **Sirocco** (State Tower, 1055 Silom Road; +66.2.624 9555; www.lebua.com/bangkok) on the 63rd floor of The Dome at Lebua. You will dine here at the world's highest al fresco rooftop restaurant. And if attention is taken away from the food, which is mostly Mediterranean, you will be mesmerised by a breathtaking theatre of Bangkok and the Chao Phraya river unfolding below. The restaurant also has an amazing open-air **Skybar** on the same level, located on a heart-stopping precipice of a platform.

Seafood lovers will find plenty to choose from the menu here,

THIS PAGE: *The Vertigo Grill and Moon Bar on the 61st storey of the Banyan Tree Bangkok is designed with escalated platforms and low walls, to allow diners a dizzy 360-degree panorama of the city below.*

OPPOSITE (FROM TOP): *100 Century Avenue Restaurant at the Park Hyatt Shanghai is currently the world's highest restaurant; The Sky at Hotel New Otani offers wonderful revolving views of Tokyo from its windows as the restaurant slowly turns.*

high-altitude dining

such as pan-fried scallops with Riesling butter, Alaskan king crab cake with a light mustard cream sauce, and unusually, a stir-fried black pepper crab casserole, giving a fresh take on a classic Asian dish. The restaurant, which also offers live jazz music, made it to *Conde Nast Traveler's* "Hot Tables" and "Hot Nights" list in 2005. Well worth a visit, especially for the views. Be warned, however, that there is a dress code and prices are equally breathtaking. And yes, it can be very windy up in the clouds.

The **Vertigo Grill & Moon Bar** (21/100 South Sathon Road, Sathon; +66.2.679 1200; www.banyantree.com) actually sits on a former helipad, hence its lofty height. Located on the rooftop of the 61-storey **Banyan Tree Bangkok**, it is named after Alfred Hitchcock's famous thriller and is probably not advised for those, well, suffering from a severe case of vertigo.

The restaurant's architecture is designed to take advantage of the views. With its escalated platforms and low walls, it gives the diner a dazzling 360-degree panorama of the city below, dotted with glittering landmarks such as the Grand Palace, Royal Chapel, Chao Phraya River, Wat Pho temple, the National Museum and the Emerald Buddha.

There are three sections—a dining courtyard, a private party lounge and the **Moon Bar**—where you can dine or drink under a canopy of stars. Signature dishes include marinated tuna tartar with salmon roe and grilled sea bass with citrus salsa and cilantro. And yes, despite being located in a frenzied metropolis, it is very quiet up there.

singapore

If you spot a queue at **Swissotel The Stamford**, it is almost certain the people in line are waiting to go up to the **Equinox Restaurant** (2 Stamford Road; +65.6837 3322; www.equinox complex.com). Located on level 70 of the hotel, they are there not only for the brunches, tea and lunch buffets that the iconic restaurant offers, but also for its killer views.

Through its dramatic floor-to-ceiling glass windows, you can see the historical Singapore River winding its way through the city, and on a clear day, even parts of Malaysia and Indonesia. At night, the city turns into a glittering jewel below your feet. Chef Hugh Styles helms the restaurant and he offers exotic flavours and produces signature dishes such as a sashimi of yellowtail kingfish with warm smoked eel, salad of Asian cresses with Kabayaki sauce; an unusual Nova Scotia lobster tartar with salt-cured Tasmanian salmon and a smoky ancho chilli gazpacho with avocado ice cream.

Indeed the restaurant has a multi-faceted appeal. During the afternoons, it is bright and airy as the sun shines through the large expanse of its glass windows. In the evening, it becomes a romantic haven as the nocturnal city comes to glittering life. ~ ST

Dining in the Air

If dining on the rooftop of a building does not appeal, Singapore offers two funky sky dining options—dining in a cable car strung high above Mount Faber (www.mountfaber.com.sg) or in the capsule of the Singapore Flyer (www.singaporeflyer.com), the world's highest observation wheel at 165 m (52.5 ft) above sea level. Personal butler service, gourmet menus and exclusivity is part of the deal. Another exciting option: not dinner, but champagne and breakfast in a hot-air balloon over Jaipur (www.skywaltz.com).

THIS PAGE (CLOCKWISE FROM TOP LEFT): The ambience at the Sirocco bar at Lebua State Tower in Bangkok is romantic and magnificent when all lit up; One of the mouthwatering dishes by Chef Hugh Styles at Swissotel The Stamford— twice baked Manjari chocolate pudding with Kirsch liqueur Sabayon Morello cherry sorbet; Singapore by night from the floor-to-ceiling windows of Equinox at Swissotel The Stamford.
OPPOSITE: The Sky Bar at Sirocco— the spot to admire the winding Chao Phraya River 63 floors below.

highaltitudedining 59

romantic escapades

A romantic experience can be enjoyed in the most unlikely places. You can order such escapades in a padi field, on the beach or even in the heart of a tropical rainforest, at some of the best resorts and hotels in Asia.

Dinner for two is no longer a simple candlelight dinner at a luxurious location. Today, romantic dining can come under many guises, not least of which is eating a meal in bed. This experience can be ordered at least in two different places: one by the beach in Bali at the Four Seasons Resort at Jimbaran Bay and the other, at the Bed Supperclub, right in the heart of Bangkok, where you dine reclining on outsized pillows on mattresses.

Hoteliers and restaurateurs are wooing couples with innovative and thoroughly romantic ways of having that intimate dinner. There are common features to such an experience: al fresco dining amidst dramatic natural scenery; proximity to the ocean or stunning views—whether of a temple, of sweeping natural vistas or of the city lights. A table for two can even be arranged in a rice field, in the middle of a forest or just over a pool deck to create a magical evening, often with the help of tasteful lighting, pampering staff or live entertainment which may include in one case, a storytelling session! And to put you in a romantic mood, the meal may come after a yoga session, as at Banyan Tree Bintan or a foot massage, as at Ubud Hanging Gardens in Bali.

Innovation does not end with the location. The menus that come with such romantic dining packages are often as creative, with unexpected combinations, titillating the senses in more ways than one.

bali, indonesia
The **Ubud Hanging Gardens** (Desa Buahan, Desa Payangan;

+62.361.982 700; www.ubudhanginggardens.com) is set high above the gorge through which runs the Ayung river at Ubud. The hotel is terraced right onto the hillside affording guests panoramic views of the valley and a scenic backdrop of the temple on the opposite side of the gorge.

And if dining against this dramatic backdrop is not enough, you could also opt for dining arrangements at various equally stunning locations. Book a picnic in the middle of a rice field, be led by children to a Balinese village where dinner entertainment is a Balinese *legong* dance, or take a walk through the rainforest to a holy water temple. Here, you will undergo a purification ritual after which you will receive a foot massage before dinner. If all that proves too strenuous, you could just ask for a quartet of *keroncong* musicians to play for you while you dine at a specially set up table at the pool deck. Dining arrangements have to be booked in advance, but that's all it takes to organise romance in paradise.

"Beds on the Beach" is the tantalisingly named gastronomic adventure which **Four Seasons Resort Bali at Jimbaran Bay** (Jimbaran; +62.361.701 010; www.fourseasons.com/jimbaranbay) has created. Literally laidback refined dining, this intimate experience comprises just 25 canopied beds strategically positioned for privacy and great views upon the sands of Jimbaran beach.

To the mellow strains of live jazz music, couples dine in the light of countless candles, interspersed with original Balinese paintings. The five-course dinner includes highlights such as green tea soba sushi rolls and foie gras, and crabmeat and Chorizo risotto. Booking a day ahead is advised.

bintan, indonesia

At **Banyan Tree Bintan** (Jalan Teluk Berembang, Laguna Bintan; +62.770.693 100; www.banyantree.com/bintan), romance begins early at dawn. Couples can enjoy yoga-breakfasts at **One Degree North**, a rustic *balau* wood pavilion located on a mangrove beach area. The programme combines a one-hour yoga session followed by a delicious Indonesian breakfast.

The hotel itself is set right beside the water, so where else but at the beach would you find other romantic dining options? "Massage of the Senses" combines massage with dining. Guests enjoy a pampering body massage by the beach, followed by dinner, all conducted in a private cabana. Otherwise, opt for a live storytelling experience before dinner. "Dinner of the Legend" is an Indonesian *rijstafel* meal inspired by dishes described in the *Violet Rainbow Goddess*, an Indonesian folk tale. This is also set on the beach.

Equally dramatic is "Dinner on the Rocks", dining at a table set high above the rocks to the sound of crashing waves. Golf-loving couples need not even leave the course. "Dinner at Eight" can be set up at the club's signature eighth hole overlooking the South China Sea, complete with a waiter and a chef.

THIS PAGE (FROM TOP): An utterly sensual dinner by the beach at Banyan Tree Bintan; Ubud Hanging Gardens can help organise dinner for two in the padi fields; Or for a change from the mundane indoors, a quiet and cosy meal by the river.
OPPOSITE: A romantic dinner while watching the sunset by the water's edge can be had, also at Banyan Tree Bintan.

romantic escapades

As dusk approaches, a floating platform can be built over the Rock Edge pool to accommodate a table for two, surrounded by reflections of majestic trees. This "Reflection Dinner" is available only for one couple a night.

bangkok, thailand

Truly, what could be more romantic than eating in bed with a loved one, except that here, you do it in the full view of other guests! In the all-white futuristic interior of Bangkok's **Bed Supperclub** (26, Sukhumvit Soi 11, Sukhumvit Road, +66.2.651 3537; www.bedsupperclub.com), you and your partner are invited to kick off your shoes and recline on comfortable mattresses lined with oversized pillows while you dine.

In addition, the themes and entertainment at the club vary every three weeks—it could well be *Karma Sutra* one time and Shanghai Cabaret another. The food is good, too, with heady Thai flavours given an American vibe.

And as befits sleepy-time activities, the experience has been touted as strange but utterly blissful and dreamy.

shanghai, china

The glittering view of the famous Bund may well take your attention away from the food, which is Hong Kong celebrity chef Jereme Leung's take on traditional Shanghai cuisine.

If not, the stylish Art Deco dining room will certainly take your breath away. Located on the fifth floor at the famous Three On the Bund complex, **Whampoa Club** (3 Zhong Shan Dong Yi Road, 5th Floor, Three on the Bund; +86.21.6321 3737; www.threeonthebund.com) is special for its sumptuous rich décor.

A large chandelier greets you at the end of the entrance hall, which is lit by jewel-like emerald green wall lamps. The entire air is that of romance, sophistication and elegance. You will feel pampered, cosseted and certainly be seduced by the meal to come—modern Shanghainese dishes that exemplify Chinese classics with a contemporary twist. Romantic dining does not come any better.

singapore

Mount Faber in Singapore was long a lovers' haunt, so it is fitting that **The Jewel Box** (109 Mount Faber Road; +65.6377 9688; www.mountfaber.com.sg) was built to take advantage of its lush greenery and outstanding views of the city. There are five dining outlets at this iconic hilltop destination, all named after gems—Empress Jade, Sapphire, Emerald Lodge, Moonstone and Black Opal. Managed by Mount Faber Leisure Group, they offer different cuisines and dining styles, but the best must be its newest addition, **Empress Jade**, actually an airy dining platform built around a giant Angsana tree. The restaurant also offers an unsurpassed view of the harbour and the city skyline.

For a more unorthodox way to dine with your loved one, you could also book a sky-dining experience in a cable car. Currently being refurbished, the cars will be ready in the first quarter of 2010. The highly popular three-course meal takes one-and-a-half hours, enough time to pop that question incidentally!

the maldives

A table set over water and under the stars—you don't need much more than this for romantic dining in the Maldives. First, get yourself in the mood at **Sip**, **W Retreat & Spa's** (whotels.com/Maldives) superbly located open-air cocktail bar. Here as you recline on loungers, you can catch the best sunset views while sipping bubbly with caviar and oysters.

Then mosey over to **Fish**, its signature seafood restaurant, with both indoor and outdoor seating, where you can enjoy seafood with an Asian flair, such as ikura sushi with caper berries on a kimchi emulsion.

The resort is set on private Fesdu Island, in North Ari Atoll in the Maldives. And yes, it is common to see shooting stars here. ~ ST

Oysters, a Food for Love?

Oysters have long been labelled an aphrodisiacal food. While the belief had Italian lover Cassanova gulping down a dozen oysters every day or so the story goes, truly there is no proven link between oysters and romance.

Its reputation as an aphrodisiac probably came about because of the similarity of its flesh to a certain region of the female anatomy. But there is a more prosaic connection—zinc. Oysters contain large amounts of zinc and this element helps counter a falling sperm count, which is probably how oysters became known as aphrodisiacs.

THIS PAGE (FROM TOP): *Diners can recline on loungers and catch the best sunset views at Sip, W Retreat & Spa; An intimate dinner at W Retreat may well include bubbly cocktails with caviar and oysters.*

OPPOSITE: *Feel pampered, cosseted and certainly be seduced by the sumpuous art deco space and by the modern Shanghainese meal to come in the VIP room, Whampoa Club in Shanghai.*

organic food + spa cuisine

There is no need to eat junk food while on vacation. You can now find holiday destinations dedicated to health—where the cuisine is prepared following various health principles, or even left raw.

When supermarkets dedicate a section of their shelves to purely organic vegetables, you know that the concept has taken hold. Some may argue, however, that this is not new to Asia, where organic eating has always been the norm in rural villages. There the chickens still roam free and the vegetables are grown on soil that has not seen any commercial pesticides nor fertilisers.

Despite recent research findings questioning the perceived benefits of organic food, the belief that it is better for health is not going to go away. In many Asian cities today, you will find households relying on regular organic vegetable deliveries and a proliferation of organic cafés. Some countries have even set aside plots of land for organic or at least pesticide-free farming. Today, retail organic markets and shops can be found in cities ranging from Bali to Bangkok to Singapore.

In Bali, there are at least three organic stores. Ubud started its first Organic Farmers' Market in November 2006, selling fresh produce and other locally produced goodies. There are similar markets in Sanur and Kerobokan. In Kerobokan, the Sunrise Market is where you find many new, organic locally produced items. Selling fruit and vegetables from four farms, it also offers herbs, free-range eggs, breads, fertilisers, neem tree saplings, neem oil, sea salt, coffee and preserves.

In Bangkok, Lemon Farm is the best-known health food co-operative in Thailand. Established in 1999, it has been helping small farmers grow and sell organic produce. It also sells organic and pesticide-free products such as jams, nuts, teas, salad dressings and the like.

At Bon Marche, an upscale outdoor market located in northern Bangkok away from the tourist trek, local farmers have set up stalls selling fresh produce. And at probably Bangkok's largest farmer's markets, Talat Aw Taw Kaw, you can buy just about any organic fruit and vegetable, as well as dried foods too.

People are increasingly concerned about their health and well-being, and are conscious about what they eat. Many are making changes to eating habits, albeit small, to their diet—whether it is eating brown rice, using healthier oils or removing obvious fat from meats. While carbohydrate intakes are reduced, more white meat such as fish is consumed.

In Singapore, the two major supermarket chains, namely Fairprice Finest and Cold Storage, have organic sections devoted to fruit, vegetables and even meat, while independent shops such as Supernature in Park House and Brown Rice Paradise at Tanglin Mall offer dedicated shop space for such products. New entrant Himalaya Organic Farm even holds an organic vegetables sale every Thursday and Friday afternoon from their Hume Heights location. For a list of vegetables available, email cynthiahoefer@mac.com. It behoves the best chefs therefore to take note of such a concern. Hotels such as the Four Seasons in Singapore have started eco-vegetable patches to supply ingredients for their tables.

Indeed if you are running a restaurant, let alone a spa café, it makes sense to think seriously about spa cuisine, which is organic food prepared according to healthy principles, be it low-fat, low-carb, low-sugar or even left raw, to preserve the nutrients.

At the other end of the spectrum, some people also believe in eating according to one's Ayurvedic body type or one's blood group. Aware of this growing concern over nutrition, Singapore hotelier Christina Ong's chain of Glow Juice Bar and Café offers spa cuisine in the cities where her COMO hotels are located. Being standalone outlets, they make it easy for those committed to health to eat a guilt-free diet even when not at a spa.

batangas, philippines

Eating at **The Farm** (119 Barangay Tipakan; +63.2.696 3795; www.thefarm.com.ph) is a revelation. Yes, you still get pastas and cream soups, cookies and ice-cream, but little has been cooked. To be accurate the ratio of raw-to-cooked foods at every meal is 85:15, hence the restaurant name, **Alive!** And this principle is followed religiously because raw foods contain enzymes that cooked foods do not.

Here, the dishes are composed of almost entirely uncooked fruits, vegetable, grains and nuts. Using methods such as soaking, blending, dehydrating and culturing, the kitchen is able to transform vegetables, nuts, seeds and fruits into appetising culinary offerings.

A centre for holistic healing and wellness, this sprawling complex,

THIS PAGE (CLOCKWISE FROM TOP LEFT): *At Singapore's Glow Café, you can order organic juices; Glow Café's tofu burgers; Chef Bruno Correa from Four Seasons Singapore makes use of the organic herbs and vegetable grown in the hotel's garden; The Farm in the Philippines uses methods such as dehydration to make fruit and nuts crunchy.*
OPPOSITE: *Farmers' markets such as this abound in Asian cities.*

organic food + spa cuisine

just two hours outside Manila, has been described as a life-changing retreat. Guests can expect customised wellness and detox treatment programmes that include "living food", a plant-based, primarily raw-food diet. As you dine at the open-air terrace within the lush jungle at The Farm, you will agree that it is an experience you have to taste to believe.

bali, indonesia

It is fitting that one of the most committed health retreats in Asia should be sited in Ubud, the spiritual heart of Bali. Here, on a sprawling forested estate of architectural award-winning luxury villas, never far from the sound of falling water—the mighty Ayung River thundering in the valley below—is the **COMO Shambhala Estate** at Begawan Giri (see pages 120–121). It offers a holistic approach towards nutrition, matching lifestyle, health and goals with recommended programmes where the core emphasis is cuisine.

Upon arriving, a resident nutritionist assesses the guest's diet. Recommendations are made, working with the executive chef and an Ayurvedic doctor (if on an Ayurvedic diet.) The prescribed therapy could include detox, body treatments, yoga and meditation, and a reworked diet.

Here the cuisine is organic, sourced locally and delivered from field to table with minimum delay. Tastes are catered for with a variety of cuisines appearing on the menu, from Indian to Balinese to Italian, with even a raw food diet. The menu accommodates all kinds of food intolerances (soy milk instead of cow's milk and yeast-free breads) and feature little salt. Raw honey replaces sugar, and raw fruit and vegetables are important. Dishes might include a lime leaf, chilli and coconut curry of fern tips and cherry tomatoes, and seared mahi-mahi with baby zucchini, chickpea and mint salad with preserved lemon and sumac dressing. Dining in paradise is probably much like this.

For a less austere approach towards healthy eating, head for Bali's award-winning **Maya Ubud Resort & Spa** (see pages 124–125). Leisurely spread over hillside gardens, located between a steep river valley and green rice fields, it is a combination of contemporary style and ethnic chic.

The **Spa at Maya** offers exotic and invigorating treatments in thatched pavilions overhanging the fast flowing Petanu River which runs through the valley below. Complementing the treatments is the exquisite spa cusine served at the **River Café** with its timbered floors and open kitchen design. The indoor-outdoor café offers both healthy fusion and spa cuisine based on a selection of low-calorie and vitamin-rich food such as tofu, green asparagus, salmon, scallop and seaweed. The vegetables on the menu are taken from selected organic farms in Bali and as far as possible, the restaurant substitutes more healthy ingredients such as unrefined sugars, fresh fruit nectars, natural Balinese sea salt and extra virgin olive oil in its dishes.

hua hin, thailand

You could call **Chiva-Som** (73/4 Petchkasem Road; +66.3.253 6536; www.chivasom.com) a healing hotel, albeit a luxurious one, offering award-winning cuisine. Sited on the beachfront of Hua Hin just three hours south of Bangkok by car, the resort offers unique Thai hospitality and luxurious accommodation, nestled within lush tropical gardens.

Widely regarded as one of the leading destination spas in the world, Chiva-Som offers extensive fitness, spa and holistic health facilities to help its guests relax, restore and rejuvenate. Its personalised programmes and treatments blend Eastern philosophies with Western diagnostic skills.

Renowned for its spa cuisine, the food is so delicious that you will not notice that it's healthy. The flavours come from a judicious use of fresh herbs and spices, and well-chosen produce. While restraint is called for in the ingredients used in some recipes, its philosophy is that taste ought not to be compromised.

Those on diet plans can choose from low-fat, lower-calorie and vegetarian options, while wheat-, gluten-, dairy- and sugar-free dishes are integrated into the menus. Most dishes are suitable for diabetics or vegans, unless otherwise stated. Dishes that contain wheat or dairy products are also clearly indicated, as befits a place of healing.

uttaranchal, india

Food tailored just for the guest is an integral part of the treatment at the **Ananda Spa** in **Ananda-in-the-Himalayas** (Narendra Nagar, Tehri

THIS PAGE (CLOCKWISE FROM TOP LEFT): At Chiva-Som, menus offered are not only healthy, but also delicious; While there may be restraint in the ingredients used, there is none in the tastes served up, such as these exquisite leaf wraps at Chiva-Som; guests of the resort can also attend cooking classes on healthy cuisine.

OPPOSITE (FROM TOP): At COMO Shambala, the cuisine is tailored to individual guests' health needs; The spa menu of the Maya Ubud consists of nutritious juices; A healthy seared fish dish available at the Maya Ubud.

organicfood+spacuisine

organic food + spa cuisine

Garhwal; +91.137.822 7500; www.anandaspa.com). Located in the heart of the picturesque Himalayan mountains, just 260 km (162 miles) from New Delhi, the resort, once the residence of the Maharaja of Tehri Garhwal, now sees tourists from all over the world.

Aside from its menu of body and beauty treatments that integrate traditional Indian Ayurvedic systems with contemporary Western spa approaches, its food philosophy is based on the idea that everyone needs a customised diet. Instead of generic low-fat, low-carbohydrate or low-sugar meal plans, diets are fashioned according to the Ayurvedic body types that each of us belong to—*vata* (air and space), *pitta* (fire and water) or *kapha* (water and earth). While menu selections can be Indian, Asian or Western, the food is always exotically flavoured, but low-calorie and highly nutritious, all cooked with less salt and spices.

The spa cuisine menu also restricts food high in cholesterol and relies on wholegrain and high-fibre carbohydrates. Freshness is of the essence—the chefs source fresh fish from the river and vegetables from their own herbal garden.

krabi, thailand
The towering majestic limestone karsts or outcrops make **Phulay Bay, a Ritz-Carlton Reserve** (111 Moo 3 Nongthalay; +66.7.562 8111; reserve.ritzcarlton.com/phulay_bay/) in Krabi a natural wonder. The first Ritz-Carlton Reserve property in the world, its premium label for one-of-a-kind boutique resorts in unique settings, it is clear why this southern Thailand location was chosen. It is a captivating corner of the world, where glistening sands and blue skies converge with the Andaman Sea. Add to it a coastline flecked with more than 200 islands, surrounded by a national forest with rugged rock formations and hidden waterfalls, Phulay Bay is a gem of a place.

But there is more to it than its spectacular setting. Its spa, **ESpa**, employs an "Inside Out" approach towards health where you complement your therapies by taking care of yourself from the inside.

At its spa café called **Raw**, the cooking methods employed make sure that the natural attributes of food are preserved. By serving most of the food raw or cooked very slowly at very low temperatures, all the nutrients remain intact. And of course organic and fresh produce are used to create tempting, healthy and incredibly tasty menus as befits a spa located in such a beautiful and natural setting.

> **Eating Right for Your Blood Type**
>
> Advocates of this dietary approach claim that there is no one diet that fits one and all as an individual's blood type will determine which foods are neutral, beneficial or even harmful to the body.
>
> Created by naturopath Dr Peter D'Adamo who describes the diet in his book *Eat Right For Your Type*, people with blood type A have a digestive system intolerant to animal proteins, while those with blood type O need to consume red meat to maintain good health. See www.dadamo.com for more information.

phulbari, nepal

For a totally rustic retreat, the Nepalese farmhouse, **Organic Himalaya Pvt Ltd** (Phulbari-5, Kavre; +65.6468 3127; cynthiahoefer@mac.com/lian8700@singnet.com.sg; www.apavilla.com) run by a Singapore-based couple, Hans and Cynthia Hoefer, offers a charming back-to-basics experience. Their hilltop farmhouse at Phulbari is situated on the loftiest point at 1,800 m (5,906 ft) in the district of Kavre, southeast of the Kathmandu Valley. Naturally it offers some of the best views of the Himalayan peaks.

Their property sprawls over 10 acres (4 hectares) of organically prepared land, filled with marigolds, dahlias, rhododendrons, wild weeds and orchids. In and around the hill are five ponds, fruit trees and plots that yield a mixed variety of radish, pumpkin, carrot, leeks, eggplant and other vegetables. Guests at the farm eat whatever is grown on the land.

The meals are best described as Nepali-vegetarian, but guests can also order free-range chicken from another village. Already the farm produces its own buffalo milk, duck's eggs, oils, grains, bread and soon, its own butter and olive oil. Best described as a farm stay, guests put up in rustic cottages and can either cook their own meals using the organic farm produce or rely on the farm's cook to prepare nutritious Nepali food throughout their stay. ~ ST

THIS PAGE: A back to basics experience: Nepali women are winnowing grain in the villages set against picturesque mountains.

OPPOSITE: In Ayurveda, spices complement diets tailored for specific body types.

organicfood+spacuisine 69

plating + food styling

Culinary experts in Asia share tips on how to set off dishes to their best advantage, making them a feast for the palate and eye. Complex plating styles with dramatic embellishing are giving way to natural, fresh elements, topped with edible garnishing.

Food styling has slowly evolved from stark, traditional assemblies on oversized white plates and skyscraper-high stacks of towering food to simple deconstructed dishes. These days, classic tableware has been replaced by unconventional "plates"—usually made from textured stones and wood to glass and even tiles—as a canvas to flaunt food art. Essentially, plating and food styling is all about respect for ingredients and the food as well as the ability to deliver the wow factor when the masterpiece finally arrives at your table.

asian inflections

Tung Lok restaurants were the first to introduce individual plating for modern Chinese dishes in Singapore. **Sam Leong**, Corporate Chef/ Director of Kitchens, **Tung Lok Group** (www.tunglok.com) says: "When we started the trend about a decade ago, other restaurants were still using traditional presentation or communal plating methods."

He adds that modern Chinese presentation is going back to the basics. "We are putting more emphasis on using garnishes on the plate not only to improve the look of the dish visually, but also to complement the taste. More efforts are put into plating to ensure everything on the plate is edible and also looks appealing. The trend is towards less frills and more emphasis on the main ingredient."

At **Yan Toh Heen** (18 Salisbury Road; +852.2313 2323; hongkong-ic.dining.intercontinental.com), **Intercontinental Hong Kong**, the Chinese cuisine is simple yet elegant, displayed on expensive chinaware to tease the eye and the palate. **Lau Yiu Fai**, Chinese Executive Chef shares his view: "While a great deal of our menu focuses on traditional Cantonese cuisine, we like to introduce modern presentation for many of our dishes. For this, we use a variety of contemporary chinaware. I also like dishes which are colourful. Some of our items are meant to 'wow' our guests. For example, our chilled mango soup with pomelo is served in jade bowls with dry ice, creating a billowing cloud-like effect."

Instead of garnishing the dish heavily, **Siu Hin Chi**, Executive Chinese Chef of **T'ang Court** at **The Langham, Hong Kong** (see pages 108–109) prefers to keep it clean and neat. He brings out the best flavour and appearance of the ingredient using his finely honed cooking techniques. Good Cantonese dishes are meant to be served at the right temperature—fresh, flavourful, aromatic and aesthetically pleasing. Chef Siu notes that it takes great experience to understand the characteristics of each ingredient. His secret to a perfect dish is to ensure that the momentum is not interrupted in the middle of cooking because it may sometimes change the texture and taste of the food due to poor timing and uneven temperature.

Chef Siu's classic Chinese garnishes in the past have included intricately carved items such as carrot, turnip, tomato and radish, and even the use of orchids. These are usually not eaten. However, over the years, Chef Siu has abandoned these traditional decorations in favour of edible garnishes like flash-cooked mustard leaf or crab roe.

In Kuala Lumpur, **Bijan Bar & Restaurant** (see pages 140–141) is one of the few places that serves fine Malay food plated in a modern style. Chef de Cuisine, **Zulkifli Razali** is of the opinion that there should be no crowding of food on the plate. Separation between items allow the inherent beauty of each item to shine through. "For curry dishes, if possible, the main meat should be elevated by placing it on other starch items or pineapple chunks so that the meat does not sink below the curry. Sauces are served separately in ramekins which allow the meat's crust to stay crisp while offering a contrast to the other items."

When **Shinji Morihara**, Executive Chef of **Inagiku** at **Fairmont Singapore** (see pages 170–171) plates his dishes, the ingredients always strictly follow the traditional and authentic Japanese style of presentation. For example, there must always be red, yellow and green vegetables accompanying red meat *teppanyaki*. "These guidelines will help define the 'seasonal image' of every meal—vegetables are used to reflect the changing seasons, and garnishes such as cherry blossoms and autumn persimmon leaves will set the tone for diners to understand the seasonal change in flavours," he says.

Morihara adds that a sense of modernism is incorporated by the use of plates made of materials like glass and ceramic. "I have refined the way each of my dishes is presented to reflect the seasons in a subtle and elegant manner." Using modern

THIS PAGE (CLOCKWISE FROM TOP): Inagiku's elegant winter kaiseki sashimi platter; Bijan's steamed palm sugar sponge cake is served with homemade coconut ice cream and palm sugar syrup on the side; Tang Court's baked seafood rice in crab shell is simply presented sans heavy garnishing.
OPPOSITE: Tung Lok's crispy-fried oyster glazed with champagne mousse and crispy bean crumps.

plating + food styling

style service ware (some not specifically designed for Japanese cuisine) allows the creative chef to explore new and innovative ways of plating the ingredients.

au naturel

Many chefs choose a minimal style of presentation instead of overloading the plates with heavy sauces and heaps of ingredients. They do not, however, compromise on the food's integrity. **Norbert Kostner**, Executive Chef of **Mandarin Oriental Bangkok** (48 Oriental Avenue; +66.2.659 9000; www.mandarinoriental.com) is one of them. His presentation style is elegant but simple, clean but not stark. "The best food is still the one that comes from the pan to the serving plate and then quickly served," said the experienced chef.

Meanwhile, over in Bali, Executive Chef **Philip Mimbimi** of **nutmegs restaurant – dining at hu'u** (see pages 128–129) believes that if the product comes from a good supplier, and it's fresh and seasoned or cooked properly, it will present itself. "I take advantage of as many quality local ingredients and resources as possible. I use the passion of the fisherman, the herb gardener, glass artisan and ceramic craftsman, and in turn create a plate that will make an impression on the person who is paying you to cook for them."

Executive Chef **Darren Lauder** of **Nusa Dua Beach Hotel & Spa** (see pages 130–131) echoes this sentiment. The way he styles his food is to let the food speak for itself. "I like to keep it simple and I don't want too many things to confuse you. Whatever garnish I use on the plate represent and enhance the dish." For him, as long as it is the best, freshest produce he is serving, the rest of the plate will fall into place.

contrast + balance

Marrying flavours, colours and textures are styling requisites for many chefs. Chef **Chris Salans** of **Mozaic** (Jln Raya Sanggingan, Ubud; +62.361.975 768; www.mozaic-bali.com) says that one needs to take into account the textures of different ingredients when plating. For instance separate crispy items from wet ones so that each remains intact, and layer certain items to make sure that a soft element is married with a crispy one. He continues: "Then comes flavour, which is the most important. Imagine a dish with six different flavours. Think about how to layer or separate various items so that when a guest eats the food, the flavours meld together."

According to Italian Chef **Fabrizio Bigi** of **Prego** at **The Westin Beijing Financial Street** (9B Financial Street, Xicheng District; +86.10.6606 8866; www.starwoodhotels.com), plating is all about balancing various shapes and colours. It must be clean and neat, and the focus of the diner should be drawn directly to the main ingredient presented with the dish.

For instance, for his signature dish, risotto with scallop and wasabi, the chef plates the risotto using a ring to create a perfect round shape. He then places a slightly blackened pan-seared scallop on top and then dabs it with a spot of green wasabi to sharpen the flavour. Then he finishes the dish with flourish of leek chips for a crispy bite.

Richard Millar, Chef De Cuisine at **Conrad Bali** (see pages 132–133) says that he always starts simple, and considers the main attributes of the dish—colours, textures, space on the plate, and most importantly, the flavour profiles. "I am a big believer in visual appeal; the dish has to be designed with the diner in mind. The food cannot be stacked too high on the plate so that it splatters on the diner if it falls. Also, you have to keep in mind that once the diner puts his fork into the dish, the look of that pretty dish is really going to change. Basically I stick to around three to five different flavours on each plate and try to have a variety of textures and tastes."

He points out that the environment too helps to define a successful dish. "I take into consideration the restaurant's interior design: contemporary, classic or Asian. Also, I don't want the diner to look at a dish and think that eight people have had their hands over his food. The plate's main element is to highlight the ingredients of the dish and not confuse it with the overuse of colours or flavours."

Executive Chef **Ronald Ngan** of **Jewel** at **The Westin Beijing Financial Street** (9B Financial Street, Xicheng District; +86.10.6606 8866; www.starwoodhotels.com) puts it more simply: "The key element in plating is the thought process. A chef needs to think out of the box in terms of the way the ingredients are cut, the combination of ingredients, colour of food, and shape of cutlery among others. There is no one way to plate your dish, and inspiration will be drawn from all the above factors."   ~ AV

Plating Trends

Many chefs are eschewing old school plating where dishes are garnished with a single sprig of parsley. Chefs today strive to make their dishes look as good as they taste. Sometimes their culinary artwork may even be too beautiful to eat. Many artistic chefs use the plate as a canvas for their ephemeral masterpiece, using tools such as tiny offset spatulas and tweezers to embellish the dish with precision. To create a lasting impression, however, sound techniques, top quality ingredients and excellent flavour profiles are still vital.

THIS PAGE: Westin Beijing Financial Street Prego's food presentation is all about balancing shapes and colours.

OPPOSITE: (CLOCKWISE FROM TOP): Mandarin Oriental Bangkok's Executive Chef Norbert Kostner prefers a simple, clean and elegant plating style; Conrad Bali's chef considers the colours, textures and flavour profiles for his dishes; Nutmegs' Chef Philip Mimbimi chooses to focus on fresh produce to make an impression.

food festivals + gourmet summits

One common bond unifies the glittering chain of Asian cities such as Hong Kong, Singapore, Kuala Lumpur and Bangkok—the ability to satisfy, even satiate, the most discerning gourmets. To show off their culinary pedigrees, annual food festivals and gourmet summits are organised at these cities, drawing celebrity chefs as well as avid foodies and wine buffs.

singapore

Singapore has always prided itself as a gourmet hub; its multiracial culture happily brewing culinary heritages drawn from its first immigrants. In its last few decades as a bustling financial and business centre, Singapore has created a sophisticated veneer of polished representations of the best Asian and Western cuisines. Round-the-clock, food can be found at its famous food courts serving the best of heartland favourites. Five-star degustation meals by award-winning chefs are available at any of Singapore's countless luxury hotels. Globalised fast-food chains, casual coffee shops, haute-cuisine eateries, boutique restaurants—all these and a lot more make Singapore a veritable gourmet paradise.

There are two major events on the Singaporean culinary calendar. The first is the **World Gourmet Summit** (WGS) (www.worldgourmetsummit.com)—a line up of gastronomic spectaculars showcasing fine cuisine, celebrated wines and unique dining experiences. First mooted a decade ago by a chef-entrepreneur to recognise the skills and talents of his colleagues in the region and beyond, the World Gourmet Summit has grown far beyond that mission. It has garnered the support of the Singapore Tourism Board (STB) which promotes it as part of its annual festival calendar.

The World Gourmet Summit is now more than a food festival platform for *haute*-cuisine in Singapore. It is also a networking opportunity for celebrity television chefs, food and beverage industry leaders as well as budding chefs who compete for its prestigious awards. Established chefs rate inception into the World Gourmet Summit Hall of Fame as a notable achievement. Events at the World Gourmet Summit now include gourmet safaris, vintner dinners, celebrity dinners, chef master classes, seminars and workshops.

Some of the celebrity chefs inducted into the WGS Hall of Fame include Singapore's own Justin Quek and Sam Leong, while guest chefs have included such luminaries as the emissary of Chinese cooking Martin Yan, Bob Blumer of *Surreal Gourmet* fame, culinary veteran Charlie Trotter and Australia's Tetsuya Wakuda.

In 2010, London's latest Michelin-starred Alex Chow and Australia's wunderchefs Greg Doyle and Grant King took the stage and showed off the latest Asian fusion trends and the skills and talents of the increasingly younger master chefs.

The annual **Singapore Food Festival** (www.singaporefoodfestival.com), organised by the STB, is designed as a tourism tool. It aims lower rather than higher, setting it apart from WGS. The month-long festival uses weekly core events, themed celebrations, culinary workshops and competitions to celebrate the local perennial favourites Singapore is famous for.

The tourism board has actually drawn up a list of Singapore favourite foods, and the food festival tends to revolve around the famous 10: *bak kut teh* (herbal pork rib "tea"), carrot (or radish) cake, *char kway teow* (fried rice noodles with cockles), chilli crab and black pepper crab, fish head curry, Hainanese chicken rice, Nonya *laksa*, *rojak* (fruit and vegetable salad tossed in an aromatic prawn-paste dressing), *roti prata* (Indian savoury pancakes) and satay (Malay meat kebabs).

In 2009, the Singapore Food Festival adopted Straits Chinese or Peranakan food as its theme. Peranakan cuisine is unique to the region and is the fusion food of Chinese settlers who inter-married into the native Malay community from 1400s onwards.

kuala lumpur
Kuala Lumpur's food scene is just as diverse, and because Malaysia has a larger and more free-ranging cultural hinterland, food in this country taps on both immigrant Chinese, Indian and Eurasian communities as well as dialectic Malay groups drawn from both Peninsular and Borneo Malaysia such as those from Aceh, Negeri Sembilan, Kalimantan and even the predominantly Muslim islands off the southern Philippines. East Malaysian food has been influenced by various tribes such as the Iban. Even the Chinese cuisines of Sabah and Sarawak are uniquely their own, having adapted to the plentiful spices of the land, in particular, pepper.

Peninsular Malaysia's west and east coast are again divided by more than the central mountain range, and Indonesian, Thai and Pacific island influences can be detected in its village kitchens. In the city, localised regional dishes are enjoying a renaissance, with a constant crop of restaurant and food-stall owners ever proud to show off the cooking of their hometowns. From the food courts in

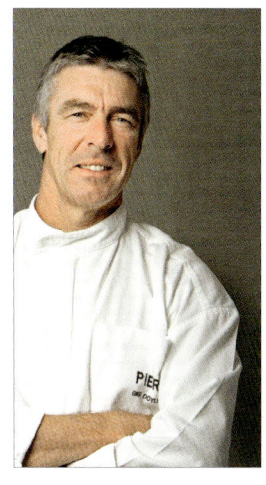

THIS PAGE (CLOCKWISE FROM TOP LEFT): Executive Chef Grant King (left) and Three Hats Chef Greg Doyle (above) are some of the talents who will show off their culinary innovations at the WGS 2010; The Song of India's Chef Milind Sovani (left) has been a regular in Singapore's past WGS and will be showcasing his talent again in 2010.
OPPOSITE: One of Singapore's favourite local fare—satay with peanut sauce.

food festivals + gourmet summits 75

food festivals + gourmet summits

the city centre to smaller restaurants in exclusive food and entertainment enclaves in the suburban outskirts, a year-round celebration of Malaysian cuisine is sustained and maintained.

Kuala Lumpur, like its neighbour Singapore, also enjoys the patronage of world-class restaurants and international chefs. These culinary masters congregate every year at the **Malaysian International Gourmet Festival** (MIGF) (www.migf.com), usually held in November, to create an event to remember for a glittering gathering of local royalty, business aristocracy, stars on the jet-set register, as well as celebrities and entertainment moguls from film and television. This has become both a social as well as a culinary event.

The MIGF proclaimed its mission from day one—to grow the local fine-dining population; to create a sustained interest in the local fine-dining scene; and to establish Malaysia as an international culinary tourism destination. The festival is almost one decade old, so it has enjoyed success in a city known for its devotion to eating.

While the MIGF mostly lauds local talent, its list of guest chefs each year reads like a who's who of the *haute*-cuisine arena. Almost all of the top hotels in Kuala Lumpur are represented, with their executive chefs showing off the best skills found in their kitchens.

Some of the more high profile chefs who have taken the stage during the Festival include the baby-faced Chef de Cuisine Khairul Ghazali of Bunga Emas restaurant in the Royal Chulan Kuala Lumpur hotel.

Chef Khairul is recognised as one of the more influential in introducing local Malaysian elements into fine dining. Another well known local chef is Ibrahim Salim, the chef who helms Tuscany, the Italian restaurant at Putrajaya Marriott Hotel. He is another home-grown chef who has shown exceptional talent in crossing and blurring the boundaries between local and Western cuisine.

thailand

Thailand is another country where excellent street food and exotic shopping bargains enjoy a global following. Here, too, a perennial feast is found in its city streets day and night, all year round. Thailand's only formal food festival, the **World Gourmet Festival** (WGF), is devoted to fine-dining establishments, with multinational hotel chains such as the Four Seasons Bangkok taking the lead in organising an annual gathering of visiting chefs to conduct workshops and master classes.

The WGF has been held for over a decade now, and some of the world's best chefs have gathered under one roof to celebrate more than one night in Bangkok. Visiting chefs in 2009 included Australia's Christine Manfield from the Universal Café. An outstanding chef, Christine Mansfield has also written several books on spices and herbs, including the Asian ones so loved in Thai cuisine.

In 2009, the festival also invited David Thompson—the doyen of Thai cooking who has been conferred many awards and much honour. Chef Thompson has done more than

THIS PAGE (CLOCKWISE FROM TOP LEFT):
Australian Chef Christine Mansfield (top left) wows with her Asian-inspired dish (right); Chef Graham Elliot Bowles (centre right) and Chef Francois Payard both participated at Bangkok's WGF 2009; A creation by Chef Bowles.
OPPOSITE (FROM TOP): The annual Hong Kong Food Festival attracts foodies and gourmets alike; The Hong Kong Food and Wine Year 2009 event at the West Kowloon Waterfront Promenade.

anyone to bring Thai cooking to an international audience, both with his Michelin star-awarded restaurant in London and his Sydney restaurants.

His definitive cookbook, *Thai Food*, has been universally recognised as the ultimate tome on Thai culinary knowledge—a fact that the Thai authorities also appreciated by making him, officially, an ambassador of the Thai culinary arts.

hong kong

In Hong Kong, the government and tourist association have taken great pains to promote and push the city as a major gourmet holiday spot. The annual **Hong Kong Food Festival** (jointly organised by the Hong Kong Convention and Exhibition Centre and Hongkong-Asia Exhibition (Holdings) Ltd) is a binge-fest of offers, promotions, tours and master classes put together with finesse and good taste. Almost every major hotel and restaurant in the city participates, and the choices of both high food and low food are bewildering.

Not satisfied with a gourmet gathering of just one month, the organisers marked 2009 as the **Hong Kong Food and Wine Year** (www.discoverhongkong.com/hkfoodandwineyear) from 30 Oct to 1 Nov, and officially made the city's favourite pastime an all-year-round period of indulgence.

Hong Kong also organises regional gatherings for everyday foodies and dedicated gourmets, wine-lovers and grape connoisseurs, and amateur cooks and professional chefs. In addition, there are industry gatherings such as the Food and Hotel Asia conventions, and newer shows such as Wine for Asia.

The well known **Food and Hotel Asia** (www.foodnhotelasia.com) is a popular trend-spotting event and this exhibition, established since 1978, is a launching pad for many new gourmet products, equipment and even cooking techniques. It is also the major sourcing platform for hospitality trade buyers, popular with both professionals and the curious public. Food and Hotel Asia also presents **Wines & Spirits Asia** every year in tandem with its food shows. The latter, however, faces a strong challenge from **Wine For Asia** (www.wineforasia.com), currently noted as arguably the most comprehensive international wine exhibition in the region, although it is a relative newcomer.

These wine shows are very much a reflection of the budding appreciation for wines in Asia and the events take pains to make wine-pairing and wine education workshops accessible to the general public. The **Hong Kong International Wines and Spirits Fair**, on the other hand, organised by its trade and development council, tends to veer towards suppliers and vendors.

If you like to eat, cook and drink well, your calendar can be filled to the brim with city-hops in search of the best food and wine festivals. Asia is waking up to its own excellent cuisines, and it wants to share this with the rest of the world. ~ PDL

cookery schools

Signing up for a cookery lesson while on holiday is a good way of getting under the skin of a destination. Cooking is much more than just learning a new recipe, it opens a window into a country's history and culture.

When you've seen all the sights and lazed long enough on the beach, the next thing to do is to sign up for a cookery class. They are all the rage these days—especially if sited at a memorable location—as holidaymakers look for something more meaningful to take away from their visit.

For the serious cook, there are full-blown specialist holidays that include intensive cookery classes combined with visits to produce markets and purveyors of food. But even for the casual visitor, cooking opportunities abound and classes can be taken at dedicated schools, at someone's home, or even the hotel or resort that one is staying at.

At Kumarakom in Kerala, the cook on board the houseboat is regularly prevailed upon to show within the narrow confines of the boat how to turn out a mean Keralan chicken curry; the Chinese chef at a hotel in the ex-Portuguese colony of Macau can demonstrate, of all things, *caldo verde*, a green kale and potato soup, for guests; while the Culinary Academy at Singapore's Raffles Hotel (www.raffles.com) offers classes not only in Asian cooking, but also Italian, French and Mediterranean.

For the non-professional gourmet traveller, attending a cooking lesson can prove to be thoroughly fulfilling as classes often go beyond mere instruction to offer a complete gourmet experience. While these classes generally teach the cuisines of the city or country that they are in—Thai cooking in Bangkok and Balinese in Bali—other characteristics may make the lesson unforgettable.

In Beijing, for example, you can learn Chinese cooking techniques in an old *hutong* (alley) house. In Bangkok, the lesson could be had in a Thai family home complete with a herb garden, while in Bali, the cookery lesson may be preceded by a visit to the local produce market. An appreciation of the destination's history, environment and its heritage all merge as part of the experience.

The move towards healthier, even raw cuisines is not ignored in the kitchen classrooms of Asia. The ardent followers of raw cuisine can learn this skill in at least three Asian countries—Thailand, Philippines and Bali (rawfoodbali.com/raw-food-retreats) where health and spa resorts advocating the benefits of raw cuisine have started. Advocates believe that beneficial natural enzymes in food are destroyed with cooking and promote what they call living food where nothing is heated beyond 47°C (118°F).

singapore

Unusually for urban Singapore, this cooking studio is housed in a black and white colonial building within a green and leafy suburb. Inside however, **Palate Sensations** (1 Westbourne Road, Wessex Estate, #03-05; +65.6479 9025; www.palatesensations.com) offers a state-of-the-art open concept kitchen where hands-on cooking lessons for up to 25 participants are held.

Reflecting the multiracial nature of Singapore society, the regularly scheduled classes feature not only Asian but also Western cuisines. Hence, classes on Singapore, Chinese, Malay, Peranakan, Indian and Thai cuisines with classic dishes such as *ayam buah keluak* (chicken with black Indonesian nuts) and chilli crab are regularly featured together with Swiss, French, Italian and even macrobiotic dishes. And depending on which one you choose, you could be learning how to cook a fancy four-course dinner or just baking cookies or cupcakes for friends. The teachers include experienced chefs, some of whom are affiliated with Singapore's finest restaurants.

Coriander Leaf by the Singapore River (3A River Valley Rd, Clarke Quay, #02-03, +65.6732 3354; www.corianderleaf.com) has a well equipped cooking studio that takes in small groups of up to 10 students. Chef-owner and restaurant entrepreneur Samia Ahad's cooking classes feature a complete menu of appetisers, sides, mains and dessert; and each class presents an integrated menu of eight to 10 recipes. She places emphasis on home-style cooking so that even novices can easily replicate the dishes at home.

Samia shows participants how to prepare the dishes from scratch and offers tips as well as background information about the different cuisines, comprising a diverse range of Asian to Middle Eastern to Western dishes. Comprehensive recipe booklets are provided too.

ho chi minh city, vietnam

If you've always enjoyed the fresh flavours of Vietnamese cuisine, be sure to sign up for the cookery classes at **Park Hyatt Saigon** (2 Lam Son Square; +84.8.3824 1234;

THIS PAGE (FROM TOP): *A well equipped kitchen space at Palate Sensations; At Palate Sensations, students are exposed to a range of classic as well as contemporary dishes across cultures and tastes.*
OPPOSITE (FROM TOP): *The state-of-the-art Raffles Culinary Academy; Students learn cooking and interact with Chef-owner Samia Ahad at Coriander Leaf.*

cookery schools

THIS PAGE (FROM TOP): Students at the Thai cooking class conducted by Mandarin Oriental Bangkok are taught how to use the ingredients in dishes; The chef shows a participant the way to handle dough; Before the cooking begins, students are brought to the local market to learn about the ingredients.
OPPOSITE: The dining area in the kitchen where cooking classes are held at the Four Seasons Chiang Mai; Cooking demonstration by the chef.

www.saigon.park.hyatt.com). They are organised at Square One, the hotel's premier Western restaurant every day from 3 to 5.30pm. Each class usually fits between two and 10 people. Nguyen Ngoc Hien, the Executive Sous Chef, or the Vietnamese kitchen's Chef de Partie will first bring students on a tour to the bustling Ben Thanh Market. Participants will get to soak in the sights and sounds of this iconic market and also select fresh herbs and ingredients for their dishes. Back at Square One's show kitchen, students will learn about traditional Vietnamese cooking. Recipes include fresh spring rolls, fried seafood spring rolls, lotus stem salad, sweet-and-sour seafood soup and wok-fried garoupa with black pepper sauce. Participants will go home with a recipe folder, a Vietnamese cookbook, a set of chopsticks and a Park Hyatt Saigon apron.

hanoi, vietnam
Sofitel Metropole Hanoi (15 Ngo Quyen Street; +84.4.826 6920; www.sofitel.com) has been drawing foodies to its cooking classes since 1998. First introduced by Sofitel Metropole's trailblazing former executive chef and culinary author Didier Corlou, the classes are now conducted under the watchful eye of the new Executive Chef, Andre Bosia. Sofitel guests are invited to join in the hotel's guided cooking tour and class, priced from US$55 per person.

The morning class kicks off at 10 am. Participants will be brought to Hanoi's spice and produce market via traditional cyclos to learn more about the variety of fresh ingredients. After the hour-long visit, students will head back to the hotel's kitchen for a hands-on cooking workshop and practical demonstration. This is followed by a "Hanoi Street lunch" at Sofitel's Spice Garden Restaurant. Bookings are essential (at least one day prior), and class sizes are generally kept small and personal (maximum of 10 students).

bangkok, thailand
The Oriental Thai Cooking School at **Mandarin Oriental Bangkok** (48 Oriental Avenue; +66.2.659 9000; www.mandarinoriental.com/bangkok), established in 1986, was the first cooking school in Thailand. The hands-on classes from 9am to 1pm, Monday to Saturday, welcome everyone, including non-hotel guests. Additional supplementary courses are available upon request from 2 to 5pm. The courses also include fruit and vegetable-carving and making Thai dessert (mock fruits made of mung bean).

Participants are divided into groups of four. The instructor first demonstrates how to cook a dish and allows the students to taste it. Different dishes are taught daily. Dishes include spicy grilled beef salad with grapes, spicy herb sea bass soup, stir-fried clams with roasted chilli paste, deep-fried taro with crab filling, Thai fish cake and more. The participants then return to their stations to cook, after which they sit down and taste their own cooking. At the end of the class, participants are presented with a certificate and a set of souvenir (consisting of an apron, sachet of herbs and a shopping bag).

chiang mai, thailand

The **Cooking School at Four Seasons Resort Chiang Mai** (Mae Rim-Samoeng Old Road, +66.5.329 8181; www.fourseasons.com/chiangmai) is a free-standing facility whose design is inspired by the ancient Lanna Kingdom. Overlooking mountains, gardens and a waterfall, the venue features an air-conditioned kitchen and an open-air dining pavilion for students to savour their own creations.

The school features four double cooking stations where eight students can cook at any given time. Chef Pitak Srichan first demonstrates at his own station and then the students go back to their stations and fire up the woks. From Monday to Saturday, the class kicks off at 7am with a tour of a local food market followed by a traditional Thai spirit-house blessing, an introduction and demonstration. Participants get to prepare a variety of Thai dishes such as spicy salads, appetisers, curries, soups and noodles with guidance from the school's chefs.

Although popular Thai dishes are taught, the focus is largely on Northern Thai cuisine. For those interested, there is a one-hour vegetable carving lesson after lunch. Depending on the day you join, the classes may include a tour of the resort's herb and spice garden; a walk through the terraced rice paddies; an introduction to the history of celadon or traditional Thai kitchen utensils as well as other activities.

hua hin, thailand

If you want to learn how to cook spa cuisine at home, head for **Chiva-Som** (73/4 Petchkasem Road; +66.3.253 6536; www.chivasom.com) in Hua Hin, Thailand. The food served at the resort is low in fat, made with local, seasonal produce and with minimum oil or salt, as the spa believes that wellness begins from within.

Cookery classes at Chiva-Som are hands-on. Before the class begins, you may invited to accompany the head chef to Chiva-Som's organic garden to pick up useful tips. There you will learn how to recognise vegetables and herbs in their best condition and select seasonal produce to cook in class.

At their "lunch-and-learn" class, launched in 2009, you first decide on the menu with the chef, watch her prepare three courses using different techniques and have lunch at the chef's table. A private one-hour session, it gives you the chance to interact with the chef one-on-one.

Demo or hands-on?

Do your research on cookery schools before you leave home and place a booking in advance. Many cookery schools only run lessons when there is a minimum number of students. Booking in advance gives the school enough time to round up the requisite numbers on the day you wish to have your lesson.

Ask if the lesson is a demonstration class or hands-on. A demo class means the students watch while the chef cooks, and then everyone sits down to try the food. More experienced cooks will benefit from a hands-on lesson where you cook the dishes under the supervision of the instructor.

cookery schools

krabi, thailand
For a more traditional approach towards Thai cooking, **Sri Trang** at Krabi's **Phulay Bay** (111 Moo 3 Nongthalay, Muang, +66.7.562 8111; reserve.ritzcarlton.com/phulay_bay), a Ritz-Carlton Reserve, offers hands-on classes in southern Thai cuisine. The lessons are hosted by the resort's executive chef in either English or Thai, using easy-to-follow, step-by-step methods that introduce techniques and fresh produce.

The classes take place in the resort's Thai Kitchen. Guests cook their own meals, according to authentic recipes, and eat their efforts at the chef's table afterwards.

If guests are interested in learning about about spa cuisine, optional classes can be held at the resort's Spa Café, **RAW**. Upon request, a trip to the local market with the chef to pick up produce for the class can also be arranged. The Reserve's tries to offer its guests in-depth experiences of Thai culture and believes that food is the perfect way to do this.

phuket, thailand
If you've had your dose of sun and sand, make your way to the **Ginja Cook Cooking School** at **JW Marriott Phuket Resort & Spa** (231 Moo 3, Mai Khao; +66.7.633 8000 ext 3748; www.marriott.com), a contemporary learning facility featuring Thai cooking classes and personalised courses. The sprawling resort's cooking school is designed in the style of a typical Thai *sala* (wooden pavilion). With a backdrop of the stunning Andaman Sea, the standalone building is adjacent to the Ginja Taste Thai restaurant. The kitchen has four cooking stations, each for two students and a spacious station for the instructing chef.

A Ginja Cook Day (8am to 2.30pm) starts with a culinary tour of the local market. Back at the resort, there will be traditional spirit-house blessing and introduction to the class. Students get to learn about different

Thai herbs and spices, as well as cook and sample their own meal. Thai favourites such as spicy green papaya salad, and other Ginja signatures like *goong som* (poached white prawns in a rich coconut and lime broth) are taught. At the end of the class, every participant is presented with a Thai cookbook, a Ginja Cook souvenir apron and a Ginja Cook master certificate. In the afternoon, the facility is transformed into a private cooking school offering a range of personalised courses. Expect to pay higher prices for these specially tailored classes.

beijing, china

At **Hutong Cuisine** (Jiaodaokou South Street, Dongmien, Hua Hutong, Courtyard 15; +86.10.84014788; www.hutongcuisine.com), you learn how to cook Chinese food in an authentic *hutong*. Classes here offer a window into traditional Chinese life as it is lived deep inside Beijing's fast disappearing traditional neighbourhoods.

Run by Chunyi Zhou, a Guangzhou native who speaks fluent English, Zhou conveys a rich understanding of local ingredients and seasonings through lots of hands-on practice. Her classes are mostly based on the cuisines of Guangzhou and Sichuan.

In each class, she demonstrates five dishes, and students cook two or three of them. The menu is structured around a specific cooking technique, such as steaming or stir-frying. Stir-frying, for example, features dishes such as *gongbao* chicken and pork with broadbean chilli sauce. Classes are held in a small open courtyard space (covered and heated in winter) and end with a shared meal under the shade of a pomegranate tree.

bali, indonesia

A typical day in a Balinese home begins with an early morning visit to the market to buy fresh food and spices for the day's meals. And cooking lessons at **Bumbu Bali Restaurant & Cooking School** (Jl Pratama, Tanjung Benoa, PO Box 132, Nusa Dua; +62.361.771 256; www.balifoods.com) try and replicate the same experience. The day starts at 6am with a visit to the local produce market, followed by an Indonesian breakfast of sweet rice dumplings, black rice pudding and fruit, just as the Balinese would do. But first, you stop off at the beach to buy fish from the returning fishing fleet. The classes, limited to 12 participants, offer a fascinating introduction to the exotic ingredients and culinary heritage of Bali.

After breakfast, the grinding of spice pastes for a whopping 22 dishes begins at the open Balinese kitchen, after which participants will learn how to cook typical Balinese dishes such as *ayam betutu* (roast chicken in banana leaf), *sate lilit* (minced seafood satay) *urap jaggung* (sweet corn with grated coconut) and *kambing merkuah* (lamb stew with cardamoms). Most lessons (on Monday, Wednesday and Friday) are hosted by Heinz von Holzen, author of five cookbooks on Indonesian and Balinese cuisine, aided by his friend, the talented Balinese chef Pak Bagus. ~ ST + AV

THIS PAGE (FROM TOP): Cookery utensils ready for the participants at the Ginga Cooking School in JW Marriot Phuket; Students are having a hands on lesson at Bumbu Bali.
OPPOSITE: The well-equipped kitchen of the Ginga Cooking School.

gourmet foods + speciality shops

There is a growing awareness for good food and esoteric ingredients taking place in Asia's booming economies. As the world becomes a smaller place, the global villager turned epicurean can enthusiastically pick from artisanal bread, cheeses and chocolate to jasmine tea and fair-trade coffee.

Maine lobsters, Maryland soft-shell crabs, Queensland Wagyu beef, Gower salt marsh lamb, Perigord foie gras, Gascony magrets de canard, Belon oysters, truffles from Provence, Yunnan Matsutake mushrooms, Hokkaido scallops, Pacific monkfish, Canadian arctic char, Alaskan king crabs, and wine lists which may include bottles of Opus One or a magnum of Château d'Yquem. These mouthwatering treasures can often be found under one roof in many cities in Asia—neatly showcased in speciality food stores and gourmet markets.

From Beijing to Bangkok and Shanghai to Singapore, the rejuvenated cities this side of the globe are catching up so quickly that suppliers can barely keep up. It is no coincidence that Hong Kong has now got its own Michelin restaurant guide and that there is now a Maison Daniel Boulud comfortably ensconced in the old American embassy right beside Tiananmen Square in Beijing. In Shanghai, celebrity chefs Jean-Georges Vongerichten, Jereme Leung and David Laris have congregated at the art-deco Three On The Bund building to feed Shanghai's elite.

china

Carrefour and **Walmart** may be staples in their countries of origin but here in China, they are foreign names that have a certain cachet among China's middle class. These large mega-market chains carry a selection of gourmet food not available in China previously. Specialist groceries like **Jenny Lou's** (www.jennyshop.com.cn) in Beijing are no longer confined to the embassy or expatriate districts.

Jenny's clientele has now spread over the huge Chao Yang district, and is headed towards the suburban luxury housing enclaves with such unlikely names like Napa Valley and Yosemite Park. Jenny Lou's used to be the only place you could get double cream or Parma ham, but similar supermarkets with their own boulangeries or charcuteries can now be found in the basement levels of Wangfujing shopping malls, or the suburban malls in Beijing's Third or Fifth Ring Roads.

Gourmet globalisation is not limited to commercial enterprise. It is invading homes as well, as a new generation of Internet-savvy young Chinese adults share recipes and track food trends online. With television chefs showing the way, young foodies in China are experimenting in a big way with specialist ingredients their parents have not even heard of. More are learning to enjoy pastas, sauces and all sorts of cold cuts.

And to cater to these new gourmets, supermarkets in China's major cities are stocking up on freshly baked bread such as foccacia, ciabatta and Lebanese flatbreads, and offering fresh pasta coloured with squid ink, spinach juice and sun-dried tomatoes. Milk, butter and cheeses, so much part of the daily shopping list in the West, are only now becoming popular here. Yogurts, especially, have taken off in a big way, with exotic fruit-flavoured tubs leading the way.

But long before these European providores became known to the gourmand in Asia, other household names have long ruled—the traditional specialists. In Beijing, **Liu Biju** (www.liubiju.com.cn) is a centuries-old pickle shop which started business during the Ming Dynasty and have miraculously survived changes of dynasty, state philosophies, wars and revolution. Newly re-branded and enjoying a celebrity status worldwide thanks to Anthony Bourdain's televised visit to Beijing, the shop moves something like two thousand tonnes of pickled cucumbers, cabbages, radishes and other root and leafy vegetables. It also makes incredibly aromatic virgin-pressed sesame oil, and boldly charges double what the average Beijing housewife will pay for an unbranded bottle.

Even China's third echelon cities are getting their own Western speciality shops. In Kunming, German speciality butchers are teaching the people who cure China's best hams how to extend their small goods repertoire. And often right next door is an outlet of the Singapore-founded bakery chain **BreadTalk** (www.breadtalk.com), which is spreading its franchise stores nationwide, introducing new breads to the fascinated Chinese public almost every week. To a general public used to simple unleavened breads, BreadTalk's floss-coated buns has become the rage of the moment, and crowds queued at the first shop at Kunming's Jin Ma Biji Square.

thailand

Thai supermarkets and speciality food stores are increasingly tapping into the gourmet provisions market. Right in the city centre, **Siam Paragon** has one whole level devoted to premium grocery shoppers. On the

THIS PAGE (CLOCKWISE FROM TOP): The Gourmet Market at Siam Paragon offers a treasure trove of ingredients for discerning Thai gourmets; Its adjoining Food Hall takes the foodie on a tasty trip around Asia; Chunks of "black gold", truffles from the Mediterranean; Exotic seafood such as the Hokkaido spider crabs are now available all over the world, at a price.
OPPOSITE: Chocolate truffles are the choice of new gourmets.

gourmet foods + speciality shops

ground level occupying over 3,000 sq m (32,292 sq ft), **Gourmet Market** (991/1 Rama I Road, Pathumwan; www.gourmetmarketthailand.com) offers exotic fruits and organic vegetables, from feijoa to radicchio, doughnut peaches to tiny champagne grapes, wild rocket and baby spinach. While local delicacies take up sizeable space, the supermarket features culinary delights from all over the world—effectively offering Thai gourmets and foreign visitors a one-stop shop for international groceries.

Paragon's **Food Hall** and food court on the same level attract dedicated gourmets in search of the exotic or the unexpected in Thailand. The Food Hall is extremely well-organised, featuring local as well as regional fare. At the food court, one can select from the numerous mouthwatering Thai dishes all in one place.

Another excellent supermarket attracting those after good food and fine wines is the **Central Food Hall** (Rama 1 Road; ww.centralworld.co.th) at the site of the old World Trade Centre. The building has been taken over by one of Thailand's largest departmental chains and has been renamed Central World Plaza, more affectionately known as Central World. Catering to Thailand's increasingly sophisticated young gourmets, the supermarket offers gourmet selections as lofty as its seven-level architecture.

singapore

Singapore's grocery business, dominated by two major players (Cold Storage and NTUC Fairprice supermarkets), is following the same trend in supplying gourmet foods and ingredients. Each has designated "fine food" markets, and the battle has raged from the residential heartlands right to the centre of the tourist district. Cold Storage recently opened an upmarket gourmet outlet, **ThreeSixty MARKET PLACE** at one of Singapore's latest shopping haunts, ION Orchard (2 Orchard Turn, #04-21; +65.6509 8434). It brings in a wide range of brands, such as Albert Menes, Dean & Deluca, Fauchon, Valrhona (its first store-in-a-store concept in Southeast Asia) and Waitrose.

A few doors away on the same floor at ION Orchard is **Vom Fass** (#04-25; +65.6509 8409), a store dedicated to speciality vinegars and oils. Bottles of fruit vinegars, the best Modena balsamic, exotic liqueurs and quality oils including the finest olive, grapeseed and even rare argan oils are filtered straight from the casks into carefully crafted bottles with jewelled-toned stoppers. The bottles are as much appreciated as the contents, and customers are encouraged to bring them back for refills.

Singapore's fine foods supermarkets also include specialist stores such as **Jones The Grocer**, an Australian gourmet chain which first started in Sydney's bohemian neighbourhood of Woollahra. Jones has two stores (Block 9, #01-12 Dempsey Road, +65.6476 1512 and 333A Orchard Road, Mandarin Gallery Lvl 4, #21-23; www.jonesthegrocer.com). One is located in the trendy gourmet enclave of Dempsey Hill, where old army barracks house boutique boulangeries, wine cellars and now, one of the largest temperature controlled cheese rooms in Singapore.

Jones also has an extensive deli and a charcuterie offering a range of small goods all under one roof, as well as gourmet coffees. It is also one of the first lifestyle grocers with cooking classes, educational wine and cheese tastings, as well as a little café area for breakfast, lunch and dinner.

This new crop of speciality shops has upped the ante for the supermarket trade, but has also made gourmet shoppers a lot happier. Previously, determined epicureans had to hunt down hotel suppliers hidden deep in the industrial parks to get their duck breasts, fresh oysters and foie gras. You also had to have the right contacts or the insider tip to get your Alaskan king crab legs or marron glace. These days, you just pick them off the shelves.

hong kong

The older gentlemen from Hong Kong believe in getting their *pu'er* or jasmine tea from trusty old shops like Ying Kee Tea House (2–4 Hysan Avenue, Causeway Bay; +852.3579 2357; www.yingkeetea.com). Precious handfuls of leaves are kept in beautifully crafted metal containers decorated with Chinese motifs. These are then faithfully brought to two-hour tea drinking sessions at local dim sum restaurants and enjoyed in the company of friends and the daily newspaper. Having seen that people like to enjoy their tea with a group of friends, Ying Kee now has a few outlets which serve its special brews.

Then there are the tried and trusted gourmet speciality places, such as Yung Kee Restaurant (32–40 Wellington Street, Central; +852.2522 1624; www.yungkee.com.hk), whose main claim to fame is their mouthwatering liquid-centred "century" eggs. These black-yolked eggs were originally served as appetisers at Yung Kee, whose signature dish is supposed to be their Cantonese roast goose. These days, the century eggs are specially packed for air travel, together with vacuum-packed pink pickled ginger, so that Hong Kong residents and visitors can deliver them to homesick friends abroad, if custom regulations allow these to be brought in. Since 2002, Yung Kee has received numerous awards, and in 2010, it was awarded one star in the Michelin guide to Hong Kong and Macau.

The best dried Hokkaido scallops are not found in Japan, but in the "southern goods" shops in Hong Kong's western and Wanchai districts. Here, dried abalone, whelk, birds' nest and bêche de mer compete for space with dried shiitake or Chinese mushrooms, bamboo boletus and other exotic mushrooms from Yunnan, and sharks' fins ranging in size from baby combs to broadsheet-sized fans.

Fresh seafood, on the other hand, draw gourmet chefs to the Outer Islands like Cheng Chau, Lamma and Lantau. The more well-heeled point their yachts southwards and head for the remote Po Toi island, where the thrashing catch comes fresh off the boats and the laver farms serve up fresh seaweed. ~ PDL

THIS PAGE (CLOCKWISE FROM TOP LEFT): Stackable bottles show off the liqueurs from Vom Fass, while a beribboned decanter may hold a cherished gift of aged balsamic or a fine oil; Ying Kee, a venerable old Hong Kong tea shop now also caters to the new generation of gourmet tea drinkers; A "flowering" tea ball with carefully stitched jasmine tea leaves or a bloom of globe amaranth.

OPPOSITE (FROM TOP): ThreeSixty MARKET PLACE by the Cold Storage Group in Singapore; Australian specialist store Jones The Grocer brings in the fine foods and also the coffee break lifestyle.

gourmet foods + speciality stores 87

new latitude wines

With the advancing invasion of Asian flavours in kitchens worldwide, sommeliers are hard put to find perfect wine matches for the strong spices and herbs that dominate fusion menus. They may do better to take a closer look at Asian vineyards.

While restaurant wine lists have been conveniently divided into Old World and New World wines previously, sommeliers in the know may soon be adding a third section on New Latitude wines—from vineyards out of India, China, Thailand, and even equatorial Bali. Unconventional terroir for wines, no doubt, but these vineyards are producing vintages that are making appreciative epicureans sit up. Often specifically grown and aged to match the particular paradox of spicy but subtle flavours of the exotic cuisines this side of the world, these "new" wines are the result of hard work by Asian winemakers taking huge leaps up the learning curve.

bali, indonesia

In Bali, on the northern hills, grapes are grown on trellises so they are shaded from too much sun and rain, and the resulting mildew, rot and disease. On the cooler slopes of this beautiful island, vintners have managed to produce award-winning vintages from evergreen vines that produce fruits all year. And, these were originally table grapes.

Hatten Wines (www.hattenwines.com), the main cultivator on the island, has successfully turned this table grape into rich, fruity vintage. The main varietal is a black grape from France, the Alphonse-Lavallé, quite simply known as "Alfonso" among growers. They also grow a Muscat grape for the white wines. White wines, red wines and sparkling rose from Hatten are featured on the wine lists of many of Bali's spas, resorts and hotels, and just as often recommended for the Asian-inspired, Balinese-influenced dishes created by its talented master chefs.

The success of the vineyard in producing excellent vintages from such non-traditional terroir is mainly due to decades of experimenting, trials, tests and persistent effort in identifying the right varietals, the proper growing methods and the control of diseases and the micro-climates. Bali benefits mainly from Australian wine-growing expertise, with many of its winemakers coming from Down Under, just like most of the island's executive chefs and a major part of its tourist market.

thailand

In Thailand, the same trials and errors were repeated by local vintners, but with more successful results and on a much larger scale. This country has a slight natural advantage in that its rolling highlands are cool and dry, creating an almost temperate climate perfect for nurturing wine grapes. This is especially so in the Asoke Valley, 350 m (1,148 ft) above sea level, although just two hours away from the capital, Bangkok. Here, in the shadow of the UNESCO World Heritage Khao Yai National Park, vineyards are changing the landscape. Sugar canes, banana trees and bamboo form a backdrop for rows upon rows of neatly trimmed vines, while hornbills and mynahs fly low among the tropical tree tops. It is an almost surrealistic picture.

A lot of the pioneering work was done by one vintner with an established history in brewing beer. Other growers also came from beverage conglomerates, including that which owned the famous Thai tonic-turned-cocktail mix, Red Bull. These converted Thai brewers all applied their basic beer-brewing knowledge to wine-making, with varying results.

The largest vineyard here, **PB Valley Khao Yai Winery** (www.khaoyaiwinery.com) started about 20 years ago, when the owner acquired 320 hectares (791 acres) of land that was surrounded by mountains and with the right microclimate for viticulture in Khao Yai. More than 50 types of grapes from Germany, Italy, France, Spain and Australia were tested for two years and finally, Shiraz, Tempranillo, Chenin Blanc and Colombard were chosen for cultivation. It was an eclectic mix which filled these rolling hills.

In 1994, a young winemaker named Prayut Piangbunta returned from a study mission in Germany, and by 1997, was putting together the finishing touches to a 3,000-sq m (32,292-sq ft) wine factory with climate control cellars and imported French oak barrels. The oak barrels cost twice as much as stainless steel vats, but no expense was spared, mainly because the ex-brewer owner appreciated the subtle nuances French oak would give the final vintages. And, by investing in its vineyards and by sending its winemaker to Germany to learn from vintners there, the learning curve was shortened considerably.

Khao Yai Winery's philosophy is to produce wines that will go with Thai cuisine, and at its vineyard restaurant and cellar, day-trippers

THIS PAGE (CLOCKWISE FROM TOP): PB Valley Khao Yai Winery is set in the shadows of a UNESCO World Heritage park; Khao Yai Winery's Sawadee premium range is popular with connoiseurs of Thai cuisine; Samut Sakorn's unique floating vineyards on the Chao Phraya river basin.

OPPOSITE: Wines from grapes have been produced in China's Xinjiang province from as far back as the times of the ancient Silk Route.

new latitude wines

THIS PAGE (CLOCKWISE FROM TOP): *Yunnan Hong's grape arbour shows off their table grapes, while an experimental station nearby tests out varietals suitable for growing; A varietal named Black General grown at the same vineyard; In a tasting room, a woman pours out glasses for the gourmands.*
OPPOSITE: *Yunnan is a province in the south of the Peoples Republic of China, one of the few wine-producing areas in China.*

and tourists alike happily experiment with fruity reds paired with Thai beef salad, or a spicy red fish with a well-chilled Chenin Blanc. It is now arguably the largest and most prolific producer in Thailand although the numbers are still mere drops compared to the larger Western producers. But the beachhead has been made and its 2004 Pirom Khao Yai Reserve Chenin Blanc and Tempranillo are excellent vintages much sought after by connoisseurs.

Other Thai wineries are following hard on the heels of Khao Yai, some with even more unconventional cultivation. **Siam Winery** (www.siamwinery.com), for example, grows its grapes on "floating vineyards" near Samut Sakorn where the vines are separated by canals, and are harvested by boat. The grape varieties here are Pok Dum and Malaga Blanc, used to make light white wines that are again designed for spicy Thai food.

china

While Bali and Thailand had little baggage to deal with in wine-growing, the vineyards in China and India had to deal with historical hiccups, failures and successes. Yunnan, in south-western China, was historically cut off from the country's ancient capital. Its sturdy little horses were plying the ancient Tibetan Tea Horse Caravan Route long before its merchants travelled eastward to Chang'an or Beijing. The alternative Silk Route also branched off to Kunming, its capital, and through these channels, Yunnan first knew grapewine brought in by Persian traders.

Nearer the present, Yunnan's proximity to Vietnam, with which it shares common borders, exposed it to Jesuit wine-growers. Vines from Bordeaux and other regions of France were brought into Yunnan via Vietnam and took root in Mile, a rich plateau in the Central Highlands. As wars and political tremors shook China, these vines were neglected and soon forgotten. Until recently, that is, no one even remembered these ancient vines. With the opening of the Chinese economy, the **Mile Yunnan Hong Vineyard** conglomerate was revived.

Geographically, central Yunnan is ideal for viticulture. It enjoys a Mediterranean-latitude climate tempered by a 2,000-m (6,562-ft) high altitude, making the summers warm and wet but mild, and its winters dry and cool, with no severe frosts. The Yunnan-Guizhou plateau has organically rich and well-irrigated soils, and the areas around Mile, Mengzi and Chenggong county comprise limestone-rich karst, all of which make for excellent conditions for the vines.

There are now several larger vineyards in operation here, such as **Yunnan Hong Wine Co Ltd**, **Yunnan Gaoyuan Wine Co Ltd** and **Yunnan Shenquan Wine Co Ltd**, mostly fermenting dry reds which are the current favourite among wine connoisseurs in China. For more information, see www.chinawine.com.

The Yunnan vineyards are just the tip of the iceberg for what may become one of the largest wine markets in the world. As Chinese wallets bulge in tandem with the

new latitude wines

burgeoning economy, palates are also undergoing a global metamorphosis.

From the initial French-chateau consciousness to real appreciation of the finer vintages to an awareness of native wines that go with native cuisine, the learning curve for the Chinese growers is a long and steep gradient, weighed down by traditional allegiance to beverages such as the white and yellow "wines" brewed from grains and cereals. With characteristic determination, however, Chinese wine-growers, vintners, sommeliers and wine connoisseurs are learning with a vengeance. A time-lapse look at wine store and supermarket shelves show the number of local vintages increasing every month. Already, brands such as Changyu, Dynasty and Yunnan Hong have become household names, aided by aggressive advertising and promotion on TV and billboards, and motivated by foreign partners ranging from French, Italian and Australian vintners to the World Bank's financial corporation.

india

India, the other Asian giant, is also waking up to the popularity of the grape. Past colonial masters such the relatively transient Portuguese and the longer-lasting British *pukka sahibs* all introduced wine drinking to India. However, these were limited to mainly fortified wines such as port and Madeira, their high alcohol contents needed to withstand the long sea voyages to India.

That was a long time ago. Now, any myth that curries kill the taste of

THIS PAGE (CLOCKWISE FROM TOP): *A worker harvests grapes at Grover Vineyards, one of the first in India to grow French varietals in South Asia; A sampling of Cabernet Sauvignon taken from a barrel with a "thief" and poured into a glass for tasting; New Latitude wines match the changing tastes of those seeking more perfect food and wine pairing.*
OPPOSITE: *Oak barrels add depth to the fermentation process, and many New Latitude vintners will go the extra length and cost for their vintages.*

wine or that wines deaden the subtleties of spices has been wiped clean off the slate and India produces both reds and whites in reasonable abundance. Compared to some Western averages of five bottles per head, however, the South Asian public is imbibing mere sips in comparison. Still, it is a market growing at a rate of 30 per cent per year, according to industry reports, and young wine lovers from Delhi to Mumbai are enjoying anything from Riesling to Pinot Noir to the ubiquitous Cabernet Sauvignon, home-grown or imported.

Wine tourism is also a growing sector of the industry and regions such as Nasik, Sangali, Bangaire and Himatchal are all exploiting this potential in tandem with the wines they are producing. The largest concentration of vineyards in India is positioned slightly off centre to the left of the sub-continent, in the state of Maharastra. This is Nasik, an area which includes Pune, Nasik and Ahmed Nagar. Here, at about 800 m (2,625 ft) above sea level, the gentle climate is kind to the vines and several top vineyards can be found here, including industry leaders **Chateau Indage** (www.chateauindage.com) and **Sula Wines** (www.sulawines.com). Further towards the tip of the peninsula, the Nandi Hills just north of Bangalore also produces wine. Himatchal is the third major wine producing region, nestled in the Himalayan foothills, specialising in the cool climate varietals.

As India, like China, sees growing prosperity and more disposable income, the market for local and imported wines is expected to bloom. The forecast for domestic wines, especially, is optimistic, and recent market surveys have shown a definite slant towards wines made in India. Again, credit goes to the producers such as Indage, Sula, Grover Vineyards, among others, who have diligently promoted their wines as best suited for Indian cuisines.

In the case of the **Grover Vineyards** (www.groverwines.com), one of the first wine-growers in India, it only took a few generations for viticulture to take root. Founder Kanwal Grover made his fortune in the importing and selling of space and defence equipment. His frequent trips in France led to an unexpected bonus. He developed a passion for fine wines. At the age of 60, Grover decided to turn his passion into a mission, and he took on the challenge of growing French grape varieties in India at what was to become the country's first premium vineyard.

His son, Kapil, became the guardian of his father's legacy, continuing the business and increasing its acreage four times. Kapil's daughter, Karishma, studied viticulture at the University of California, Davis, and is now the estate's wine-maker. She is also the first female wine-maker in India.

It is stories like this that best showcase the dedication of India's fledgling wine industry, and guarantees a continuity that may make these New Latitude wines a challenge to existing vintners.

Wine and food are inseparable, and in the age of the new gourmet, New Latitude wines are set to take the stage in a big way. ~ PDL

gourmet cocktails

No one asks for a regular gin and tonic anymore. More than just opening a good bottle, the choice and exotic mix of ingredients, and the skills employed in making a drink are as important as the person making it.

Even the ice makes a difference in a good cocktail. Singapore's Tippling Club for example claims that its ice is hand-chipped from mineral water-filtered blocks that chills drinks for longer periods. Similarly in the best Tokyo bars, the ice is sent back if it is not good enough. At these places, the best ice is washed, then refrozen to get a hard clear block that shows off its natural icy grain.

Beyond ice, the newest trend in cocktails is to source for the finest ingredients—as in the culinary world. The bartender or mixologist as he (or she) is called now, sources for the best herbs, spices or fruit to flavour the drinks. Like a food menu, the best drinks menu is seasonal: so in Japan, you might be served a pomelo champagne cocktail in winter, but only during the fruit's short two-week season. In summer, rum may be paired with ripe Okinawan mango. No wonder Tokyo is dubbed the cocktail capital of the world, such is the precision of the craft practised there.

When Hidetsugu Ueno, head bartender at the Star Bar Ginza, makes a martini, for example, he uses both chilled and room temperature gins. And for certain shaken cocktails, he chooses a plastic shaker to keep the ice from chipping too much.

But beyond drinks, what is it that makes a great bar? Celebrity chef Tetsuya Wakuda in an interview with *Gourmet Traveller* said: "I just want somewhere simple, with a personal approach... I like the Observatory Hotel bar in Sydney—because the atmosphere is warm without being noisy. I want to be able to talk, and that's very hard to find."

new delhi, india

One of the most famous bars in the city, **Rick's** at the **Taj Mahal Hotel** (1 Mansingh Road; +91.11.2302 6162; www.tajhotels.com) is inspired by the movie *Casablanca*. Also known as "slick Rick's" for its easy-going ambience, it is a magnet for beautiful people, with as many yelling into their mobile phones as they are talking to one another on a typical night.

Cocktails are the drink of choice here. The bar, dubbed Delhi's latest sizzle, is famous for its vodka-based cocktails, the guava berry martini, the Cosmopolitan and the Bacardi-based mojito. Rick's also has a good selection of spirits (101 martinis, and 43 single malts and vodkas to be exact).

singapore

At cutting-edge **Tippling Club** (8D Dempsey Road; +65.6475 2217; www.tipplingclub.com), the food pairing is with cocktails, not wines. In their tasting menu, a dish called vegetable garden with porcini soil is matched with a Bax Beet Pinot 2008. With no grape in sight despite the reference to Pinot, it is instead a mixture of beetroot, Italian bitters and liqueurs, served in a wine glass.

Helmed by Melbourne mixologist, Matthew Bax and Chef Ryan Clift, the two operate out of a cavernous space in Singapore's hip Dempsey neighbourhood where restaurants, shops and bars have taken over the barracks vacated by the British army. Diners look out to verdant views from the bar and restaurant, which draws young professionals and foodies, attracted both by the cocktails and the food.

There is only one place in Singapore where you can litter without qualm. At the **Long Bar** of **Raffles Hotel** (1 Beach Road; +65.6412 1816; www.raffles.com), guests are even encouraged to throw peanut shells on the floor. But the bar has another claim to fame—the legendary Singapore Sling was born here. Invented by Ngiam Tong Boon, a bartender working there before 1910, recipes for this cocktail have varied over time.

This said, the gin cocktail at the hotel remains essentially the same. The original recipe uses gin, and, importantly, fresh juice from pineapples as it creates a foamy top. Today, club soda gives the fizz.

The bar is also worth a visit, not least for a feel of the plantation days in 1920s Malaya. It is a truly nostalgic experience, reclining in a cane chair with palm fans above, nursing a *stengah*, that is, a half measure of whiskey and soda served over ice.

shanghai, china

100 Century Avenue Bar at the **Park Hyatt Shanghai** (100 Century Avenue, Pudong New Area; +86.21.6888 1234; shanghai.park.hyatt.com) is the highest bar in the world. The bar is part of the complex occupying the 91st to 93rd floors of the World Financial Centre in Pudong. The Western-style Music Room has a lively ambience and the quieter Shanghai Lounge opposite is where you can watch 1930s-style Shanghai ballroom dancers sway to music.

The bar offers a Western and Chinese selection of whiskey, wines and of course, creative cocktails. To

THIS PAGE (FROM TOP): At Singapore's Tippling Club, you get classics such as a Negroni; As well as new creations such as their signature Smokey Old Bastard; Long Bar at Raffles Hotel where the famed Singapore Sling was born.

OPPOSITE: Matthew Bax, the Melbourne mixologist, one of a two-men team who's shaking things up at the Tippling Club located at Dempsey Park. His concoctions are as much showpieces as they are cocktails.

gourmet cocktails

make its ginger pina mojito, Cuban rum is infused with ginger before being muddled with roasted pineapple, kaffir lime and organic mint leaves and topped up with ginger ale. The bloodless martini, which incorporates pepper-infused vodka, uses clear "tomato water" obtained from the transparent drippings of chopped tomatoes.

When temperatures soar in Shanghai, everyone wants cool summer drinks. And who better than a Southeast Asian restaurant to know their tropical fruit, lemon grass and limes or coconut? **Simply Thai** (159 Ma Dang Road at corner of Xing Ye Road, Xintiandi; +86.21.6326 2088; www.simplylife-sh.com/simplythai) serves summer drinks that has exactly these ingredients. Its mango mojito adds fresh mango to the lime, mint and rum mix while the actual fruit goes into its lychee martini. Its mocktails also take inspiration from familiar recipes. After all, who living in Southeast Asia has not resorted to an iced longan, lemongrass or fresh coconut drink on a hot day?

Simply Thai opened in 1999 as Shanghai's first Thai restaurant in its former French concession. Today, it has restaurants at Xintiandi, Hongmei and Jinqiao, with the outlet in Xintiandi boasting an uber-chic bar and lounge.

bangkok, thailand
Touted as the highest al fresco bar in the Asia Pacific, who would not enjoy sultry Bangkok while perched 61 storeys high on the roof of the **Banyan Tree Hotel**, with cool drink in hand? **Vertigo Grill & Moon Bar** (21/100 South Sathorn Road; +66.2.679 1200; ww.banyantree.com) offers a great open-air position from where to enjoy the tumultuous cityscape and the great Chao Praya River meandering far below.

And if your poison is a fine cocktail, ask for a Moon Romance. This is a fruity mix comprising melon vodka with crème de menthe, peach and lemon juice. Or else order a bright red Vertigo Sunset, its most popular drink where Malibu rum is topped with cranberry and pineapple juices, perked up by lime and topped with fresh pineapple.

ho chi minh city, vietnam
For a watering hole with a history, you cannot do better than to visit the rooftop **Saigon Saigon Bar** at the **Caravelle Hotel** (19 Lam Son Square; +84.8.823 4999; www.caravellehotel.com), where journalists reporting on the Vietnam War gathered. The historic hotel celebrated its 50th Anniversary in 2009.

According to press releases, the bar was "the centre of operations—both professional and social—for the international media. From their 10th-floor perch, cold beers in hand, journalists could, by the war's closing days, see the front line from their bar stools." Indeed if you look out from the balcony, you can still see colonial and wartime landmarks dotting the city.

Today, the historic bar has transformed itself into an upscale spot with a chic-colonial ambience and ample armchairs, greenery and ceiling fans. And of course, the bar now offers more than cold cold beers.

hong kong, china

Grilled fruit cocktails are the thing at the **Lotus Restaurant & Cocktail Lounge** (37–43 Pottinger Street, Central; +852.2543 6290; www.lotus.hk). The establishment is divided into three sections— a terraced bar in the front, followed by the dining area with another cocktail bar complete with a DJ booth, and a private dining room. Celebrity Head Mixologist Grant Collins' cocktails are based on the molecular science of their ingredients leading him to even grill the fruit for a toasted pink grapefruit martini. His is one of the more innovative drink lists in the city, offering concoctions such as a grilled pineapple and cracked pepper martini, and a burnt lemon and vanilla margherita.

Collin's liquid creations are matched by the equally creative renditions of Thai food cooked by his partner, Executive Chef Will Meyrick. Meyrick puts a twist on the Thai betel leaf appetiser by serving smoked trout and trout roe as well as dried shrimp and galangal on the leaf wrap.

Located in the hip NoHo district, you might miss the unassuming entrance of this Australian-owned establishment. You will need to climb some steep stairs to arrive at a stylish Asian-inspired interior.

tokyo, japan

If you want original cocktails, **Peter** at **The Peninsula Tokyo** hotel (24F, 1-8-1 Yurakucho, Chiyoda-ku; +81.3.6270 2763; www.peninsula.com) serves them. Dubbed Tokyo's hippest restaurant and bar, this was where the famed Tokyo Joe cocktail, Japan's answer to the Singapore Sling, was born.

Created by bartender Mari Kamata, the drink has a Bombay Sapphire base, mixed with aromatic umeshu plum liqueur, cranberry juice, Drambuie and lemon, resulting in an electric pink cocktail. Its name was inspired by the 1949 Humphrey Bogart movie of the same name. Kamata clearly enjoys creating inventive cocktails, and you can taste her latest concoctions while enjoying views of Tokyo and the Imperial Palace Gardens through the bar's floor-to-ceiling windows.   ~ ST

Origins of the Cocktail

It was probably the Americans who created the cocktail. A cocktail was originally a mixture of distilled spirits, sugar, water and an alcoholic beverage known as "bitters". Today, the word has gradually come to mean almost any mixed drink containing alcohol. Although the origin of the mixed drink is clouded in controversy, it is said that cocktails began as a result of the Prohibition (1920–33) in America when liquor was not allowed and there were only dubious spirits available. People had to add something to make the concoction drinkable. And so the cocktail was born!

Early cocktails were just fruit juice added to hard liquor. What else is a daiquiri than lime juice to which rum was added? Then something good arose in those dark years halfway around the globe—the Singapore Sling was born at the renowned Raffles Hotel Singapore, before 1910. The rest, as they say, is history.

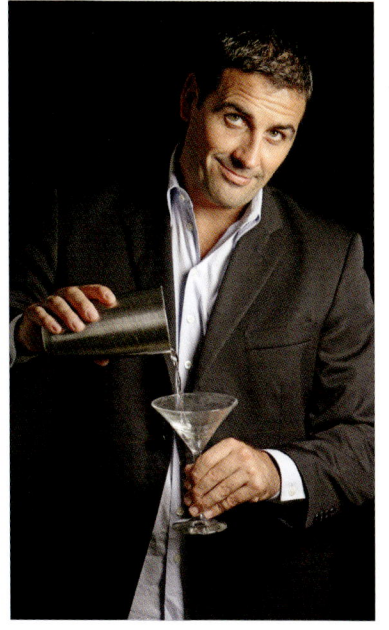

THIS PAGE (CLOCKWISE FROM TOP LEFT): Great views of Tokyo's Imperial Palace through the windows at Peter, The Peninsula hotel in Tokyo; Tokyo Joe, Tokyo's answer to the Singapore Sling; Grant Collins, celebrity mixologist at Hong Kong's Lotus Cocktail Lounge.

OPPOSITE (CLOCKWISE FROM TOP LEFT): Outdoor fountain at the Simply Thai outlet, Xintiandi, Shanghai; Tropical cocktails such Vertigo Sunset, Caipirina and Mojito are all-time favourites at the Vertigo Bar & Grill in Bangkok.

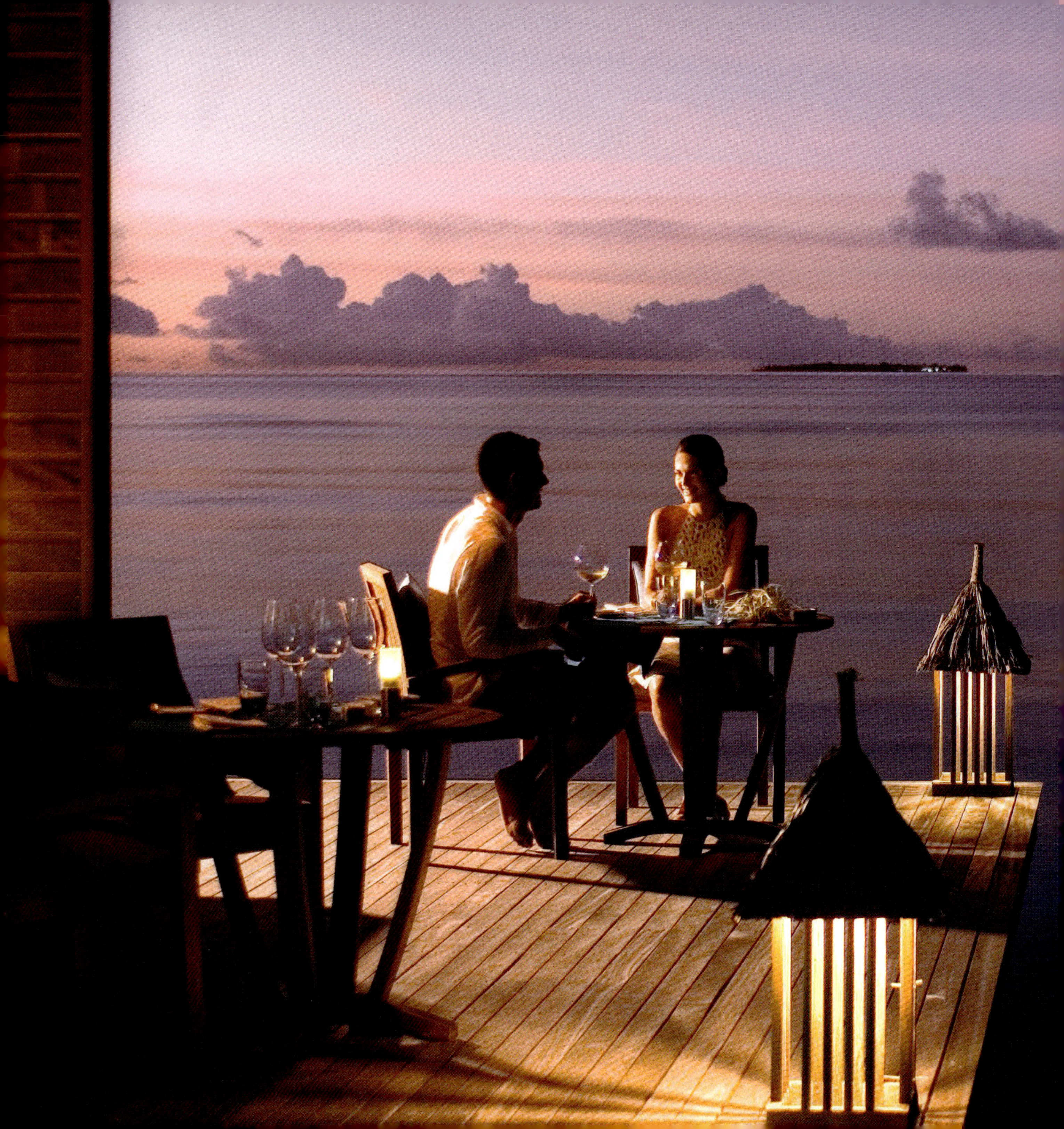

gourmetrestaurants

Whether you are dazzled by restaurants perched on skyscraper rooftops or suspended underwater, or awed by chic and minimalist interiors, and unsurpassed levels of service, the unifying thread that links all the restaurants listed in this section is the excellent food whipped up by some of Asia's most talented chefs. Apart from a summary of dining highlights, the restaurants featured here also share their recipes for selected signature dishes—for guests who want to replicate the sublime experience at home. Bon appétit!

café cha shangri-la hotel, beijing

If you are in search of a defining gastronomic experience, make a trip to **Café Cha** at the **Shangri-La Hotel, Beijing**. Café Cha offers an international buffet spread that is prepared fresh from the open kitchens, promising to offer something for every taste and fancy. Set beside a soothing garden, Café Cha is the perfect choice for a relaxed meal.

At the entrance is a pastry and bakery station, where the smell of freshly baked desserts entices passers-by. At breakfast, an array of pancakes, muffins, waffles, breads and pastries is offered. During lunch and dinner, more elaborate confections take centrestage, with soufflés, mousses, cream cakes, cookies and chocolates crowding the counter.

Once you tear yourself away from the sweets, you will see a seafood bar and a sushi and sashimi counter. Watch as the chefs show off their knife skills as they make sushi, and indulge in the freshest selection of oysters, mussels, crayfish, prawns and crabs that fight for attention. There is a real sense of performance here, and it is clear that Café Cha places importance on ensuring that only the freshest food is served to its guests.

Another prime feature is the sheer variety of food that is served. The café offers a milieu of cuisines, and besides a wood-fired oven that serves up pizza and grilled vegetables, there is an Asian Noodle station where chefs from Hong Kong prepare timeless noodle dishes. Here, you can find the signature slow-braised *udon* noodles with soya sauce, *char kway teow* or wok-fried flat rice noodles and Nyonya curry *laksa*—thick rice noodles in a coconut-based curry soup.

The restaurant's décor is classy and modern, creating a casual ambience for its diners. Designed by Hong Kong's John Chan Design, the colour palette is neutral and hues of beige and cream are complemented by glass tables and walls. All these features work to engender a vibe of tranquility. Bay windows grant picturesque views of the hotel's beautiful garden, making Café Cha a perfect place to just while away the afternoon, in the midst of good company and good food.

Of course, no one leaves without a glass of "silk-stocking tea", after which the café is named. Complete your epicurean journey with this sweet and satisfying ending, in the cool comfort of Shangri-La Hotel, Beijing.

THIS PAGE (FROM LEFT): **There are chefs stationed at different counters to prepare food freshly for diners on request;** **The chic ambience of the restaurant is perfect for a relaxed, delicious meal.**
OPPOSITE (FROM TOP): **Signature dish, the sumptuous slow-braised udon noodles with soya sauce;** **Authentic Southeast Asian delicacies that present a multiplicity of flavours.**

beijing **china**

slow-braised udon noodles with soya sauce

serves 4

4 portions *udon* (about 150g each)
4 cloves garlic, finely chopped
½ brown onion, finely chopped
100ml cooking oil
4 rashers smoked bacon
60g cooked fish cakes, finely sliced
16 tiger prawns, cooked and shelled, with tail on
1 cup Chinese white cabbage, sliced and blanched
4 cups stock
4 tbsp dark soya sauce
4 tsp light soya sauce
4 tbsp oyster sauce
2 tbsp sesame oil
white pepper

For Garnish
2 tbsp fried shallots
spring onions, finely sliced
1 red chilli, finely sliced

Method:
1. Heat some oil in a wok and add the bacon, onions and garlic. Cook on low heat until the mixture becomes fragrant and golden brown.
2. Add stock and oyster sauce and stir. Bring the mixture to a boil.
3. Put *udon* noodles in the stock and add the seasoning sauces and sesame oil. Simmer for about 4 minutes.
5. Cook on low heat until the sauce becomes thick.
6. Divide noodles into 4 portions. Arrange the cabbage, prawns and fish cakes on top of the *udon*. Garnish with spring onions and chilli. Scatter fried shallots on the top and serve.

Notes:
This is a classic braised noodle dish in a thick soya sauce. The sauce-braised gravy coats the noodles and provides both flavour and texture. You can garnish the noodles with your choice of ingredients. Apart from this seafood version, you can also try adding braised meats such as stewed pork or *char siew* (barbecued pork).

restaurant + address
Café Cha
Shangri-La Hotel, Beijing
Garden Wing 1st Floor
29 Zizhuyuan Road, Beijing, China
telephone: +86.10.6841 2211 ext 6715
email: restaurantsrsvns.slb@shangri-la.com
website: www.shangri-la.com

cuisine
international buffet

signature dishes
slow-braised *udon* noodles with soya sauce • *char kway teow* (wok-fried flat rice noodles) • Nyonya curry *laksa* (noodles in coconut-based curry soup)

opening hours
6am–midnight daily

other f + b outlets
Blu Lobster • Shang Palace • Nishimura

what's nearby
Summer Palace • Zhongguan Technology Park • Financial Street

nishimura shangri-la hotel, beijing

THIS PAGE: The minimalist design of Nishimura is classy and simple, consisting of clean and sleek lines.

OPPOSITE (FROM TOP): Chef Yoshinori Mizutani's signature dish, torched nigiri sushi; The spacious design of Nishimura is the ideal space for an elegant meal.

Visitors to Beijing know they can find a piece of heaven at the **Shangri-La Hotel, Beijing** not only because it has a reputation of being a world-class, award-winning hotel, but also because of the multiplicity of gourmet choices available. There are seven exceptional bars and restaurants to choose from depending on your flavour of the day, and it is no surprise that Shangri-La Hotel, Beijing has played host to countless tourists and dignitaries from all over the world.

Nishimura is the hotel's signature restaurant that serves authentic Japanese food in a fine-dining atmosphere. Its design consists of sleek and clean lines which are in sync with the restaurant's concept of presenting unadulterated Japanese food. The restaurant is a tranquil refuge in the heart of the Chinese capital, and its cool dining room incorporates the feng shui elements of wood, stone, glass, water and metal. The principles of *yin* and *yang*, of balancing colours, aromas, shapes and sounds, govern both décor and food at Nishimura.

The restaurant is divided into three main areas, with both *kantou* (sushi) and *kansai* (hot) styles of cuisine served at the open area, *teppan* tables and a sushi bar. Incidentally, a sake bar hosts an excellent collection of the best brews, and guests can choose to enjoy their sake hot, cold or blended in one of Nishimura's signature sake cocktails.

It comes as no surprise that Nishimura's impeccable food and service have earned the establishment numerous accolades in recent years. The restaurant was named Best Japanese Restaurant by *Time Out Beijing* in 2010, and Best Restaurant Selection by *Modern Weekly* in 2009. It was also awarded Best Japanese Restaurant by *City Weekend* in the same year. The awards reflect Nishimura's culinary prowess, making it the benchmark for Japanese cuisine in Beijing.

Another recommended restaurant at the hotel is Shang Palace. Here you can experience Chinese fine-dining at its best, renowned for the refined Cantonese cuisine and *dim sum* served. Shang Palace's kitchen is led by Chef Chau Oi Fong, who prides himself on using only top quality ingredients to create classic dishes such as abalone and sea cucumber.

beijing **china**

torched nigiri sushi

serves 4

80g top quality tuna belly (*toro*)
4 live fresh scallops, cleaned and thinly sliced
80g top-grade fresh salmon fillet, thinly sliced
180g cooked sushi rice (for 12 pieces)
30g sea urchin roe
40g salmon roe (*ikura*)
½ stalk leek, thinly sliced
4 tsp grated white radish (*daikon*)
4 slices of lemon, cut into thin slices
onions, thinly sliced
2 tbsp mayonnaise
40g pickled ginger
4 tsp *wasabi* powder
sushi soya sauce
4 bamboo leaves
4 tsp *ponzu* vinegar

Method:
1. Slice fresh *toro* and salmon fillet into 4 portions each.
2. Divide sushi rice into portions of 15g each to make 12 pieces of sushi.
3. Mix *wasabi* powder and a little water to make a paste.
4. Put a dab of *wasabi* on top of each sushi and place fresh *toro*, salmon and scallops on top to create 3 different types of *nigiri*.
5. Lightly grill the *nigiri* using a chef's blowtorch.
6. Season *toro nigiri* with grated radish, *ponzu* and leek slices.
7. Season scallop *nigiri* with sea urchin roe, salt and lemon slices.
8. Season salmon *nigiri* with mayonnaise, sliced onion and top with the salmon roe.
9. Arrange the *nigiri* and condiments for presentation and serve.

Notes:
There are many types of sushi which have recently gained popularity among gourmet diners all over the world. However, the ingredients do not vary much—it is the combination and style of presentation that make all the difference.

Nigiri sushi is topped with mostly raw or cooked fish and garnished with thinly shredded ingredients. *Chirashi* sushi literally means "loose sushi", with various layers of raw fish or roe served on a bowl of rice.

Fotomaki is a large roll with various ingredients wrapped in *nori*, a dried seaweed. It is similar to *temaki* or the cone-shaped handrolls.

restaurant + address
Nishimura
Shangri-La Hotel, Beijing
Garden Wing 2nd Floor,
29 Zizhuyuan Road, Beijing, China
telephone: +86.10.6841 2211 ext 6719
email: restaurantsrsvns.slb@shangri-la.com
website: www.shangri-la.com

cuisine
authentic Japanese

signature dishes
salt-grilled seafood selections • torched *nigiri* sushi

wine list
broad selection of sake and Japanese wines served hot or cold, or blended in signature cocktails

opening hours
11.30am–2.30pm daily
5.30–10pm daily

rooms
670 rooms • 30 suites

features
CHI, The Spa • swimming pool • gym • business centre • shops

other f + b outlets
Blu Lobster • Café Cha • Shang Palace

what's nearby
Summer Palace • Zhongguan Technology Park • Financial Street

senses the westin beijing financial street

THIS PAGE (FROM TOP): The open kitchen at Senses has alluring displays and a modern design; The pristine white palette of the interior is chic and inviting.

OPPOSITE: Seneses' signature dish, marinated salmon with Sichuan peppers, is a delicious mouthful not to be missed.

Epicureans in Beijing are known to head to **Senses** at **The Westin Beijing Financial Street** for its weekly champagne Sunday brunch—a winner in every sense of the word. Apart from offering an award-winning gastronomic spread that makes every diner a self-professed glutton, the brunch buffet also features free-flow of champagne, a fine selection of red and white wines, beers, martinis, vodkas, freshly squeezed exotic fruit juices and the most creative cocktails.

The Westin's signature restaurant presents a myriad of Chinese, Asian and international fare in the wide variety of food offered. Its open kitchen has won many awards for this famous champagne Sunday brunch, which brings in family diners as well as a regular business clientele. Although the restaurant brands its cuisine as contemporary fusion, its Executive Chef was actually classically French-trained. Canadian Chef Stéphane Tremblay has won many accolades for his French cuisine in his native Quebec. He gained invaluable experience from stints in prestigious five-star hotels in France, Canada, Japan and other parts of Asia, and has now distilled this into his innovative creations.

Local publications such as *Time Out Beijing* and *The Beijinger* agree that Senses is an excellent choice for dining. In just three years, from 2007 to 2009, the restaurant has collected countless awards. Senses promotes the Westin's "Super Food" concept where only the freshest local and imported ingredients are used. This is showcased in dishes like grilled cajun spiced salmon pita with crisp lettuce, tomatoes and cilantro lime mayo or vegetable fajitas on a sizzling skillet with broccoli, peppers, spinach and mushrooms. The menu features Asian favourites such as authentic Malaysian *bak kut teh* or braised pork spare ribs with Chinese herbs in a claypot and *char kway teow*, Penang's wok-fried flat rice noodles with prawns, crabmeat, Chinese sausage, bean sprouts and chilli.

The Westin also plays host to the annual Hats Off culinary celebration. Every November, Michelin-starred chefs from around the world converge in Beijing for a grand cook-off. This is an event that is an adventure for the senses, not to be missed.

beijing **china**

marinated salmon with orange and sichuan peppers

serves 4

For Salmon
400g salmon fillet
4 tbsp coarse sea salt
2 tbsp sugar
10–12 Sichuan peppercorns
1 tsp whole white peppercorns
4–6 juniper berries
1 piece dried Australian orange peel

For Garnish
1 bunch mint leaves
1 tbsp whipping cream
1 lemon
1 orange
1 tbsp olive oil
1 tbsp diced carrots
1 tbsp diced zucchini
1 tbsp sliced leeks
1 tbsp diced celery
salt and pepper
2 endive leaves, shredded
spring onions
orange segments

Method:
1. Heat up 3 tablespoons of coarse sea salt and crush in a mortar and pestle with the sugar, peppers and juniper berries. Set aside.
2. Peel the oranges and reserve only the peel. Mix the peel with a little salt and marinate for 2 hours. Rinse and then dry in a very low heat oven at 50°C (120°F) until the peel is very dry and crisp.
3. Crush the peel and mix into the first mixture.
4. Cover the salmon with the sea salt mixture, wrap in plastic film and leave for 2 days.
5. Before serving, rinse the salmon, pat dry and drizzle the olive oil over the top. Slice thinly.
6. Squeeze the juice from the orange and lemon, and add the olive oil, salt and pepper to make a dressing.
7. Shred the mint and mix into the whipping cream. Season with salt and pepper to taste.
8. Dice the carrots, the zucchini and the leeks, and then lightly blanch in some salted water.
9. To serve, plate salmon slices, drizzle dressing over and serve with mint cream, salad leaves, diced vegetables and orange segments.

Notes:
Salt and sugar curing is a common way to prepare salmon. Often, strong spices or herbs are added to the curing mix to flavour it. Some common herbs that are added are dill or coriander. Sometimes, vodka or another strong liquor hastens the curing process, which basically firms up the fish by drawing out its moisture. This gives the characteristic chewiness of well-made cured salmon such as gravlax.

restaurant + address
Senses
The Westin Beijing Financial Street
9b, Financial Street, Xi Cheng District
Beijing 100140, China
telephone: +86.10.6629 7810/11
email: f&b.beijing@westin.com
website: www.westin.com/beijingfinancial

cuisine
contemporary fusion

signature dishes
grilled cajun spiced salmon pita with lettuce, tomatoes and cilantro lime mayo • vegetable fajitas on a skillet with broccoli, peppers, spinach and mushrooms • *bak kut teh* (braised pork spare ribs with chinese herbs in a claypot)

wine list
there are both Old World and New World wines on the wine list • the restaurant hosts monthly wine promotions and also wine education classes

opening hours
breakfast 6–10.30am daily
lunch 11.30am–2.30pm daily
dinner 5.30–10pm daily
supper a la carte 10pm–midnight daily

rooms
486 rooms • 205 residences

features
Heavenly Spa • gym • swimming pool • business centre • executive lounge • Zen Garden • taichi, yoga and pilates classes

other f + b outlets
Jewel • Prego • Buzz Bar • Daily Treats • Plush Lobby Lounge • Shui Bar

what's nearby
The Forbidden City • Tiananmen Square • Seasons Mall • business, shopping, and entertainment districts

mandarin grill + bar mandarin oriental, hong kong

The **Mandarin Grill + Bar**, housed in Hong Kong's **Mandarin Oriental** hotel, has retained its position as one of the city's top restaurants for more than 40 years. The restaurant won its first Michelin star in 2009, and its success can easily be credited to its ability to constantly re-invent itself over the decades, updating its menu according to the latest culinary trends.

Executive Chef in residence is Uwe Opocensky, who serves up many exciting grill specialities. The chef prides himself on featuring quality organic produce and using seasonal ingredients. The Grill first opened in 1963, and was given a complete facelift in 2006 by one of Britain's most famous restaurateurs and designers, Sir Terence Conran. The designer decided to exploit the natural light of the space, and chose a neutral colour scheme for the interior. With Hong Kong's skyline as its backdrop, the Mandarin Grill fosters a relaxing vibe and possesses effortless charm, playing host to food aficionados from around the world. The sophisticated décor and an enticing menu makes dining at this illustrious institution a popular choice, reserved only for the crème de la crème of Hong Kong's society.

Chef Opocensky has an extensive resume, having worked with culinary luminaries such as Ferran Adria at El Bulli, Anton Mossiman in London and other great chefs such as Alain Ducasse. The chef has chosen to take the contemporary European route, adding touches of progressive gastronomy that point to his stint at El Bulli and his molecular gastronomy training. But the chef still appreciates traditional and uncomplicated cuisine, and has introduced a Crustacea Bar where diners may enjoy a selection of the finest oysters. Signature dishes at this restaurant include black cod, classic onion soup and a traditional lamb dish called 17th-century lamb. Another special feature at this restaurant is the popular four-course tasting menu which changes weekly.

Mandarin Oriental, Hong Kong, is the epitome of modern luxury and Oriental opulence. Conveniently located in the central business district, the hotel is a prime choice for those who have a penchant for impeccable food and world-class service.

THIS PAGE (FROM TOP): The lavishly adorned presidential suite represents ultimate luxury; The soothing décor of Mandarin Grill is perfect for a relaxed and unhurried meal.

OPPOSITE: Mandarin Grill's signature dish, pork loin with croqueta, apple jelly and mushroom quinoa.

hong kong **china**

pork loin with croqueta, apple jelly and mushroom quinoa

serves 4

For Croqueta
80ml melted butter
80g cake flour
250ml milk
150ml chicken stock
8 gelatin leaves
50g Parma ham, finely chopped
1 white onion, finely chopped
1 tbsp chopped chives
120g Parmesan cheese

For Apple Jelly
4 green apples
300g castor sugar
1 cinnamon stick
4 tsp *agar agar* powder

For Quinoa
200g quinoa
320ml mushroom stock

For Pork Loin
4 pork loins, about 160g each
salt and pepper to taste

Croqueta Method:
1. Melt the butter in a pan and sprinkle cake flour over to create a roux. Add milk and stir well to make a béchamel sauce.
2. Sauté the onions in a little olive oil, add ham and then chicken stock.
3. When the stock has released its flavours, add the gelatin sheets.
4. Allow to cool and add the béchamel sauce, followed by the cheese, chives and seasoning.
5. Pour into trays, freeze until firm and then cut into squares.
6. Breadcrumb each piece and deep-fry till golden brown.

Apple Jelly Method:
1. Peel, quarter and core apples.
2. Place apples in a pan with sugar and cinnamon stick. Cover with just enough water and slowly cook until apples are firm but make sure that they are not mushy.
3. Drain the apple pieces and blend into a purée. Pass through a fine sieve and then pour back into a pot.
4. Heat up the purée until it simmers, and then add the *agar agar* powder. Stir well until the powder completely dissolves.
5. Place the mixture in a flat tray or in moulds. Chill until firm.

Quinoa Method:
Cook quinoa in mushroom stock until tender. Cool on flat trays.

Pork Loin Method:
1. Place seasoned pork loin in a roasting bag and cook in a water bath at about 55°C (130°F) for 40 minutes or until cooked.
2. Remove and fry in a hot pan with olive oil until lightly browned on both sides. Allow to sit for about 4–5 minutes for the meat to rest.

Assembly:
Plate the pork loin on top of the mushroom quinoa, serve with *croqueta* and green apple jelly.

---

restaurant + address
Mandarin Grill & Bar
1st Floor, Mandarin Oriental, Hong Kong
5 Connaught Road, Central, Hong Kong
telephone: +852.2825 4004
email: mohkg-grill@mohg.com
website:
www.mandarinoriental.com/hongkong

cuisine
contemporary European

signature dishes
black cod • onion soup • 17th-century lamb

wine list
extensive wine list with a large selection of wines and champagnes by the glass

opening hours
breakfast 7.30–10am Monday–Friday
lunch noon–2.30pm Monday–Friday
dinner 6.30–10.30pm Monday–Saturday
dinner 6.30–9.30pm Sunday and public holidays

rooms
501 rooms and suites

features
spa • fitness centre • Mandarin Barber • Mandarin Salon • swimming pool

other f + b outlets
Man Wah • The Krug Room • M Bar • Captain's Bar • Pierre • Café Causette • Clipper Lounge • The Chinnery • Cake Shop

what's nearby
Chater Square • Landmark • shopping at Central • IFC Mall • Star Ferry • Lan Kwai Fong district • Peak tram

t'ang court the langham hong kong

In a city where good food and gourmet meals are such an integral part of everyday life, **The Langham Hotel**'s **T'ang Court** is a stellar gem among diamonds. The best testimony to this fact is the two Michelin stars that it won in 2008, hanging proudly on the wall. The restaurant showcases authentic Cantonese dishes, and serves up a repertoire of time-tested classics in a luxurious ambience reminiscent of the glory days of the Tang Dynasty. The restaurant is exquisitely clad in red and gold silk and adorned with contemporary sculptures. Its five private dining rooms are named after Tang Dynasty poets—Tai Bai, Le Tian, Zi Shou, Bai Yu and Zi Mei—and only accessible by a spiral staircase.

Executive Chef Siu Hin Chi is a traditional practitioner and master craftsman, having started his career as an apprentice at the early age of 17. He has served under many renowned Chinese chefs and has distilled more than 20 years of culinary expertise into the restaurant's elegant menu. His award-winning dishes include sautéed prawns and crab roe with golden fried pork and crabmeat puffs and stir-fried fresh lobster with spring onions, red onions and shallots. These dishes are all inspired by traditional Cantonese flavours. The chef's epicurean creations marry conventional methods and ingredients with his own creative touch, creating a fusion that delights the senses.

T'ang Court also prides itself on offering two unique menus which appeal especially to ladies who dine. An eight-course Nourishing Skin Menu is specially designed for those who believe that beauty is more than skin-deep. Using traditional Chinese ingredients known for their medicinal properties, this menu incorporates luxurious ingredients that are valued for their skin nourishing value. Abalone, *beche de mer* (sea cucumbers), shark's fin, garoupa, snow fungus and bird's nest are rich in Vitamin E, collagen and protein. Another exclusive menu caters to women in need of post-natal pampering, with special ingredients that are chosen for their recuperative and nourishing properties.

T'ang Court has chalked up many accolades from international media, including American *Food and Wine Magazine*'s list of "293 Outstanding Places to Eat" in the May 2008 issue. The hotel is right in the heart of Kowloon, and houses three other award-winning restaurants under its roof, promising something for every taste and fancy.

THIS PAGE (FROM TOP): *Guests are greeted by the luxurious lobby of the hotel; The opulent interior of T'ang Court is the perfect setting for authentic Cantonese cuisine.*
OPPOSITE: *Chef Siu's signature dish, pan-fried crab claw with celery and bell peppers.*

hong kong **china**

pan-fried crab claw with celery and bell peppers

serves 4

4 fresh crab claws
227g fresh shrimp paste (minced shrimps)
113g red bell pepper, diced
113g yellow bell pepper, diced
76g celery, diced
76g conpoy (dried scallops), soaked, drained and shredded
38g Japanese crab roe
salt, sugar, chicken bouillon powder, sesame oil to taste
cornstarch

Method:
1. Deep-fry the shredded conpoy until golden and crisp. Set aside.
2. Shape the shrimp paste around each fresh crab claw.
3. Pan-fry the stuffed crab claw until golden. Drain and set aside.
4. Lightly blanch the diced red and yellow bell peppers and diced celery.
5. Heat up some oil and stir-fry the peppers and the celery. Season to taste, and place on a dish.
6. Return the stuffed crab claws to the pan and braise with stock and seasoning. Thicken sauce with a little cornstarch.
7. Garnish the crab claw with the deep-fried shredded conpoy and crab roe, and serve.

restaurant + address
T'ang Court
The Langham Hong Kong
8 Peking Road, Tsim Sha Tsui
Kowloon, Hong Kong, China
telephone: +852.2375 1133
email: tlhkg.info@langhamhotels.com
website: hongkong.langhamhotels.com

cuisine
classic Cantonese

signature dishes
sautéed prawns and crab roe with golden fried pork and crabmeat puffs • stir-fried fresh lobster with spring onions, red onions and shallots

wine list
an extensive list of wines with a sommelier on-hand for recommendations

opening hours
lunch noon–3pm Monday–Friday
lunch 11am–3pm Saturday and Sunday
dinner 6–11pm daily

rooms
495 rooms and suites

features
Health Club • 24-hour gymnasium • jacuzzi and sauna • the Langham Club business facilities

other f + b outlets
L'Eclipse • The Bostonian Restuarant • Main St. Deli • Palm Court

what's nearby
shopping at Tsim Sha Tsui

fresh mandarin oriental, sanya

Sanya is the only place in China which has beautiful warm beaches, swaying coconut palms and a semi-tropical monsoon climate. Its salubrious weather and unspoilt beaches have earned it the moniker—Hawaii of the East. This resort town on the island of Hainan is attracting much attention these days, and has become a popular destination for hosting a wide spectrum of events, from beauty pageants to world economic forums. The sea, sand and palm trees are the perfect backdrop for the natural attractions of Hainan, just off the coast of Vietnam. At the southernmost tip is Sanya, a port city that has become a holiday base for those keen on water sports. This is where you can set off on a fishing expedition or go diving in the South China Sea.

The **Mandarin Oriental, Sanya** is a new gem in the glittering chain of international hotels springing up along the coast. **Fresh**, its signature restaurant, serves some of the best seafood on the South China coastal rim. The restaurant is situated on the beachfront and offers al fresco dining. Guests can enjoy the chef's seafood creations while basking in the magnificent view and cool sea breeze. The cuisine at Fresh is touted as new eclectic, blending the best of cooking traditions of Southeast Asia and Europe. The menu features Asian and French Provençal appetisers and exotic seafood platters which will take you on a global culinary adventure. Choose your seafood from the fish tanks, and while you wait, Fresh will whet your appetite with a complimentary amuse-bouche.

A striking feature of this restaurant is its unique wood-and-coconut fired grill where fish and lobsters are grilled to perfection. Fresh lives up to its name by serving up some of the freshest seafood infused with a musky and fruity flavour. The restaurant also offers an interesting selection of cocktails, premium malts as well as speciality beverages to complement your meal. Cooking classes and culinary demonstrations led by the Executive Chef are also available on request.

THIS PAGE (FROM TOP): At Fresh, bask in the sweeping views of the ocean while you dine; A picturesque and extensive view of the resort from an aerial perspective.
OPPOSITE (FROM TOP): Try the signature dish of marinated blue-shelled yabbies for a real taste of the sea; Relax by the sea at Sanya's beautiful pristine beaches.

hainan china

marinated blue-shelled yabbies

serves 4

For Stock
3 stalks onions, cut into 8 pieces
2 leeks, cut into 8 pieces
2 stalks celery, cut into 8 pieces
10 cloves garlic
juice from 2 lemons
water, enough to cover all the ingredients
white wine (optional), a splash
800g yabbies
1cm ginger, finely sliced

For Jelly
1 sheet gelatin
2 tomatoes, finely diced
½ stalk celery, finely diced
1 leek, finely diced
1 onion, finely diced
5 cloves garlic, minced

For Marinade
50ml olive oil
50ml lemon oil
salt, pepper and honey to taste

For Assembly
Swiss chard leaves, blanched
1 young leek, cleaned, rinsed and blanched

Method:

1. Blanch the yabbies in the boiling stock, and remove after 3 minutes or till just cooked. Reserve 200ml of stock for the jelly.
2. Shell the yabbies, and reserve the tail meat.
3. Line a small terrine mould with cling film and then layer with blanched Swiss chard leaves. If you do not have Swiss chard leaves, you can use large spinach leaves instead.
4. Soak 1 sheet of gelatin in cold water for about 5 minutes. Remove and squeeze out all the excess liquid before stirring it into the reserved boiling stock.
5. Add the finely diced vegetables to the jelly stock and set aside.
6. Place cooked yabbie tails on the Swiss chard leaves in the prepared terrine mould and ladle over a spoon of jelly stock. Place the blanched young leeks over each layer of yabbies. Repeat until ingredients are used up, ending with a layer of Swiss chard.
7. Allow the terrine to chill for 2 hours.
8. Meanwhile, prepare the marinade by stirring the olive oil, lemon oil, honey and seasoning together.
9. To serve, unmold the terrine and slice with a sharp knife into 1cm (0.5in) slices. Remove the plastic film and serve with a drizzle of marinade.

Notes:

Blue-shelled yabbbies are small fresh-water crustaceans whose natural habitat is Australian ponds and rivers. They look like and are related to lobsters, although they are much smaller. They are widely cultivated for their sweet meat.

restaurant + address
Fresh
Mandarin Oriental, Sanya
12 Yuhai Road
Sanya 572000
Hainan, China
telephone: +86.898.8820 9999
email: mosan-fresh@mohg.com
website: www.mandarinoriental.com/sanya

cuisine
modern eclectic seafood

signature dishes
seafood sharing platter • marinated blue-shelled yabbies

wine list
a master wine list with more than 200 labels • eight bottles are offered by the glass

opening hours
dinner 6–10pm daily

rooms
297 rooms

features
spa facilities • fitness centre • watersports facilities • MoMo kids club • flood-lit tennis courts • steam and sauna facilities • outdoor infinity pool

other f + b outlets
Yi Yang • Pavilion • Mee & Mian • Sunset Bar • Wave • MO Blues • Breeze

what's nearby
Summer Mall • Da Dong Hai Square

kathleen's 5 rooftop restaurant + bar

Shanghai is a city known for gourmet decadence, and restaurants often outdo each other in the quest to attract the city's rich and famous. For **Kathleen's 5 Rooftop Restaurant & Bar**, its unbeatable location instantly sets the restaurant apart. Perched on the fifth floor rooftop of the Shanghai Art Museum, diners are offered a full frontal view of the clock tower. As you step through the old wooden doors and stained glass façade of the restaurant, you are immediately reminded of Old Shanghai. It is no coincidence that this is where the prestigious Shanghai Racecourse Club used to be located, and the modern restaurant pays homage to its heritage in the name it has chosen in Chinese, which is Horse Racing Restaurant. Here, it is easy to imagine perfume and cigar smoke wafting through the air back in the day, amidst silhouettes of *cheongsams* and fedora hats.

Today, the elegant décor transforms the restaurant as nostalgia gives way to sleek modernism. Kathleen's 5 has refrained from the over-the-top opulence that characterises so many other Shanghai eateries. Instead, the understated interior allows the panoramic view to take centrestage. From the terrace, guests can look onto People's Square while they enjoy their food and bask in the glow of neon signs on this side of Nanjing Road.

The food is enjoyed by locals and expatriates alike for its emphasis on quality and in-season produce. An Australian chef oversees a kitchen that boasts a unique and ever-changing menu, which offers classic, unadulterated Western cuisine. The braised giant octopus with chorizo or pigeon and artichoke terrine are both inspired appetiser choices. The steamed ocean trout with prawn mousse and chilli jam, or the pan-fried tuna steak with braised globe artichoke and carrot purée are other delectable treats for mains. You may choose to indulge in their signature dish, suckling pig served three different ways.

An award-winning Hong Kong mixologist presides over the Backroom Lounge, which offers wines and some very ingenious cocktails, including lychee and kaffir lime martini and apple chili cucumber martini. If you prefer something more sinful, do not miss the succulent dessert platter that includes a roast apple soufflé with burnt caramel sauce and a special vanilla bean pannacotta with honey-poached pear in sweet wine jelly.

THIS PAGE (FROM TOP): *K5's glass pavilion allows patrons to dine in full sight of the historical clock tower; The open air terrace grants panoramic views of the city's modern landscape.*

OPPOSITE: *Signature dish, the savoury braised lamb shanks with gremolata; The delectable spiced house-made chorizo served with braised lentils.*

shanghai china

braised lamb shanks with gremolata

serves 4

4.5kg lamb shanks
all-purpose flour
4 tbsp olive oil, duck fat or dripping
2 carrots, roughly chopped
2 stalks celery, roughly chopped
1 leek, roughly chopped
2 onions, roughly chopped
1 head garlic, broken up into cloves
1 sprig thyme, leaves picked
1 sprig rosemary, leaves finely chopped
2 bay leaves
6 anchovy fillets
2 tbsp tomato paste
675ml dry red wine
675ml beef, chicken or lamb stock

For Gremolata
3 cloves garlic, finely chopped
5 tbsp chopped fresh parsley
2 lemons, grated zest only

Method:
1. Preheat the oven to 140°C (290°F).
2. Season the lamb shanks with freshly ground black pepper and dredge lightly with flour. You will not need to add salt, as the anchovies are salty enough.
3. Heat a little fat in a casserole, and brown the lamb shanks evenly. Remove and set aside.
4. Add the anchovies, carrots, celery, leek, onions, garlic cloves and herbs and cook over high heat, stirring continuously until the vegetables are caramelised and browned.
5. Add tomato paste and cook for 2 minutes, stirring all the time.
6. Deglaze the casserole by adding red wine. Reduce the juices to a third and scrape up the residue from the bottom of the pan.
7. Add stock, place shanks on top of the vegetables, and cover with a tight-fitting lid. Cook in the oven for about 3½ to 4 hours.
8. After 2 hours, turn over the meat and top up with extra stock or water to ensure that meat is completely submerged. Return to oven.
9. When the lamb is cooked, remove the shanks and keep them warm.
10. Strain the cooking liquid into a wide pot and place on medium-high heat to reduce to a thick sauce.
11. To make the gremolata, mix the chopped ingredients.
12. To serve, place a lamb shank on a plate, coat with sauce and then sprinkle with gremolata. Serve.

Note:
Gremolata is an Italian mixture of chopped parsley, garlic and lemon peel that is added to stews to give pungency to the dish.

You may choose to serve this dish with some potato gnocchi and cooked broad beans. Or, you can plate the lamb on a bed of horseradish potato mash or soft polenta enriched with mascarpone, butter and Parmesan cheese.

restaurant + address
Kathleen's 5 Rooftop Restaurant & Bar
5th Floor, Shanghai Art Museum
325 Nanjing Xi Lu, Shanghai, China
telephone: + 86.216.327 2221
email: info@kathleens5.com
website: www.kathleens5.com

cuisine
modern continental

signature dishes
suckling pig three ways • grilled king prawns with master stock pork terrine and sweet tamarind jus • k5 dessert sampler platter

wine list
an eclectic wine list featuring both Old World and New World wines • a sommelier is available to recommend wines to complement the food

opening hours
lunch 11.30am–2.30pm Monday to Friday
brunch 10.30am–4.30pm Saturday and Sunday
tea 2.30–4.30pm daily
dinner 5.30–11.30pm daily

what's nearby
Grand Theater • People's Square • Nanjing Road malls • Shanghai Museum

simply thai

If you are looking for good Thai cuisine in Shanghai, food aficionados will point you in the direction of **Simply Thai**. With scores of awards and testimonials to boast, the restaurant has a reputation for being the authority on Thai food in China. Food critics from the country's top magazines and newspapers agree, regularly paying homage to the restaurant's culinary prowess.

Simply Thai began as a single restaurant in the old French Concession, and over the last 10 years has expanded to four outlets strategically located across the city of Shanghai. The secret of Simply Thai's success is, as their name suggests, keeping it simple. The restaurant commands a large team of Thai chefs, supported by a pool of waitstaff who stay true to the Thai ethos of friendly hospitality. The menu offers genuinely authentic Thai cuisine with no compromises to the local palate other than opting to make the dishes less spicy, on request.

The restaurant's Head Chef is Bangkok native Sukit Niramitcharoenwong, a pioneer who has seen the chain through its decade of transformation. Chef Sukit oversees the kitchens, and his team of Thai chefs ensure that the quality and standard of food are maintained across the board. The culinary expertise of the chefs at Simply Thai lies in their ability to transform ordinary Thai street food into fine-dining delicacies that make it to the tables of the restaurant.

The chefs at Simply Thai recommend their best-selling dishes such as the classic *tom yum* seafood soup and the green papaya salad. Other favourites include the Simply hors d'oeuvre platter, barbecued chicken, crispy fish in sweet-sour sauce and fried prawns in curry sauce.

THIS PAGE (FROM TOP): *A sense of grandeur is created with red velvet chairs complemented by teak fixtures at Simply Thai; An austere Buddhist statue stands serenely, and represents the official Thai religion.*

OPPOSITE (FROM TOP): *The rich and creamy green curry chicken; An authentic Thai sculpture.*

shanghai china

green curry chicken

serves 4

For Green Curry Paste
1 stalk lemongrass, finely chopped
2–3 green chillies
3–4 shallots, or 1 small red onion
4–5 cloves garlic
5cm length of *galangal*, chopped
1 cup packed fresh coriander leaves and roots
½ tsp ground cumin
½ tsp ground coriander
½ tsp ground white pepper
3 tbsp fish sauce
1 tsp shrimp paste or *belacan*

For Green Curry Chicken
1 cup green curry paste
3–4 tbsp fish sauce
1 litre coconut milk
25g palm sugar
500g chicken, cut into bite-sized pieces
1 eggplant, cut into chunks
100g pumpkin, boiled and cut into chunks
½ red bell pepper, sliced into strips
½ green bell pepper, sliced into strips
1 stalk basil leaves
2–3 kaffir lime leaves

Method:
1. Make green curry paste. Place all the ingredients in a blender and pulverise to a fine paste.
2. Heat some oil in a pan and sauté the green curry paste until the mixture becomes fragrant.
2. Add the coconut milk, fish sauce and palm sugar. Stir to blend.
3. Bring the coconut milk to a boil, and add the chicken and eggplant chunks. Simmer until the chicken is cooked and eggplant is tender.
4. Add the cooked pumpkin chunks, red and green pepper strips and the kaffir lime leaves.
5. Season to taste. Just before serving, add some basil leaves and mix them into the curry.
6. Serve with hot rice.

Notes:
Green curry paste uses fresh herbs and spices that are easily available. This is a recipe that will yield about one cup of paste, enough for a large bowl of curry. Use more or fewer chillies, according to the level of heat desired. Traditionally, Thai cooks would pound the ingredients of the green curry paste in a mortar and pestle, starting with the garlic, onions, chillies and shrimp paste, adding the fresh herbs and roots before finally adding the spices. If you cannot find *galangal* (also known as blue ginger), you can substitute with fresh ginger.

restaurant + address
Simply Thai Xintiandi
159 Ma Dang Road, corner of Xing Ye Road
Shanghai 200021, China
telephone: +86.40. 800 7729
email: enquiry@simplythai-sh.com
website: www.simplythai-sh.com

cuisine
authentic Thai cuisine

signature dishes
green papaya salad • barbecued chicken • *tom yum* seafood soup

wine list
a wine list of about 60 bottles, with New World wines predominant • wine by the glass is available

opening hours
11am–midnight daily

what's nearby
Xintiandi area for shopping

bale sutra hotel tugu bali

THIS PAGE (FROM TOP): *The Puri Le Mayeur villa, dedicated to the love story of painter Adrien-Jean Le Mayeur de Merprès and Legong dancer Ni Polok; Bale Sutra's opulent red room.*

OPPOSITE (FROM TOP): *Signature dish sesame-coated crab claws; Enjoy a romantic picnic in bed by the sea at the resort.*

The Chinese first settled in the Malay Peninsula and Indonesian Archipelago in Southeast Asia as far back as the 15th century. These new settlers married local women, adopted the cultural practices of their new home and infused the Chinese cooking they were accustomed to, with local herbs and spices. Peranakan-style cooking was thus born, reflecting a synthesis of Chinese and indigenous culture, also known as Babah Peranakan in Indonesia.

Original Chinese cooking methods and recipes were adapted so that a completely new taste emerged when ingredients such as coconut milk, lemongrass, turmeric and tamarind were incorporated. These exotic ingredients were unique to the native land, and were used to flavour many dishes.

Bale Sutra, the signature restaurant at the **Hotel Tugu Bali**, has dedicated its menu to authentic Peranakan cuisine. Diners can experience the best examples in an equally authentic and historical setting—a 300-year old Javanese temple painstakingly moved to Bali and restored to resplendence.

The restaurant's best-selling dishes show off the perfect marriage of Chinese and Indonesian gastronomy. Some examples are *lumpia udang*, crisp-fried bags of plump tiger prawns tied with leek, and flavoured with rice wine and sesame sauce; and lobster *bumbu rujak*, or lobster in light tomato, tamarind and coconut stew. *Babi masak kecap* is a classic pork stew which uses a sweet soya sauce that is typically used in many Indonesian dishes.

Bale Sutra's commitment to tradition and heritage is exhibited in its special multi-course Babah Peranakan, China Imperial and Summer Palace menus. The food here is served on antique silver and Ming-style tableware, presented on a long dining table that is draped in 18th century embroidered silk.

As lilting music from traditional Chinese instruments plays in the background, diners may feast on exotic creations such as the "pearl ball" (steamed prawn ball with glutinous rice) and the "eye of dragon" (steamed stuffed zucchini with prawn). Bale Sutra also provides the appropriate cultural backdrop with *wayang golek* (Javanese Wooden Puppet) and *wayang kulit* (Javanese Shadow Puppet) fixtures embellishing the restaurant, while a papier maché longevity goddess sits at the head of the table. At Bale Sutra, dine in complete comfort as you taste a slice of living history.

bali **indonesia**

sesame-coated crab claws

serves 4

2 fresh crabs (to yield about 200g of crabmeat)
100g breadcrumbs
1 whole egg
40g sesame seeds
1 large leek, white parts finely chopped
100g fresh shrimps, peeled
2 tbsp sesame oil
150g flour
1½ tsp salt
1 tsp sugar

For Sauce

5 red peppers, about 30g each
4 small red chillies
2 tsp sugar
2 cloves garlic
½ tsp salt
60ml water
60ml coconut milk

For Garnish

50g young potatoes
rice flour
500g small heads of broccoli or young asparagus
1 large onion, sliced
4–5 cloves garlic, peeled and minced
1 small red capsicum, finely diced
1 small green capsicum, finely diced

Method:

1. Bring a large pot of water to boil. Place the crabs in the water. Once the crabs are cooked or turn orange, take them out and remove the claws. This should take about 6 to 8 minutes. Set aside.
2. Carefully remove the crabmeat from the shells, making sure that no bones or shell fragments remain.
3. In a separate pot, blanch the shrimps until they just turn orange. Drain and mince the shrimps into a fine paste using a blender.
4. In a large mixing bowl, place the crabmeat, minced shrimp, chopped leek, sesame oil, salt and sugar. Mix well.
5. Take a large ball of the mixture and mould around each crab claw. Coat each claw ball with flour, egg, breadcrumbs and sesame seeds.
6. Deep-fry until the crab claws turn golden brown.

Assembly:

1. Peel the potatoes and grate into long strips. Dust lightly with rice flour, press lightly into a woven basket arrangement, and deep-fry till crisp and golden.
2. Cut the chillies lengthwise and take out the seeds. Simmer the chillies and garlic for about 15 minutes. Drain the water, then grind or blend. Add about 4 tablespoons of water as well as the sugar and salt. Heat in a pot, stirring all the time.
3. In a separate pan, stir-fry the broccoli or asparagus with the onions and season with a pinch of salt. Set aside.
4. Stir-fry the chopped garlic, diced red and green capsicums until fragrant. Add chilli sauce, coconut milk and the rest of the water, Heat on low fire. Stir and reduce the sauce slightly; season to taste.
5. Place the claws in potato basket with broccoli or asparagus on the side. Drizzle the capsicum sauce over the crab claws and vegetables.

Notes:

This is a traditional recipe that has been used over many generations by Babah Peranakan families in Java. The use of coconut milk is typical of Southeast Asian cuisine while the use of the sweet capsicum sauce is a Chinese influence.

---

restaurant + address
Bale Sutra
Hotel Tugu Bali
Jalan Pantai Batu Bolong
Canggu Beach, Bali, Indonesia
telephone: +62.361.731 701
email: bali@tuguhotels.com
website: www.tuguhotels.com

cuisine
Babah Peranakan cuisine

signature dishes
lumpia udang (crisp fried spring roll stuffed with prawns) • *udang windu bumbu rujak* (prawns stir-fried in tomato and lemongrass sauce)

wine list
there is a fairly extensive list of both Old and New World wines • wines are also served by the glass

opening hours
11am–11pm daily

rooms
21 villas and suites

features
Waroeng Djamoe Spa • Iboe Soelastri cooking class • romantic private dining by the beach

other f + b outlets
Tugu Dom • Wantilan Agung • Bale Paputan • Waroeng Tugu • Garuda Megibung • Selamatan Jaranan

what's nearby
Tanah Lot Temple • Bali Nirwana Golf • Echo Beach • Seminyak nightlife

beduur ubud hanging gardens

THIS PAGE (FROM TOP): A table at Beduur overlooking the lush valley and the Ayung River; Orchids and candles set the mood for a romantic meal.

OPPOSITE: The unique passion fruit crème brûlée, a delicious signature dessert at Beduur that should not be missed.

Beduur is situated in **Ubud Hanging Gardens** and, as its name suggests, is surrounded by sweeping jungle vistas. The restaurant overlooks the winding Ayung River and offers spectacular views of the valley. On the opposite bank of the gorge, there is a sacred temple that sits proudly on its perch.

Those who visit the restaurants at Ubud Hanging Gardens will be greeted by a flawless combination of fine-dining and beautiful scenery. They share one common feature—panoramic views of the vast valley and temple. At Beduur, the al fresco seating offers an intimate commune with nature, and the tranquil ambience is perfect for enjoying the contemporary French-Asian cuisine. A unique characteristic of the restaurant is that it features vegetables that are grown on the island itself, guaranteeing top quality.

French Executive Chef Renaud Le Rasle helms the kitchen at Beduur and his creativity is easily seen in the sophisticated menu. He has significant experience when it comes to serving the crème de la crème of society, and this is reflected in his impressive culinary resume. The chef started his career with an apprenticeship at the three-Michelin star Restaurant Pic in France. He subsequently earned fame at the prestigious Drome l'Hermitage culinary competition as the youngest ever contestant to win. Chef Le Rasle then went on to work for Alain Ducasse at Louis XV in Monte Carlo, and at Guy Savoy Bistro l'Etoile in Paris he was Chef de Cuisine.

Chef Le Rasle most recently moved to Bali to study the ingredients and culture of an island known for its exotic flavours and fusion cuisine. The result is an array of creations that is both aesthetically appealing and deliciously irresistible. The unique sake-flavoured Peking duck ballotine, Tasmanian sea trout chorizo "under the skin" and passion fruit crème brûlée are a few famous dishes on the menu.

Beduur also offers set meals apart from the a la carte menu, and there is a menu degustation that introduces Chef Le Rasle's specialities. The chef also shares his tips and secrets with cooking classes that teach students to understand Balinese ingredients and to prepare local delicacies. Students start with a tour of the local village, and then head to the hotel's Balinese kitchen where the cooking lesson begins.

bali **indonesia**

passion fruit crème brûlée

serves 4

200ml cream
200ml milk
4 egg yolks
1 fresh passion fruit
50g passion fruit purée
4 sable Breton bases
15g granulated sugar
100g strawberries
20g palm sugar
4 scoops mango sorbet
4 sprigs mint leaves
5ml passion fruit reduction

Method:
1. Boil the milk and the cream together.
2. Whisk in the eggs and sugar, the fresh passion fruit and purée.
3. Pour into moulds and bake in a bain-marie at 180°C (360°F) for about 20 minutes. Chill in the freezer.
4. Sprinkle the palm sugar on top of the crème brûlée and then sear with a blow-torch.
5. Place the crème brûlée on top of the sable Breton (French shortbread bases).
6. Slice the strawberries and place them around the pastry.
7. Finally, serve with some mango sorbet, a sprig of mint and the passion fruit reduction.

Notes:
A sable base is a French-style base made from shortbread. It is a crumbly biscuit dough that is usually rolled into a thick sausage, chilled and then cut into fluted rounds.

Sable Breton is so called because it is made from Breton butter. There are also other regional recipes such as sable Lisieux, sable Caen and Dutch sable. Sable Liseux is flavoured with cinnamon, brown sugar and cream, while sable Caen is scoured with a fork and brushed with egg yolk to give it a deep golden finish. Dutch sable is made with two doughs, one flavoured with chocolate and the other with vanilla.

To make a simple sable, rub 260g plain flour with 200g butter until the mixture resembles fine breadcrumbs. Add 50g castor sugar, a teaspoon of salt and a spoonful of vanilla. Dampen the mixture with two egg yolks and shape into a dough. Chill the ball of dough. Roll out to about 4cm (1.5in) thick and cut into rounds for tart bases.

restaurant + address
Beduur
Ubud Hanging Gardens
Desa Buahan—Payangan
Ubud, Bali 80571
Indonesia
telephone: +62.361.982 700
email: ubud@orient-express.com
Website: www.ubudhanginggardens.com

cuisine
French Asian cuisine with Balinese influences

signature dishes
sake-flavoured Peking duck ballotine • braised tender beef cheeks • Tasmanian sea trout chorizo "under the skin" • chocolate lime macaroons

wine list
extensive list of both Old and New World wines • wines are also served by the glass

opening hours
breakfast 7–10am daily
lunch noon–3pm daily
dinner 6.30–11pm daily

rooms
38 pool villas

features
two infinity swimming pools • Ayung Spa • business centre • yoga classes

other f + b outlets
Diatas Pohon Café • Bukit Becik Bar

what's nearby
mountain biking • Batur Volcano • Besaki Mother temple • painting classes • river rafting • elephant rides • Ubud markets • trekking • Land Rover tour • museums

glow como shambhala estate

THIS PAGE (FROM TOP): The stately architecture of the open air restaurant creates grandeur; Tirta Ening is one of the resort's five residences which allows visitors to bask in Ubud's luscious greenery.

OPPOSITE: Signature dish raw green curry made especially for the health conscious.

In a corner of the idyllic island of Bali, there is a sanctuary for clean, green living. **COMO Shambhala Estate** is the perfect retreat for those who have a desire for healthy cuisine with a gourmet touch. The spa resort boasts its own nutritionist who liaises between guests and the kitchen to ensure that all personal dietary needs are met. What appears on the dining tables is organic and locally sourced, delivered from field to table with minimum delay. Meat, fish and vegetables are featured equally, allowing guests to choose from an array of dishes inspired by various cuisines ranging from South Indian to Italian and of course, Balinese styles of cooking.

Guests with special diets are carefully catered to, and the resort offers choices such as soya milk instead of cow's milk, and yeast-free breads. Menus also feature low salt preparations and raw, unprocessed honey replaces sugar. The Estate's dishes highlight raw fruit and vegetables as main ingredients, all of which are rich in living enzymes. There is also an extensive juice and vegetable extract menu for guests to cleanse their systems.

COMO Shambhala's signature restaurant is **glow**—a contemporary, Koichiro Ikebuchi-designed outlet with an open-air kitchen that looks out onto sweeping jungle vistas. The emphasis is on all things natural, and guests are served healthy saté, sorbets and granitas in bamboo steamers, wooden vessels and banana-leaf wraps, keeping in line with the organic concept. At glow, some menu favourites include warm salad of roast pumpkin, parsnips and brussels sprouts with sautéed grains, nuts and seeds, and peppered tuna fillet with snow-pea shoots, quinoa noodles and lemon chilli sauce.

The resort's Australian-born Chef Amanda Gale exudes a culinary flair which combines pan-Asian influences with a deep respect for carefully sourced ingredients. She possesses a keen awareness for intelligent nutrition. Chef Gale is also the Executive Chef for COMO Hotels & Resorts, and has worked with other culinary luminaries such as Kylie Kwong and Neil Perry in Sydney.

COMO Shambhala offers individually tailored meal programmes for its health conscious guests, such as Ayurvedic, cleansing and fasting menus. A dedicated raw menu is available, and guests are encouraged to partake in this nutrition-packed cuisine.

bali indonesia

raw green curry
serves 4

1 small zucchini
½ green mango, cut into strips
6 spears baby corn, thinly sliced
3–4 sugar snap peas, cut into strips
¼ young coconut flesh, thinly sliced
1–2 stalks celery, sliced
a few sprigs coriander leaves
4–6 Thai basil leaves
1 stalk lemongrass, sliced
1 avocado, pitted
10g raw cashew nuts
juice of 1 lime
1–2 green chillies
2 stalks Italian basil, leaves only
1 tsp curry powder
20ml coconut water from a young green coconut
1 tsp sea salt

Method:
1. Mix the avocado, cashew nuts, lime juice, green chillies, Italian basil and curry powder with the coconut water.
2. Process to a smooth paste in a blender, and season to taste.
3. Wash and cut the vegetables. Toss well to mix.
4. Spoon some of the sauce onto a deep plate and place the mixed salad on top of the sauce.
5. Garnish with coriander, Thai basil and lemongrass. Serve.

Notes:
This is a recipe that exploits the freshness and natural flavours of the ingredients. It combines a variety of textures and flavours to create a green curry that is scented by the perfume of spices and herbs.

The crunch of the zucchini and baby corn is paired with the tart sweetness of finely cut green mango. Sugar snap peas, crisp and sweet, add more texture.

The sauce or curry uses avocado as a thickener and its richness is accentuated by the raw cashew nuts. Lime juice and coconut water lighten the sauce and fresh basil lends its unique aroma to make this a truly healthy, tasty recipe very representative of modern spa cuisine.

restaurant + address
glow
COMO Shambhala Estate
Banjar Begawan, Desa Melinggih Kelod
Payangan, Gianyar 80571
Bali, Indonesia
telephone: +62.361.978 888
fax: +62.361.978 889
email: res@cse.comoshambhala.bz
website: cse.comoshambhala.bz

cuisine
healthy spa cuisine

signature dishes
warm salad of roast pumpkin, parsnips and brussels sprouts with sautéed grains, nuts and seeds • stir-fried marinated *tempeh* with mushrooms, asian greens and organic red rice

wine list
in keeping with the resort's wellness theme, residents are not encouraged to consume alcoholic beverages whilst undergoing programmes • however, a good selection of wines, both red and white, are available by the glass or bottle upon request

opening hours
11am–10pm daily

rooms
30 rooms, suites and villas

features
wireless internet access • gymnasium • yoga • Ayurveda • pilates • 24-hour in-room dining • lap pool • retail shop

other f + b outlets
Kudus House

what's nearby
temples • museums • galleries • Ubud

kemiri uma ubud

THIS PAGE (FROM TOP): *Uma Ubud's pristine Terrace Room overlooking the verdant green Tjampuhan Valley; Kemiri Restaurant by the lush tropical garden and koi pond.*

OPPOSITE: *Signature dish, a healthy and inspiring king prawn, orange and pomelo salad at Kemiri.*

The **Kemiri** restaurant at **Uma Ubud** in Bali is named after the candlenut, an exotic ingredient that is crucial to many Indonesian dishes. Part of the COMO group, the restaurant offers a unique menu which has been thoughtfully conceived to maximise energy and well-being using raw, organic food rich in living enzymes, vitamins and minerals.

The restaurant was designed by Japanese architect Koichiro Ikebuchi, who has constructed an open-air dining space complemented by a waterfall-fed koi pond, creating a sense of tranquility. Inside, light airy *alang-alang* ceilings engender a cool and comfortable ambience. Kemiri is located in the heart of Bali, in Ubud. This is a small but lively town often regarded as the island's cultural hub. The restaurant is just five minutes away from the town centre, next to the Neka Museum.

The menu's Balinese and Asian dishes are inspired by seasonal ingredients grown in the neighbourhood and Executive Chef Chris Miller's creations incorporate spices found in the Indonesian Archipelago. The Australian-born chef combines pan-Asian gastronomic flavours with an emphasis on intelligent nutrition, a trademark of his cooking.

At Kemiri, some signature dishes include Sichuan salt and pepper squid salad with green mango, chilli and lime, crispy fried soft-centred duck eggs with oyster sauce and chilli, and a grilled beef tenderloin with asparagus and oyster sauce. For dessert, try the delectable warm chocolate and cinnamon fondant with Bedugul strawberries.

Kemiri offers cooking classes for those keen on exploring healthy eating beyond the menu. Special sessions can be organised to provide fascinating insights on Balinese life, beliefs and culture through learning about its food, cooking methods and culinary myths. Students will be taught to prepare a complete menu under the watchful eyes of Master Chefs, and will walk away with a whole new perspective on Balinese cuisine. Dishes taught include curried chicken and glass noodle hotpot, Balinese soya meat saté and Indian Ocean seafood in banana leaf and spicy beef dumplings.

bali **indonesia**

king prawn, orange and pomelo salad

serves 4

For Salad
4 oranges, cut into segments
½ a pomelo, cut into segments
3 apples, peeled and thinly sliced
½ bunch picked mint leaves
1 bunch coriander leaves
2 kaffir lime leaves, finely shredded
4 shallots, thinly sliced
8 shallots, sliced and deep fried
⅓ cup finely shredded young coconut flesh
2 tbsp crushed peanuts
2 red chillies thinly sliced, for garnish
4 grilled king prawns, about 20g each

For Dressing
2 tsp palm sugar
6 small pieces dried tangerine peel
1 kaffir lime leaf
2 red bird's eye chillies, seeded
soya sauce to taste
tamarind juice to taste
peanut oil

Method:
1. Prepare dressing by caramelising the palm sugar in a little water with the dried tangerine peel, kaffir lime leaf and chillies. Cook till the color deepens to a deep gold.
2. Add tamarind juice and soya sauce according to taste. Whisk to combine. Adjust consistency by adding a little water if necessary.
3. Pour dressing into a bowl and whisk with peanut oil to emulsify.
4. Mix all the salad ingredients together and toss with the tamarind palm sugar dressing. Arrange on a plate and garnish with the shredded young coconut.

Notes:
This salad uses many citrus ingredients that may not be familiar to the Western cook. Pomelo is a tropical citrus fruit that is like grapefruit but less tart, and with sacs that separate very easily. It is sweet with a slightly bitter tang and is a popular salad ingredient in Thailand, Vietnam, Malaysia and Indonesia.

Kaffir lime leaves come from another tropical citrus plant. The plant bears a wrinkled lime that is very dry and hard. The skin is used in many Malaysian curries and *sambals*, but it is the leaf, finely shredded, that is used as a herb in many dishes.

Dried tangerine peel originated in China, where the peel of the Chinese mandarin orange or tangerine is air-dried in the winter to produce a pungent peel that is used to flavour soups and desserts.

restaurant + address
Kemiri
Uma Ubud
Jalan Raya Sanggingan
Banjar Lungsiakan, Kedewatan
Ubud, Bali
Indonesia
telephone: +62.361.972 448
email: res.ubud@uma.como.bz
website: uma.ubud.como.bz

cuisine
contemporary Southeast Asian cuisine

signature dishes
Sichuan salt and pepper squid salad with green mango, chilli and lime • crispy fried soft-centred duck eggs with oyster sauce and chilli • grilled beef tenderloin with asparagus and oyster sauce

wine list
a fairly extensive list of both Old and New World wines • wines are also available by the glass

opening hours
breakfast 6.30–10.30am daily
lunch noon–3pm daily
dinner 6.30–10.30pm daily

rooms
24 rooms and 5 suites

features
COMO Shambhala Retreat • reflexology area • open air yoga pavilion • meditation bale • steam room and sauna • 25-metre (80-feet) pool • business centre facilities

other f + b outlets
Uma Pool Bar

what's nearby
Neka Museum • Arma Museum • Ubud Palace • Ubud Art Market • Tjampuhan Ridge • Sobek white water rafting

maya sari mas restaurant maya ubud resort + spa

Perched high above the Petanu River valley, **Maya Ubud Resort & Spa** affords spectacular views of luscious rice fields and hillside gardens. While this classic Balinese resort's hospitality and luxurious spa facilities are all reasons to linger, dining at its signature restaurant, **Maya Sari Mas Restaurant**, is a particularly enjoyable experience.

Maya Ubud's Director of Food & Beverage is Kath Townsend, an Australian trained chef with extensive restaurant and resort experience. She is also Executive Chef of Maya Ubud and her personal touch has left an unforgettable mark on the resort's award-winning restaurants.

Maya Sari Restaurant is the resort's premier restaurant consisting of two levels—**Maya Sari Mas** on top, and **Maya Sari Asiatique** below. Here, guests can start their day with an extensive sunrise breakfast buffet or partake in a relaxed and casual lunch. In the evening, they may dine in complete comfort while enjoying the restaurant's international selection on an open deck, where cool evening breezes ruffle elegant white drapes against a backdrop of nature.

Another highlight of the resort is the bar upstairs, **Bar Bedulu**, which is nestled under a traditional thatched roof pavilion. Enjoy the balmy weather as you sample cocktail concoctions, thirst-quenching tropical juices and icy cold beers, or select wines by the glass from a comprehensive list of both Old and New World vintages from the cellar.

In keeping with its unmistakable Balinese charm, Maya Sari Asiatique is an Asian-style restaurant that boasts an eclectic collection of gourmet treats with influences drawn from around Asia. The restaurant also has a *teppanyaki* grill, where the Japan-trained Sous Chef demonstrates his brilliant culinary and knife skills, bringing diners a unique and intimate experience. Here, specially designed set menus are available for those who cannot decide when faced with the wide variety of exotic dishes. The set menus offer a wonderful sampling of classic Balinese dishes to tantalise the senses.

It comes as no surprise that Maya Sari Restaurant has won numerous accolades and earned recognition from major tourism publications, or that its menu is deemed by many as an epicurean tour of the best of Asia.

THIS PAGE (FROM TOP): *Maya Sari Mas affords spectacular views of the Petanu River valley; Upstairs, Bar Bedulu overlooks lush gardens, while Maya Sari Asiatique below takes diners even closer to nature.*
OPPOSITE: *Balinese vanilla, coconut and kaffir lime-scented pannacotta with brûléed mango and coconut wafers.*

bali **indonesia**

balinese vanilla, coconut and kaffir lime-scented pannacotta with brûléed mango and coconut wafers

serves 4

For Pannacotta
300ml fresh milk
125ml cream
75ml coconut cream
60g white sugar
3½ sheets gelatine
1 vanilla bean, halved and seeded
4 kaffir lime leaves, torn
zest of 1 kaffir lime

For Brûléed Mango
2 firm ripe mangoes

For Palm Sugar Syrup
200g dark palm sugar
2 kaffir lime leaves
juice of ½ lime
½ cup water

For Vanilla Syrup
1 vanilla bean, seeded
½ cup caster sugar
½ cup water

For Coconut Wafers
¼ cup plus 2 tbsp clarified butter
2 cups unsweetened shredded coconut flesh
⅔ cup sugar
½ cup egg whites
⅓ cup all-purpose flour

For Garnish
4 tbsp finely diced mango
12 baby kaffir lime leaves, dipped in toffee and set firm
freshly grated coconut

Method:
1. Soak gelatine in a little cold water until soft. Heat up milk, cream, vanilla bean, lime leaves, zest and sugar until the mixture is almost boiling. Add gelatine and stir until it is totally dissolved.
2. Stir in the coconut cream, remove from heat immediately and strain mixture into a deep baking tray. Refrigerate until it sets, and cut out 12 rounds of pannacotta using a round cutter.
3. Peel mangoes and cut the flesh into 12 discs 0.5cm (0.2in) thick and 4cm (1.5in) in diameter.
4. Make palm syrup by boiling together dark palm sugar, kaffir lime leaves, lime juice and water. Bring to a boil and simmer for 10 minutes. Strain, cool and set aside for use.
5. Make the vanilla syrup by boiling together vanilla bean, sugar and water. Strain and set aside until ready for use.
6. Preheat the oven to 180°C (360°F). Line two large baking sheets with parchment paper and brush with 2 tablespoons of clarified butter.
7. Make coconut wafers. Thoroughly mix together shredded coconut, sugar, egg whites, flour and the remaining clarified butter.
8. Drop tablespoons of the coconut mixture onto the prepared cookie sheet. Shape the mixture into a thin 15cm x 8cm (6in x 3in) triangle. Repeat with remaining mixture. Bake each sheet of wafer for 12 to 15 minutes, or until they are golden. Roll up wafers and cool on tray.

Assembly:
1. Place mango discs onto a metal tray and sprinkle with castor sugar. Caramelise the top using a blowtorch or by placing under a hot grill.
2. Arrange 3 rounds of pannacotta on each plate, and top with caramelised mango discs. Place a coconut wafer on each round.
3. Swirl palm sugar and vanilla syrups decoratively around the plate. Garnish with a little fresh coconut and diced mango, and finish with a toffee-coated lime leaf.

restaurants + address
Maya Sari Mas • Maya Sari Asiatique
Maya Ubud Resort & Spa
Jln Gunung Sari Peliatan
PO Box 1001, Ubud 80571
Bali, Indonesia
telephone: +62.361.977 888
email: info@mayaubud.com
website: www.mayaubud.com

cuisine
Maya Sari Mas—contemporary international • Maya Sari Asiatique—asian gourmet

signature dishes
Maya Sari Mas—green pea cappuccino with grilled prawns • Maya Sari Asiatique—*teppanyaki* selection

wine list
selection of Old and New World wines, with an emphasis on Australian wines, by bottle, carafe and glass

opening hours
breakfast 7–10.30am daily
lunch noon–2.30pm daily
dinner 7–11pm daily

rooms
48 rooms • 60 private villas

features
Riverside spa • two pools • tennis court • pitch and put golf • yoga and meditation

other f + b outlets
Bar Bedulu • River Café

what's nearby
rice terraces • mountain bike rental • village trekking and nature walk • cultural performances • Ubud Royal Palace

nelayan restaurant jimbaran puri bali

The best seafood in Bali comes from Jimbaran where the local fishing fleet is based, and is a mere five-minute stroll from the **Jimbaran Puri Bali**. Each morning, the fleet comes back to shore loaded with the night's catch of barracuda, snapper, lobster, shrimp, squid and tuna. The morning market offers a cornucopia of treasures that will tickle the imagination of any chef. This is the reason why Jimbaran Puri's signature restaurant, **Nelayan Restaurant**, takes such pride in its seafood dishes. When you have the freshest ingredients at your doorstep, it is only natural for the chef to be inspired to create the best dishes.

The setting of Nelayan is simple and creates a relaxing ambience. Tables are set up by the beach, and you can dig your toes into the sand as you feast on delicacies that have been freshly picked from the sea. Nelayan serves locally caught fish and seafood, as well as French-Mediterranean dishes. The flawless marriage of seafood and Mediterranean-style cuisine creates a menu that presents a dazzling array of choices even for the most seasoned gourmand.

For appetisers, there is a tuna and avocado tartare, lightened with citrus juices and scented with aromatic herbs. Another outstanding choice is a steamed sweet river prawn salad served with fresh fruits and a balsamic and olive oil dressing, or the seared scallops served with spinach purée, sour cream, parma ham chips and fresh apple. For the main course, the catch of the day is served simply with rice, vegetables and finally topped with a special Balinese sauce. The more adventurous may want to try a Balinese-influenced mahi-mahi with a local prawn curry and coconut sauce. Lobsters are special no matter where you are from, and Nelayan pays tribute to the king of crustaceans with its own dedicated section on the menu. Fresh lobster and hearts of palm are dressed plainly with some lime and olive oil, while the Mediterranean influence surfaces in a pumpkin and lobster ravioli served on tomato purée in a coriander cream sauce. More sophisticated aficionados should try the sautéed lobster medallions served in a vanilla butter sauce with pink peppercorns.

There is something for everyone at Nelayan, and if it is prime grade meat you are after, choose the Australian grilled beef tenderloin, the honeyed duck breast, the pan-fried veal or the roasted lamb loin.

THIS PAGE (FROM TOP): Indulge in complete relaxation at the poolside facing the ocean; Nelayan with breathtaking views of the sunset.
OPPOSITE (FROM TOP): Signature dish, caramelised sea scallops on organic English spinach purée; Quench your thirst with freshly-made cocktails.

bali indonesia

caramelised sea scallops on organic english spinach purée with sour cream and crispy parma ham

serves 4

640g fresh organic English spinach
12 large sea scallops
100ml sour cream, plus extra for garnishing
60g butter
120g Parma ham
2 lemons
small bunch of watercress
small bunch of chervil
1 head of frisse lettuce
2 tsp *fleur de sel* (salt flakes)
1 tsp black pepper
2 tbsp extra virgin olive oil

Method:

1. Wash and rinse the spinach, then blanch in lightly salted boiling water for about 40 seconds. Plunge in ice water to stop the cooking process and to retain the fresh green colour of the spinach.
2. Purée the spinach in a processer and strain to get a smooth cream.
3. Place the sliced Parma ham between baking trays and bake in the oven at 180°C (360°F) for about 8 minutes, or until the ham is crispy.
4. Dry the scallops with kitchen paper towels then season with *fleur de sel* and freshly ground black pepper. Add a small amount of butter and olive oil in a hot frying pan and sear scallops on each side for about 20–30 seconds.
5. Dress the salad leaves with some extra virgin olive oil, lemon juice and *fleur de sel*.
6. Warm the spinach purée and mix in the sour cream. Adjust seasoning according to taste.
7. Spoon a ladle of the spinach purée in the middle of the plate and place the seared scallops on top.
8. Place dressed salad leaves on top of the scallops, and garnish with a small dollop of sour cream, crispy Parma ham and a drizzle of extra virgin olive oil.

Note:

Fleur de sel is a natural sea salt that is hand-harvested by scraping off only the top layer of salt before it sinks to the bottom of large salt pans. *Fleur de sel* is very delicate, and dissolves almost instantly. Hence, it is often used on salad or meats, usually sprinkled on just before serving.

restaurant + address
Nelayan Restaurant
Jimbaran Puri Bali
Jalan Uluwatu
Jimbaran, Bali 80361
Indonesia
telephone: +62.361.701 605
email: info@jimbaranpuribali.com
website: www.jimbaranpuribali.com

cuisine
seafood and Mediterranean cuisine

signature dishes
the lobster tasting menu • the daily catch of seafood

wine list
the list of about 40 wines at the Puri Bar includes Old World with a few Californian and Australian wines, including sparkling wine and champagne • ten bottles of wine are available by the glass

opening hours
lunch noon–5pm daily
dinner 6.30–10.30pm daily

rooms
42 individual cottages • 22 pool villas

features
spa • main pool • beach view

other f + b outlets
Tunjung Café • Puri Bar

what's nearby
Kuta and Seminyak for shopping, cafés and surfing

nutmegs restaurant – dining at hu'u

As you enter **nutmegs restaurant – dining at hu'u**, it feels as though you are walking through a secret Balinese garden. The verdant tropical greenery complemented by the lap pool is a fitting prologue to the epicurean feast that awaits. The star of this open concept restaurant is gastronomic genius and food connoisseur, Chef Philip Mimbimi. He leads a team in crafting more than 30 dishes at the restaurant, all made from Bali's finest and freshest ingredients. Often, there is a whimsical play on words in the menu, where the restaurant's name is incorporated into traditional dishes. For example, Ubud's famous roast suckling pig *babi guling* is renamed *babi huuling*, and comes dressed with the chef's signature touches.

The chef's tongue-in-cheek style is not the only attribute which makes him stand out. His ability to create a perfect union of Asian and global cuisines must be recognised, and he draws inspiration from his exposure to many regions around the world. The chef began his global culinary adventure in Phuket, and then moved to Ritz-Carlton Hotel in Montego Bay, Jamaica. Before coming to nutmegs restaurant, he was at the prestigious Four Seasons Hotel in Singapore.

With such an impressive resume, it is little wonder that the chef has become a true guru of global cuisines, and is fast earning acclaim for his innovative and inventive cooking style. His prowess in the culinary field has won the restaurant numerous accolades over the years. Under Chef Mimbimi's direction, the restaurant lives up to its commitment of providing a truly unique dining experience for all.

Attached to the restaurant is an elegant bar that boasts an impressive selection of champagnes and New World wines. Savour some very unique cocktails here, such as the signature lychee martini that is a real force to be reckoned with, and not to be missed.

THIS PAGE (FROM TOP): *Chef Mimbimi at work; White curtains and table settings are the perfect complement to lush greenery.*
OPPOSITE (FROM TOP): *The signature dish, coriander chicken with pineapple fried rice in red sambal coconut sauce; The must-try lychee martini.*

bali indonesia

coriander chicken with pineapple fried rice in red sambal coconut sauce

serves 4

For Coriander Chicken
4 pieces chicken thigh, boneless
1 tsp oyster sauce
1 tsp soya sauce
freshly ground black pepper, to taste
1 coriander root, white part, crushed

For Pineapple Fried Rice
2 cups steamed white jasmine rice
1 tsp minced garlic
1 tbsp diced white onion
1 tbsp diced carrots
2 tbsp diced pineapple
1 tbsp chopped fresh coriander leaves
1 tsp curry powder
1 tsp turmeric powder
freshly ground black pepper, to taste

For Red Sambal Coconut Sauce
1 red chilli
1 clove garlic, skinned
4 red shallots, skinned
½ brown onion, skinned
sugar to taste
1 tsp *sambal belacan* (shrimp paste)
½ cup chicken stock
kaffir lime leaf
dark soya sauce, to taste
1 cup coconut milk
vegetable oil

For Vegetable Pickles
½ cucumber, peeled, blanched, seeded, sliced thinly
3–4 shallots, peeled and halved
1 red chilli, seeded, sliced very finely
½ carrot, peeled and sliced thinly
1 cup white vinegar
½ cup white sugar

Method:
1. Marinate the chicken thighs in the oyster sauce, soya sauce, black pepper and crushed coriander root for at least 3 hours. Then, grill over a wood fire.
2. Prepare pineapple fried rice. Heat some oil in a frying pan and fry the garlic, diced onion, carrots and pineapple.
3. Add the rice and the seasoning, including curry and turmeric powders. Season to taste.
4. Prepare vegetable pickles. Mix all the ingredients together and marinate overnight, keeping them chilled in the refrigerator.
5. Prepare red *sambal* sauce. Fry the onion, garlic, chilli and shallots in hot oil. Then lightly sauté the *sambal belacan* until aromatic. Add remaining ingredients and simmer over low heat. Season to taste.
6. Serve the grilled coriander chicken with the pineapple rice. Add the red *sambal* coconut sauce and vegetable pickles by the side.

restaurant + address
nutmegs restaurant – dining at hu'u
Jalan Oberoi, Peti Tenget
Kerobokan, Kuta, Bali
Indonesia
telephone: +62.361.736 443
email: info@huubali.com
website: www.huubali.com

cuisine
eclectic global cuisine

signature dishes
hot and sour prawn risotto • coriander chicken with pineapple fried rice in red *sambal* coconut sauce • nutmeg's signature dessert platter

wine list
mainly New World wines, consisting premium selections with some vintage wines

opening hours
11.30am–11.45pm daily

what's nearby
key attractions in Bali

raja's nusa dua beach hotel + spa

Balinese *ikat* and Kamasan paintings of Ramayana scenes are just some traditional touches that distinguish **Nusa Dua Beach Hotel & Spa** from other hotels. The thatched roof of the resort is perfectly complemented by immaculately landscaped gardens, both of which are nostalgic of a Balinese palace.

Nusa Dua's signature restaurant is **Raja's**, known for its traditional Balinese cuisine. Raja's is located by the hotel's pool, just metres away from the beach and the restaurant offers both indoor dining and al fresco seating. Since opening in 2001, Raja's has remained dedicated to serving authentic Balinese cuisine. The restaurant prides itself on providing classic Balinese food in a fine-dining atmosphere, and the use of traditional tableware—ornate brass plates, cutlery and food stands or *dulang*—proves that careful effort has been made to offer an authentic dining experience. The restaurant proved its worth as a hallmark of Balinese cuisine when it was given the award for Best Gastronomic Experience in Asian Cuisine at the Hospitality Asia Platinum Awards 2008–10.

Each dish at Raja's is meticulously prepared using local herbs, spices and elaborate cooking methods. A classic example is the signature dish *bebek betutu*, where a duck is marinated in 16 traditional spices and herbs, some of which can only be found in Bali. It is slow-roasted in an oven for 12 hours before it is ready to be served.

Popular dishes at the restaurant include *sambal ulam tongkol* which is a fresh yellow-fin tuna salad in a shallot and lemongrass chilli dressing and the award-winning *palem sari ulam* or steamed seafood in coconut curry pudding. Apart from these, the menu also offers an array of dishes that range from vegetarian to meat feasts. For diners who love the hot and spicy, an essential complement to the meal is the freshly made chilli *sambal* that is prepared tableside using a mortar and pestle. Finish off your meal with the desserts that are guaranteed to sate your palate. Try the *pisang rai*, poached bananas in coconut batter with honey and ginger ice cream or the classic *dadar gulung*, pandan-flavoured coconut crepes with a jackfruit and palm-sugar filling served with coconut ice cream.

THIS PAGE: *Raja's overlooking the pool of Nusa Dua Beach Hotel & Spa.*
OPPOSITE: *Balinese bebek betutu, served fresh and fragrantly from the oven.*

bali indonesia

balinese bebek betutu (balinese roasted duck)

serves 4

- 1 tsp white peppercorns
- 2 tsp black peppercorns
- 8 dried red chillies
- 2 *jinten* leaves (substitute with 1 stalk curry leaves)
- 2 *jangu* leaves (substitute with 1 stalk lemongrass)
- 2–3 kaffir lime leaves
- 2 tsp white sesame seeds
- 2 tbsp pounded fresh turmeric or turmeric powder
- 1 tbsp pounded fresh *galangal* or *galangal* powder
- 1 tsp *kencur* (optional)
- 1 tsp pounded fresh ginger or ginger powder
- 3–4 cloves garlic, peeled
- 3–4 shallots, peeled
- 4–6 fresh bird's eye chillies
- 1 tsp coriander seeds
- 1 tsp candlenuts (substitute with macadamia nuts)
- salt to taste
- 1 duck, about 1kg
- 1 palm leaf (substitute with banana leaf or aluminum foil)

Method:
1. Put all the spices and herbs into a food processor and grind until they become a coarse paste.
2. Stuff and rub the whole duck with the spice mixture, then wrap with the palm leaf and leave in a refrigerator overnight to marinate.
3. Set oven at low heat, at about 120°C (250°F).
4. Roast for about 4 hours, until cooked. Test the duck. The meat should be tender and fall off the bone easily.

Notes:
This is a very famous Balinese creation that gets its flavour from the many spices used in the marinating process. It is a classic slow-cooking dish which results in the duck meat becoming very soft and aromatic. Many of the spices and herbs used are indigenous to Bali, and you may not find them anywhere else. The herbs and spices permeate the duck meat and also tenderise it. Some herbs used in this recipe have a very unique scent. One such example is the *jinten* leaf, a local cinnamon. *Kencur*, or the lesser-known *galangal*, is also known as *cukor* in other parts of Southeast Asia. It is a tiny rhizome but packs a punch in flavour. Although it is not very common, you might be able to find it in the larger wet markets.

---

restaurant + address
Raja's
Nusa Dua Beach Hotel & Spa
P.O. Box 1028, Denpasar
Bali, Indonesia
telephone: +62.361.771 210
website: www.nusaduahotel.com

cuisine
authentic Balinese cuisine in a fine dining atmosphere

signature dishes
tambusan tahu sareng oong bali (baked tofu and mushrooms with turmeric, chilli and coconut milk sauce) • *palem sari ulam* (steamed seafood in coconut curry pudding) • *sambal ulam tongkol* (fresh yellow fin tuna salad in a shallot and lemongrass chilli dressing)

wine list
the wine list offers 10 different wines by the glass, including Balinese, Australian, French and Chilean labels • New World wines are also featured largely on the list

opening hours
dinner 6.30–10.30pm daily, except Tuesdays
reservations are recommended

rooms
381 rooms and suites

features
spa • three pools including a 20-metre (7-feet) lap pool • fully equipped fitness centre • business centre • executive floor • 150-metre (500-feet) beach

other f + b outlets
Wedang Jahe Restaurant • Sandro's Pizzeria • Maguro Asian Bistro • Chess Beachfront Restaurant • Budaya Cultural Theatre • Spa Café • Chess Bar • Pool Bar • Lobby Bar • Santi Lounge

what's nearby
shopping malls (15 minutes by taxi) • Jimbaran beach • golf course

rin conrad bali

THIS PAGE (CLOCKWISE FROM TOP): *The contemporary setting at RIN is characterised by neutral hues, warm lighting and red accents; Suku is another dining option with panoramic views of the beautiful resort and the ocean; Eight Degrees South, a stunning beachfront restaurant with private bales by the sea.*
OPPOSITE: *The innovative dessert, the sake kasu panacotta.*

The fragrance of frangipani scents the air as diners enjoy a meal al fresco at **RIN,** in **Conrad Bali**. The restaurant exudes a cool elegance and the menu delivers innovative creations specially created by its chef. Chef de Cuisine Richard Millar is known for his adventurous take on Japanese food. Traditional ingredients are specially flown in from Japan and the chef constantly experiments with new ways to harmonise the five basic tastes of sweet, sour, salty, bitter and *umami* (savoury). Chef Millar confesses to having a penchant for Japanese cuisine, and this led him to spend 18 months travelling and working in Japan. During his time there, he learned all he could about the country's food, flavours and ingredients.

The food at RIN is best described as Asian eclectic, and is created with the freshest seasonal ingredients such as herbs, spices, pickles and good oils. Chef Millar sets out to surprise and inspire with his innovative dishes. A good example of this is the way in which he incorporates *sake kasu*, the wine dregs from making sake, into a pannacotta. Another twist on a classic favourite is *chawanmushi* (Japanese steamed savoury egg custard) with foie gras blended in. This adds another dimension of flavour and a layer of silky texture. Meticulous attention is given to the smallest details, and RIN makes sure its *dashi* stock (a Japanese soup stock) is freshly made every day. It is this impeccable professionalism and dedication that makes Chef Millar stand out amongst his peers. He also has considerable experience from his work at some of Australia's top restaurants.

RIN is the star feature of the Conrad Bali, which welcomes guests to its sprawling tropical gardens and lush lagoons with cascading waterfalls. With beautiful scenery and attractive menus, every meal promises to be a truly unforgettable experience.

bali **indonesia**

sake kasu pannacotta

serves 4

175ml milk
75ml cream
75g condensed milk
50g *sake kasu*
1 gelatin leaf, softened in water
150ml water
150g sugar
200ml sake
300g strawberries
pashmak for garnish

Method:

1. Pour milk, cream and condensed milk into a saucepan and heat until it is just about to boil. Remove from heat and then add the *sake kasu* and softened gelatin. Stir.
2. Cool for approximately 10 minutes, then pour into moulds. Leave to set overnight.
3. Pour sugar into a saucepan and cook to a light caramel colour. Carefully add water, and boil to reduce by a third.
4. Add the sake and simmer for about 5 to 10 minutes. Cool and marinate the strawberries in it.
5. To assemble the dish, spoon the marinated strawberries over the pannacotta. Garnish with *pashmak*.

Note:

Sake kasu are the dregs or lees left over from sake production. It is used as a pickling agent, a food flavouring or as a marinade.

Pashmak is a Persian candyfloss made from sesame and sugar.

Pannacotta is a very well-known Italian milk pudding, very much like an English milk junket. The term itself means "cooked cream", which immediately tells you how it is made. Unlike the English milk pudding, which is set with the help of rennet, pannacotta holds its shape with the help of gelatin.

This dessert, which is said to originate from the dairy-rich Piedmont region of Italy, is often served with berries or other mixed fruits. The addition of *sake kasu*, the sweet wine dregs of Japanese sake, gives the pannacotta another layer of flavour and texture.

---

restaurant + address
RIN
Conrad Bali
Pratama
168 Tanjung Benoa
Bali 80363, Indonesia
telephone: +62.361.778 788
email: restaurants@conradbali.com
website: www.conradbali.com

cuisine
contemporary eclectic cuisine with Asian influences

signature dishes
tuna *chutoro*, *shoyu* jelly • *tamago yaki* in apple-mustard dressing • foie gras *chawanmushi* with king crab

wine list
an extensive list of wines by the glass, featuring selections from both Old World and New World wines

opening hours
6–11pm daily

rooms
360 guest rooms including 55 Conrad suites

features
award-winning Jiwa Spa and Wellness Studio • 350-metre (1,150-feet) pristine beach • 33-metre (110-feet) swimming pool and lagoons • fitness club • retail village • water sports • cultural programmes • two floodlit tennis courts • 25-metre (80-feet) spa pool • beach club • Infinity wedding chapel

other f + b outlets
Suku • Eight Degrees South • Azure • East

what's nearby
Pura Luhur Uluwatu • beaches • nightclubs • shopping • sport fishing

restaurant dewi ramona matahari beach resort + spa

THIS PAGE (FROM TOP): Bask in the sun, sea and sand while sipping on cocktails at Leon Beach Bistro; The devotion to tradition at Dewi Ramona is reflected in both its décor and menu.

OPPOSITE: Signature dish marinated barracuda in beetroot with capsicum flan.

Food is taken very seriously at the **Matahari Beach Resort & Spa**. The resort is tucked away in a secluded bay north of the lake district Bedugul where much of the island's fruits and vegetables are grown. It is in this area that Matahari grows its ingredients, ensuring that only first-grade produce make it to the table.

Matahari is the perfect escape for those seeking to indulge in complete luxury. As one of the first members of the prestigious Relais & Chateaux in Southeast Asia back in 2001, it is equipped with all the facilities you would expect to find in a world-class hotel. But the owners have stayed faithful to creating a resort nostalgic of a Balinese village. At Matahari, the antique architecture and traditional décor inspires old world charm.

The flagship **Restaurant Dewi Ramona** operates in the same vein by offering a unique menu of traditional Balinese dishes along with contemporary fusion cuisine. Some international favourites at the restaurant include a lobster bisque, made from the freshest local lobster, and the chicken breast paired with goose liver, red cabbage and red wine sauce. Dewi Ramona offers some of the best Balinese dishes on the island, paying tribute to the island's natural and exotic flavours. *Bakso ayam* is a must-try, a classic chicken soup served with glass noodles.

As no meal is complete without wine, the resort has its own wine cellar filled with a selection of more than 120 kinds of wines that complement the menu. Serious epicureans can get even closer to the source with visits to organic farms, or go on a local market tour with the resident chef, where he will share insights on creating the perfect Asian meal.

bali **indonesia**

marinated barracuda in beetroot with capsicum flan

serves 4

4 pieces barracuda fillets, about 250g each
3 small beetroots
300ml water
a few sprigs thyme and parsley
2 bay leaves

For Capsicum Flan
1 large red capsicum or bell pepper, seeded and sliced
40g cream
200ml chicken stock
1 white onion, finely chopped
3–4 cloves garlic, minced
1 gelatin sheet
1 egg white
salt and pepper to taste
olive oil
fresh lemon juice
chopped shallots
salad leaves

Method:
1. Wash and cut the beetroot into chunks. Add water and then blend the mixture into a thick purée.
2. Place the barracuda fillets in the beetroot purée. Add the herbs and refrigerate overnight to allow flavours to infuse.
3. Sauté the onion and garlic in olive oil until they soften.
4. Add the red capsicum and chicken stock. Cook until soft and till the stock is reduced. Blend until fine and pass through a sieve.
5. Return to the pan and heat. Add softened gelatin and stir.
6. Sieve again and let the mixture cool.
7. Whip the cream and the egg white, and fold gently into the capsicum mixture. Place into flan moulds.
8. To plate, remove the barracuda fillet from the beetroot purée and cut into thin slices.
9. Arrange on a plate and season with salt, pepper, lemon juice and olive oil. Garnish with chopped shallots and mixed herbs.
10. Place the capsicum flan in the middle and garnish with salad leaves.

Note:
This is an unusual ceviche of fish. The sweet earthy flavour of the beetroot permeates the fish during the long marinating process. A final squeeze of fresh lemon juice will complete the dish.

restaurant + address
The Restaurant Dewi Ramona
Matahari Beach Resort & Spa
Jl. Raya Seririt-Gilimanuk
Ds. Pemuteran, Kec. Gerokgak
Kab. Buleleng 81155
Bali, Indonesia
telephone: +62.362.92 312
email: info@matahari-beach-resort.com
website: www.matahari-beach-resort.com

cuisine
fusion European/Indonesian

signature dishes
seafood carpaccio with herb salad and sauer cream • snapper under coconut crust and saffron sauce

wine list
a unique selection imported from Europe, South America, California, South Africa, Australia and New Zealand

opening hours
lunch noon–2pm daily
dinner 7–11pm daily

rooms
16 bungalows with 32 rooms

features
Parwathi Spa • beauty salon • gymnasium • library • Padi diving school • swimming pool • tennis courts

other f + b outlets
Leon Beach Bistro • The Wayang Cocktail Bar

what's nearby
Menjangan Island • Bali Barat National Park • Pulaki Temple • Melanting temple

the restaurant the legian

THIS PAGE (FROM TOP): The Restaurant's open concept creates a soothing atmosphere; Rattan chairs and umbrellas create the perfect setting for a leisurely meal by the sea.

OPPOSITE: Signature dish the delicious slow-cooked petuna ocean trout with marinated fennel and parsley oil.

What sets **The Restaurant** at **The Legian** apart from other resort restaurants is the presence of Master Chef Dorin Schuster. Crowned San Pellegrino Chef of the Year at the 2007 World Gourmet Summit, Chef Schuster is a true gourmet force to be reckoned with. He distills years of classical European training with an Asian perspective that he honed as a chef at one of Asia's top restaurants, Iggy's at The Regent in Singapore. At The Restaurant, Chef Schuster demonstrates his forte of combining the best of the East and West, with a menu that is an epicurean adventure even for food connoisseurs. His mastery of fusion cuisine can be attributed to his ability to tantalise palates with fresh Asian flavours, while retaining a comfort level for Western appetites and sensibilities.

The Restaurant at The Legian is located in Seminyak and offers sprawling views of the beach and the Indian Ocean. A climate-controlled wine cellar impresses diners as soon as they enter, but the highlight of the restaurant is its open kitchen in the centre of the dining room. Guests will enjoy an intimate and unique gastronomic experience as they watch the chef prepare their meals.

The Restaurant is mostly known for its seafood and wine-tasting dinners, and in order to truly experience Chef Schuster's culinary skills, choose the Tasting Menu. This menu features a mesmerising selection of seafood that is alluring in both presentation and taste. The ceviche of pearl meat with cauliflower cous cous, lime vinaigrette and fresh herbs is a delicate creation that resonates with the chef's global influences. Another masterpiece is the marbled goby tempura with Japanese herbs and watercress, tempered with a soya and tarragon sauce that explodes with flavour in your mouth. As if to pay tribute to his Asian sojourns, Chef Schuster also offers an array of traditional dishes for diners seeking local flavours.

The Restaurant's wine cellar is just as enticing. For two consecutive years, the establishment has won the *Wine Spectator*'s Award of Excellence. This award is accorded to restaurants whose wine lists present interesting collections appropriate to the style of cuisine, while also appealing to a wide range of wine lovers.

bali **indonesia**

slow-cooked petuna ocean trout with marinated fennel and parsley oil

serves 4

4 ocean trout fillets, about 160g each
250ml olive oil
6 basil leaves
2 sprigs thyme
1 tbsp white peppercorns
8 bay leaves
1 large fennel bulb with fronds
1 bunch dill
1 bunch parsley
1 small piece *konbu*, finely chopped
Maldon sea salt to taste

For Lemon Vinaigrette
3 lemons
1 tbsp icing sugar
50ml olive oil
salt and pepper to taste

For Parsley Oil
1 large bunch parsley, chopped
100ml olive oil

Method:

1. Place ocean trout fillets in a deep baking dish together with peppercorns, basil, thyme and bay leaves. Cover fillets completely with olive oil.
2. Place baking dish in a water bath and slow-cook in the oven at 55˚C (130˚F) for about 20 minutes.
3. Make lemon vinaigrette by combining all the ingredients and mixing well. An easy way is to put the ingredients inside a capped jar and to shake them until they emulsify.
4. Slice the fennel bulb into fine julienne and marinate with lemon vinaigrette, chopped dill, fennel fronds and the *konbu*.
5. Arrange the marinated fennel on the plate.
6. Remove the ocean trout from the baking tray. Drain well. Place the fillet on top of the fennel.
7. To make the parsley oil, combine chopped parsley and olive oil and allow to infuse for 30 minutes. Strain and draw thin lines of parsley oil around the fennel.
8. Lastly, dust the trout with sea salt flakes and then garnish with fennel fronds and dill.

Notes:
This method of cooking is very similar to the French way of confiting or allowing meat to cook gently in fat. The fish is barely cooked and becomes tender. Ocean trout is a pink fish very similar to salmon, so if you cannot find ocean trout, you can substitute with fillets of salmon.

Konbu is a dried Japanese seaweed that is a natural flavour enhancer. It is deep green in colour and can be bought at any Asian supermarket or Japanese produce shop.

restaurant + address
The Restaurant at The Legian
The Legian, Bali
Jalan Kayu Aya, Seminyak Beach
Bali 80361, Indonesia
telephone: +62.361.730 622
email: legian@ghmhotels.com
website: www.ghmhotels.com

cuisine
bistro-style contemporary European with Asian influences

signature dishes
ceviche of pearl meat with cauliflower cous cous, lime vinaigrette and fresh herbs • marbled goby tempura with Japanese herbs and watercress in soya-tarragon butter sauce • fresh mussels and coriander

wine list
an award-winning list of 185 fine wines with a particular focus on Australian and French varietals

opening hours
7am–11pm daily

rooms
100 rooms

features
two swimming pools with whirlpool • fitness centre • tennis and squash courts • The Spa at The Legian • scuba diving • snorkelling

other f + b outlets
Intimate Dining Affair • The Lobby Lounge & Bar • The Pool Bar

what's nearby
shopping • surfing

citabria

Citabria is one of Tokyo's best kept secrets—a little piece of Napa Valley hidden in a residential enclave of the city. The restaurant stands alone on its little villa, and is just a stone's throw from the main Roppongi-dori expressway. Although Citabria is hard to find, the food keeps diners coming back for more.

Resident Chef Tsutomu Endo is the one responsible for this. He was formally trained in Italy, but his main culinary influence is Napa Valley cuisine. This is reflected in the menu he has created for Citabria, which incorporates strong Californian accents. Complementing the chef is Sommelier Kazuto Chiba, who is aptly qualified for his post. He has worked at Auberge du Soleil, one of the top restaurants in Napa. This explains the overwhelming number of Californian wines that are paired with the dishes served here.

Signature dishes at Citabria include the chef's rendition of *bagna cauda*, a traditional Italian dish. Chef Endo has updated this recipe by adding a distinctively Japanese twist. His use of sweet white *miso* neutralises the sharpness of the salty dip, and shows his flair for incorporating the best of the East and West in his cuisine. Chef Endo possesses an uncanny ability to seamlessly mix flavours while preserving the authenticity of each dish. He is also famous for his innovative degustation menus, as well as a delicately crafted pigeon pie, not for the faint-hearted.

Sated gourmets may retire to the lounge for a cigar after their meal, or enjoy a tantalising bite of dessert such as the persimmon tiramisu or pomegranate sorbet on lime macaroons. For a nightcap, have a glass of excellent wine from the cellar.

THIS PAGE (FROM TOP): *Sleek lines and crystal accents create a modern and elegant vibe; The outdoor lounge area offers panoramic views of Tokyo's beautiful cityscape.*
OPPOSITE (FROM TOP): *Chef Endo's signature recipe bagna cauda; Sophisticated table settings create a luxurious experience.*

tokyo **japan**

bagna cauda (anchovy and garlic dip with miso)

serves 4

60g anchovy fillets
80g white *miso*
60g garlic, skinned
60g unsalted butter
45g whipped cream
olive oil
2 young carrots
3–4 tender celery stalks
1 Japanese cucumber (*kyuri*)
8–10 cherry tomatoes

Method:
1. Prepare crudités. Peel carrots and cucumber.
2. Cut carrots into batons. Remove the core from the cucumber and cut into batons as well.
3. String the celery stalks and trim till they are the same size as the carrots and the cucumbers.
4. Wash and dry cherry tomatoes. Chill crudités until ready to serve.
5. Prepare *bagna cauda*. Blanch garlic in hot water and then milk to get rid of its pungency. Drain.
6. Place the garlic in a blender together with the butter, white *miso*, and anchovy fillet. Process until the mixture forms a fine purée.
7. Add whipped cream to the mixture.
8. Heat the mixture on a low fire and add enough olive oil to get it to the desired consistency.
9. Finally, serve in a deep bowl surrounded by the chilled crudités and the cherry tomatoes.

Notes:
Bagna cauda is the signature speciality of Piedmont, a region in Italy known for its sparkling white wine, *asti spumante*, Alba white truffles and rice—these account for nearly a third of the region's total output.

Normally served as a dip with raw vegetables, the dish takes its name from the Italian term "*bagno caldo*" or hot bath. It is served in the cool evenings of autumn and winter as the amount of garlic in the dip is said to warm the body.

Folklore has it that the recipe was invented out of expedience in the winter when little fresh produce was available. The salty dip, which was made using expensive salt that was scarce, was a delicacy reserved for only the most favoured guests.

restaurant + address
Citabria
2-26-4 Nishi Azabu Minato-ku
Tokyo 106-0031, Japan
telephone: +81.3.5766 9500
email: info@citabria.co.jp
website: www.citabria.co.jp/index.html

cuisine
modern French/Californian

signature dishes
roasted pork chop with soya sauce reduction, *yuzu* peppers and secret spices • bagna cauda (anchovy and garlic dip with *miso*)

wine list
an extensive list featuring a mixture of French and Californian wines

opening hours
lunch noon–2pm daily
dinner 5.30–11.30pm daily

what's nearby
Fuji Film Building • Roppongi shopping and nightlife

bijan bar + restaurant

Kuala Lumpur is a gourmet city and it is easy to find good food on every street corner. However, traditional Malay cuisine requires meticulous attention and preparation, so it is rare to find a restaurant willing to invest in the time and effort to create authentic dishes.

Bijan Bar & Restaurant is a restaurant that prides itself on serving traditional Malay cuisine. Perched on a hill in a single-storey building, the restaurant does not capitalise on the usual touristy impressions of what a Malay restaurant should be. There are no bare-footed dancers waving palm fronds or chiffon scarves—the cultural experience is in the eating, as it should be.

The restaurant is run with a refreshing consideration for its diners. The décor is simple and there is no mistaking the subtle Asian influence here. Exposed concrete walls and hints of unpolished dark wood create a vibe of authenticity and old world charm. Folding glass doors lead out to the patio for al fresco dining while the bold use of purple on the walls, a large orange dragonfly mural and a bamboo bar are some exotic touches that punctuate the understated layout.

It is the food, atmosphere and service that take precedence here, reminding you of traditional homestyle hospitality. Resident Chef Zulkifli Razali's credits his grandmother's cooking as his main inspiration, and he fiercely guards his collection of authentic recipes. The chef wisely preserves the tastes and adheres to traditional cooking methods, only conceding to modern dining in terms of portions and presentation. The menu he has created focuses on forgotten favourites, but guests will also be surprised by new flavours and textures. A prime example is the use of durian to create chocolate durian cake, a popular dessert at Bijan.

Chef Razali has been recognised by numerous awards, and was a finalist in the Best Malay Chef category at the HAPA awards of 2008. Bijan was also named the winner of Best Malay Cuisine in the *Time Out KL* Food Awards 2009. The chef recommends the dish *rusuk panggang*, which is chargrilled marinated beef short ribs served with *pegedil* (potato cake), sweet soya sauce and *sambal belacan*. *Pucuk paku goreng tahi minyak* is yet another forgotten classic. This is a dish of wild fern or fiddleheads stir-fried with chillies, caramelised coconut and shrimps.

THIS PAGE (FROM TOP): The casual chic atmosphere creates a relaxing dining experience; Bamboo fixtures and lush greenery make the perfect setting for a traditional meal.

OPPOSITE (FROM TOP): Classic masak lemak udang dengan nenas; Batik accents engender a vibe of old world charm.

kuala lumpur malaysia

masak lemak udang dengan nenas (prawns and pineapple in spicy coconut milk)

serves 4

- 4–6 shallots, skinned
- ½ a large brown onion
- 2–3 cloves garlic, skinned
- 3–4 slices ginger
- 2 slices fresh turmeric
- 1 stalk lemongrass, trimmed, using white parts only
- 2–3 bird's eye chillies, seeded
- 2 large red chillies
- 300ml water
- 50ml cooking oil
- 10 kaffir lime leaves
- 1 small pineapple
- 500g large prawns
- 250ml coconut milk
- 1 tsp salt
- 1 tsp sugar

Method:

1. Skin the shallots and garlic and cut the brown onion into chunks. Roughly chop the lemongrass.
2. Place ginger and turmeric slices in a blender and add the shallots, onion and garlic. Add the lemongrass and chillies with about 150ml water and blend into a fine paste.
3. Skin the pineapple and remove the core. Slice, then cut into chunks.
4. Heat oil in a pan and sauté the paste until it is fragrant. Add kaffir lime leaves and fry for another minute to release the oils in the leaves before adding the pineapple chunks.
5. Add the rest of the water, coconut milk and prawns.
6. Simmer until the prawns are cooked and pineapple chunks are tender. Season to taste and adjust salt and sugar accordingly.

Note:

This is a lovely mild curry that is redolent with traditional Southeast Asian herbs like turmeric and kaffir lime. The pineapple adds a fresh tangy fragrance to the sweetness of the prawns. If you cannot handle too much heat, double the amount of the larger red chillies instead of using the little bird's eye chillies. Remove the seeds, and you will get the fragrance of the chillies instead of the heat.

This dish needs to be eaten immediately as the acidity of the pineapple may affect the texture of the prawns if left overnight.

restaurant + address
Bijan Bar & Restaurant
No.3 Jalan Ceylon 50200
Kuala Lumpur, Malaysia
telephone: +60.3.2031 3575
fax: +60.3.2031 3576
email: admin@bijanrestaurant.com
website: www.bijanrestaurant.com

cuisine
traditional Malay cuisine

signature dishes
masak lemak ikan dengan belimbing (rich curry of red snapper fillets simmered in chillies, turmeric, coconut milk and sour carambola) • *masak lemak udang dengan tempoyak* (prawns and pineapple in spicy coconut milk) • chocolate durian cake

wine list
an extensive wine list of both the Old and New World wines • wines are mostly sold by the bottle, but house wines are available by the glass

opening hours
dinner 4.30–11pm daily

what's nearby
KL Tower • KLCC • Petaling Street • Lot 10 • Starhill • Pavillon • KLCC

gobo chit chat traders hotel, kuala lumpur

With a new generation of young gourmets eating out, catering to their ever-changing food trends and palates can be a challenge. **Traders Hotel, Kuala Lumpur**'s trendy **Gobo Chit Chat** manages to hold its own in a highly competitive industry because of its multi-dimensional appeal. The restaurant's décor itself is a novel attraction, with its colourful light and music displays—stylish colour animations projected on the curved ceiling are accompanied by New Age music. This sets the mood for guests who see dining as a complete sensory experience, appealing to the eyes, ears and tastebuds.

The food at Gobo Chit Chat caters to those who desire the best of all worlds. Gobo's contemporary Western and Eastern cuisine choices include a sushi bar, a Thai appetiser buffet, an open noodle kitchen and a show bakery. Open kitchens allow the chefs to showcase their culinary skills and guarantee that the food is served fresh off the stove. The restaurant offers a buffet spread that comprises international and local cuisines.

For some traditional local flavour, the very interesting *Lok Lok* or "Dip Dip" is a popular *pasar malam* (night market) treat that is fast disappearing from the streets. Gobo Chit Chat offers this dish in its traditional form—fish balls, thin slices of meat, seafood, vegetables, beancurd, quail's eggs and other dainty morsels are threaded on skewers which are dipped into a pot of boiling water to cook. The cooked skewers are then doused in a selection of sauces, including *hoisin* sauce, chilli sauce or satay sauce, completing the "Dip Dip" experience.

Gobo Chit Chat offers a wide range of cuisines, but takes care not to neglect the Malaysian dishes that are unfailingly popular. Traditional favourites like *char kway teow* and quail with roasted onions are also served here with special care taken to preserve the authenticity of local flavours. For a sweet ending to the perfect meal, try the newest addition to the dessert spread, *teppan* ice cream, where ice cream is mixed with toppings over a frozen metal table.

THIS PAGE (FROM TOP): The delicious spread of cold cuts and salad will whet your appetite; The delectable and sinful dessert buffet is the perfect ending to a delightful meal; The cool and classy interior of Gobo Chit Chat restaurant.

OPPOSITE (FROM TOP): The signature dish char kway teow is the epitome of local flavour; Sumptuous Asian favourites that are a must-try.

kuala lumpur **malaysia**

char kway teow (fried rice noodles)

serves 4

4–6 cloves garlic, chopped
12 prawns, shelled and deveined
1 squid, cleaned and sliced
120g cockle meat
4 eggs, beaten
4 tsp chilli paste
80g bean sprouts, tails removed
2–3 stalks garlic chives, cut into 4cm pieces
500g *kway teow* (flat rice noodles)

For Kway Teow Sauce

175ml oyster sauce
200ml light soya sauce
100ml dark soya sauce
100ml fish sauce
250g chicken powder
1 tbsp sugar
1 tsp salt
1 tbsp minced garlic
2 tbsp oil

Method:

1. Prepare *kway teow* sauce. Sweat the minced garlic in oil until fragrant, and add the rest of the sauce ingredients. Simmer for about 2 to 3 minutes to allow flavours to infuse. Set aside.
2. Clean the squid and open up the tube. Score one side of the squid diagonally, and again in the other direction to get a fine diamond pattern. Cut into slices. This will make the squid "flower" when it is being cooked.
3. Blanch the prawns and squid in boiling water until just cooked. Set aside till ready for use.
4. Add oil to a large pan and sweat the garlic and chilli paste.
5. Turn the heat up high and add the seafood and rice noodles. Toss to mix. Season with the *kway teow* sauce.
6. Stir in the egg, followed by the chives and beansprouts.
7. Add the cockles and give a final toss. Plate and serve immediately.

Notes:

Kway Teow is a flat noodle made of rice flour. The best *kway teow* is very smooth and thin and eaten fried or in soup. The noodles do tend to clump together, so one good way to separate them before cooking is to ease them apart with oiled hands. They will also cook faster this way.

The cockles used in this classic Malaysian hawker dish are blood cockles. Locals eat them barely blanched and still bloody, but recent concerns about hepatitis have changed that. The cockles cook very easily and may turn rubbery if left in the pan for too long—this is why they are always added at the last, heated through quickly to barely cook, and then served immediately.

restaurant + address

Gobo Chit Chat
Traders Hotel, Kuala Lumpur
Kuala Lumpur City Centre
50088 Kuala Lumpur, Malaysia
telephone: +60.3.2332 9888
email: thkl@shangri-la.com
website: www.shangrila.com

cuisine

international buffet

signature dishes

mee mamak (Indian-style fried noodles) • *spinosini* (hand-made pasta imported directly from Italy)

wine list

basic selection of wines available

opening hours

6.30am–11pm daily

other f + b outlets

Gobo Upstairs Lounge & Grill • SkyBar

what's nearby

Suria KLCC • Petronas Twin Towers • Bukit Bintang for entertainment and shopping

skybar traders hotel, kuala lumpur

SkyBar is in a league of its own when it comes to nightlife in Malaysia, and it is no wonder that it has been voted Malaysia's best bar by top socialite publication, *Malaysia Tatler*. SkyBar owes its success to its trendy ambience and unique cocktails. Maroon, purple and orange furniture are a striking contrast to the calming blue water of the pool, and the spectacular view of the Petronas Twin Towers lights up the sky at night.

The bar is housed in **Traders Hotel, Kuala Lumpur**, whose central location in the Golden Triangle of Kuala Lumpur's city centre makes it an accessible destination for the glamorous and the chic. The main allure is the creativity of SkyBar's resident and guest mixologists—the cocktail kings of Malaysia. The bar's five signature cocktails speak for themselves.

The Kiwitini is a drink that distills the essence of kiwifruit. It is paired with quality vodka and topped with champagne, and served in a tall flute garnished with a curl of lime. The Lychee Rose has the slightest tinge of pink accentuated by a single rose petal floating on the top. This cocktail is loved for its subtle aromas of lychee and rose. The golden hues of the Mata D'or make for a fruity mocktail popular with those who wish to have something alcohol-free. It is a display of the mixologist's skills as he carefully layers grenadine syrup, passion fruit pulp and Red Bull to create a lava-lamp effect.

Raised in Manhattan is SkyBar's take on a classic cocktail, with infused raisins, Martini Rosso and maraschino being the dominant flavours. Finally, there is the signature cocktail, Selangor Sling. This is a veritable mix of flavours with fruit juices kicked up a notch where Tanqueray and cherry brandy are topped off with a herbal liqueur.

Skybar also offers equally elegant tapas and snacks, as every good bar should. Bite-sized finger foods include buffalo inferno wings with blue cheese dip, crispy white bait with *wasabi* mayonnaise, yellow fin tuna tartare with tomato granita and an open-face Wagyu beef burger. Choose any of these for the perfect complement to the perfect drink.

THIS PAGE (FROM TOP): **The magnificent Petronas Towers form the perfect backdrop for a refreshing midnight cocktail; Cabana-style seating provides panoramic vistas of Kuala Lumpur's sprawling cityscape.**

OPPOSITE (FROM LEFT TO RIGHT): **Signature cocktails Kiwitini, Lychee Rose, Mata D'or and Selangor Sling; SkyBar's exterior at night.**

kuala lumpur **malaysia**

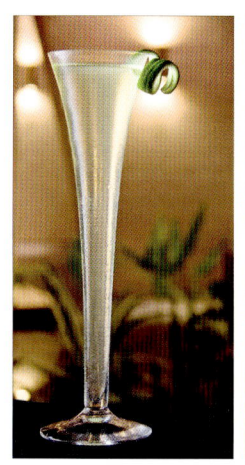

skybar cocktails

Kiwitini
1 kiwifruit, peeled
20ml Belvedere vodka
5ml sugar syrup
120ml Moet & Chandon champagne

Lychee Rose
10ml lychee liqueur
40ml Belvedere vodka
5ml rose syrup
5ml lychee syrup

Mata D'or
10ml grenadine
80ml passion fruit purée
1 can of Red Bull

Selangor Sling
30ml Tanqueray
20ml cherry brandy
25ml lemon juice
25ml pineapple juice
20ml sugar syrup
soda water
5ml Benedictine DOM

Kiwitini Method:
1. Mash up the kiwifruit in a shaker.
2. Pour vodka and syrup over the mashed kiwifruit.
3. Add the crushed ice and shake well.
4. Double strain into a champagne flute.
5. Top up with the champagne.

Lychee Rose Method:
1. Chill a martini glass well.
2. Combine all the ingredients. Add crushed ice and shake.
3. Double strain and pour into a glass.
4. Garnish with one lychee fruit and a rose petal.

Mata D'or Method:
1. Pour grenadine syrup into the bottom of a tall tumbler.
2. Add the passion fruit purée.
3. Top up with Red Bull and crushed ice and garnish with a lemon curl shaped into a rose bud.

Selangor Sling Method:
1. Chill a tall glass.
2. Combine all the ingredients, except the soda water and the DOM. Add crushed ice and shake.
3. Pour into a glass over some ice cubes.
4. Top with soda water and a layer of DOM on top.
5. Garnish with a lemon wedge and a maraschino cherry.

restaurant + address
SkyBar
Traders Hotel, Kuala Lumpur
Kuala Lumpur City Centre
50088 Kuala Lumpur, Malaysia
telephone: +60.3.2332 9888
email: skybar.thkl@shangri-la.com
website: www.skybar.com.my

cuisine
tapas and bar snacks

signature cocktails
kiwitini · raised in manhattan · lychee rose · selangor sling · mata d'or

opening hours
10am–1am Sunday to Thursday
10am–3am Friday, Saturday and eve of public holidays

rooms
571 rooms

features
fitness centre · swimming pool · jacuzzi and hot tub · spa · business centre

other f + b outlets
Gobo Chit Chat Restaurant ·
Gobo Upstairs Lounge & Grill

what's nearby
Petronas Twin Towers · Kuala Lumpur Convention Centre · KLCC Park · Suria KLCC · Pavilion Shopping Mall · Bukit Bintang · Ceylon Hill

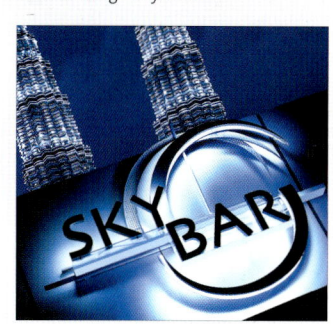

kogetsu the saujana hotel, kuala lumpur

The Saujana Hotel, Kuala Lumpur epitomises the country club lifestyle in Kuala Lumpur. Set amidst sprawling greenery just outside the city limits, the hotel is a 210-rooom retreat just next to the twin 18-hole championship golf courses of the Saujana Golf & Country Club. The hotel's own lush tropical gardens reflect its name, which is taken from an old Malay expression "*sejauh di sana*", which literally means, "as far as the eye (can see)".

Kogetsu, the hotel's signature Japanese restaurant is especially well-known for its earthy country-style cuisine. "*Kogetsu*" literally translates to "reflection of the moon on the lake" and is appropriately built overlooking the landscaped lake on the hotel grounds. The restaurant's décor complements its cuisine, and heavy timber beams combined with wooden floors evoke the charm of a traditional countryside restaurant. The use of dark blue cushions and decorative antiques, including some vintage Japanese farming equipment, are interesting accents to the interior. Wood, stone and bamboo all work to create an ambience that takes diners back to the origins of the cuisine.

Different sections allow guests to choose their style of dining according to individual preferences. At the sushi counter, they can watch the delicate preparations of skilled sushi chefs as they hand-mould each morsel. Two *teppanyaki* tables are placed by windows which provide views of the tranquil Japanese garden. Private dining is available in three *tatami* rooms, while the seating area next to the open kitchen is for guests who wish to watch the chefs prepare their hot meals.

Kogetsu offers typical country-style Japanese favourites ranging from hearty noodles such as wheat and buckwheat udon and soba, and sets like the *donburi* and *bento* boxes. *Teppanyaki* sets and sushi menus are also available for lunch and dinner.

But it's the little attention to detail that makes dining at Kogetsu so pleasurable. Japanese jazz music plays in the background and sets the mood, while attentive waitstaff dressed in traditional farmers' garb greet guests with old-fashioned country-style hospitality. The kitchen is overseen by Kyoto native Minami Taketoshi, a Master Chef who makes sure that the quality of food is top-notch, and that only the best and freshest of ingredients are used. If you are in search of some Japanese food for the soul, Kogetsu will give you an experience to remember.

THIS PAGE (FROM TOP): *The sleek design of Kogetsu ensures a tranquil dining experience; A wide variety of fresh sushi is available at the counter.*
OPPOSITE: *The perfect combination of sweet and salty in the classic tori teriyaki.*

kuala lumpur **malaysia**

tori teriyaki (chicken teriyaki)

serves 4

4 chicken thighs
  (boned, about 200g each)
2–3 tbsp soya sauce
2–3 tbsp *mirin*
2–3 tbsp cooking sake
2 tbsp sugar
salt and pepper to taste
cooking oil

Method:
1. Season chicken with salt and pepper and chill for half an hour.
2. Pour soya sauce, *mirin* and sake in a small pan and cook until the alcohol has evaporated. This should take about 5 minutes.
3. Add sugar and stir to dissolve. Reduce the sauce at a gentle simmer until it thickens.
4. Heat up the oil in a frying pan and fry the chicken, skin side down.
5. Reduce the heat to medium and fry until chicken is fully cooked and the skin is crisp and golden.
6. Keep the chicken in the pan, but pour away any excess oil. Add the prepared *teriyaki* sauce and bring to a boil, making sure that the chicken pieces are thoroughly coated.
7. Serve with a garnish of spring onions.

Notes:
Teriyaki is a popular cooking technique much loved by Japanese chefs. The word itself is derived from "*teri*" which refers to the glaze on the meat because of the high sugar content, and "*yaki*" which refers to the grilling or broiling.

The sauce itself is almost always made with *mirin*, a very sweet rice wine with low alcohol content. It is an essential ingredient in every Japanese kitchen and is often paired with soya sauce, *miso* or bean paste to give a distinct taste to many Japanese braised dishes.

Cooking sake is simply a lighter version of the traditional rice wine. Sake is a unique liquor as it is made from a brewing process that is more similar to making beer than the normal distillation method. Pure sake has a relatively high alcohol content of between 18 and 20 percent. Sake is therefore often diluted for cooking.

restaurant + address
Kogetsu
The Saujana Hotel, Kuala Lumpur
Jalan Lapangan Terbang SAAS
40150 Shah Alam
Selangor Darul Ehsan, Malaysia
telephone: +60.3.7843 1234
fax: +60.3.7846 3008
reservation fax: +60.3.7846 5443
general email: info@thesaujana.com
reservations email:
reservations@thesaujana.com
website: www.thesaujanahotel.com

cuisine
country-style Japanese

signature dishes
makunochi bento (traditional lunch box with Japanese delicacies) • *tori teriyaki* (chicken *teriyaki*)

wine list
an extensive selection of hot or cold sake, shochu and Japanese beers

opening hours
lunch noon–2.30pm daily
dinner 6.30–10pm daily

rooms
210 rooms and suites

features
business centre facilities • gift shop • medical service on call • special sightseeing tours • fitness centre

other f + b outlets
Bayu Lounge • Suria Café • Sri Melaka • Senja Restaurant • Ti Chen Restaurant • Golfer's Terrace • RP Entertainment Centre

what's nearby
The Japanese School of Kuala Lumpur

the restaurant the club at the saujana

The Club at the Saujana is right next to The Saujana Hotel, and offers some great dining choices. **The Restaurant** is the Club's signature Western dining room. It is set in the middle of beautifully landscaped grounds and overlooks the lush greenery and the soothing lake. The décor of The Restaurant is clean and classy, and has a neutral colour scheme that sets the stage for the food that is served here, defined by crisp, classic flavours.

Under the guidance of Executive Chef Nancy Kinchela, The Restaurant entices diners with a menu of modern European delights. The chef is no stranger to the gastronomic arts, and has garnered many awards during her illustrious career. Chef Kinchela is Australian-born, and has gained international exposure from her work in prestigious kitchens in the United States, Europe, London and the Middle East. As one of the best international female chefs, Chef Kinchela has won countless culinary awards, including the Waterford Crystal Promotion of The Savoy Hotel and also gold and silver medals at the culinary awards at London's famed Olympia, and the Moreau & Fils competition. Her passion for quality ingredients, fresh food and precision cooking is reflected in the menu she has created for The Restaurant.

Popular lunch appetisers exhibit the British influence on the chef's cooking. A pumpkin soup is spiced up with a hint of young ginger while a clam and potato chowder pays homage to her time in the United States. Other appetisers come from varied international influences, and there is something for every kind of diner—choose from a Greek feta salad, an oven-roasted tomato with mozzarella, an asparagus omelette and even a traditional Malaysian dish, steamed chicken rice noodle.

Dinner offers selections from the grill as well as the chef's signature dishes which include a rack of lamb, striploin, king prawns and barramundi from East Malaysian waters. The chef offers classic favourites with a twist, and her personal touch is easily seen in all of her dishes, even the side dishes. A truffled mashed potato lifts this side dish out of the ordinary, and it is little touches like this that keeps diners coming back for more.

The Restaurant's menu is truly distinct, thanks to Chef Kinchela's gourmet touch. She has redefined clubhouse dining by constantly updating her recipes, ensuring that her dishes are always fresh and new.

THIS PAGE (FROM TOP): Have a classy dinner party in The Restaurant's private room; Enjoy the soothing and tranquil ambience at the al fresco dining area by the pool.
OPPOSITE: The Restaurant's delicious dish, lobster custard, butter poached lobster and cauliflower purée.

kuala lumpur **malaysia**

lobster custard, butter poached lobster and cauliflower purée

serves 4

4 lobster claws (or large prawns), shelled
100g butter

For Custard
300ml lobster bisque
2 eggs, beaten
60ml cream
1 stalk tarragon
salt and cayenne pepper to taste

For Cauliflower Purée
100ml milk
100ml water
¼ head cauliflower
1 tbsp sour cream
1 sprig thyme
truffle oil

Method:

1. To make the custard, heat the lobster bisque and add the stalk of tarragon to infuse. Cool the bisque to room temperature, add eggs and whisk well.
2. Strain the custard mixture and then add cream. Stir well, and pour into 4 dariole moulds. Cover each with parchment paper or muslin and steam over gentle heat for about 10 to 12 minutes.
3. Set the custard aside until it is ready to be served.
4. Cut cauliflower into smaller florets and simmer in the milk and water mixture over gentle heat, with the sprig of thyme.
5. When the cauliflower is tender, remove from the pot, drain and then purée in a blender.
6. Add sour cream to the cauliflower purée and season with salt and truffle oil according to taste.
7. Place 100g butter in a pan and slowly poach the lobster claws or prawns until cooked. Do not allow butter to scorch.
8. To plate, place custard in the centre and top with a quenelle of cauliflower purée. Place a lobster claw or prawn on top of the cauliflower. Drizzle some of the cooking butter over the custard for extra flavour.

Note:
Lobster bisque is made by first sautéing lobster, crab or prawn shells in butter. The shells are pounded or ground, and then boiled. This soup is strained, after which herbs, seasoning and cream are added. Finally, a shot of cognac gives the bisque more body.

restaurant + address
The Restaurant
The Club at The Saujana
Jalan Lapangan Terbang SAAS
40150 Shah Alam
Selangor Darul Ehsan, Malaysia
telephone: +60.3.7843 1234
email: info@thesaujana.com
reservations email:
reservations@thesaujana.com
website: www.theclubatthesaujana.com

cuisine
modern European

signature dishes
confit of lamb shoulder • lobster custard, butter poached lobster and cauliflower purée

wine list
an extensive wine list featuring both red and white varieties from Australian, Argentinian and Spanish labels

opening hours
breakfast 6.30–10.30am daily
lunch noon–2pm daily
dinner 7–10.30pm daily

rooms
105 rooms and suites

features
The Club Concierge • 39-metre (130-feet) swimming pool • free form swimming pool • fitness centre • sauna and steam room facilities • The Spa & Med Beauty

other f + b outlets
The Lounge

what's nearby
The Japanese School of Kuala Lumpur

neo restaurant + luxe lounge

NEO Restaurant and Luxe Lounge is a new bar-restaurant that has instantly become a hit with the "in" crowd—it goes beyond serving just food and drink. In fact, Neo has reinvented Kuala Lumpur's night scene by designing novelty themed nights that have quickly gained popularity amongst the glamorous in the city.

Chill-out Monday, KAN PAI Tuesday, Blackberry Wednesday, Fit Freak Thursday, NEO-rotic Friday and Stiletto Saturday are daily bar specials that draw in a steady crowd. Apart from the fun and drinks, the food served is also making an impact on the local dining scene. NEO, the latest launch by the Samadhi Retreats group, has enlisted the expertise of Thai-Canadian chef Thiti Thammanatr as its Food Designer and Executive Chef. He is one of the rare Asian chefs who has ventured out of his comfort zone, exploring multi-culture cuisines with complete dedication.

Chef Thiti has introduced Western methods, techniques and presentation styles, as well as ingredients previously not commonly used in Southeast Asian cuisine. The chef's multi-culture cuisine incorporates his native Thai with Japanese influences along with Western flavours, creating what he calls "new creation cuisine". His culinary style can be best described as borderless "neo cuisine", and his unique creations have quickly earned him industry recognition and acclaim.

NEO's menu is uniquely classified into different sections. Diners can choose from Raw Agents or cold starters which include scallops marinated with a trio of caviar, fig balsamic reduction and truffle oil. Flamed Agents refer to the dishes created over an open fire grill. The classic grilled lamb chops are given a twist, served with a habanero and tomato salsa on top of curried sweet potato mash. For the mains, the Hot Metal Agent offers seared scallops topped with seared foie gras and a passion fruit reduction. The strong flavours continue with the Wagyu beef striploin served with a Gorgonzola cheese and a whole baked garlic bulb. Under Liquid Agent, there is a poached cod fillet with caramelised onions in a lavender-scented sauce. It is worthy to note that NEO's portions are served with a focus on healthy eating, perfect for the health conscious and weight-watchers.

NEO challenges diners' senses and perceptions of Southeast Asian cuisine, and judging by the restaurant's popularity, these may indeed be the flavours of the future.

THIS PAGE (FROM TOP): The modern and sleek lounge area at NEO is both trendy and stylish; The zen-style private dining area is set amid lush greenery.

OPPOSITE: NEO's signature dish pan-roasted lamb loin, pumpkin mashed potatoes, balsamic reduction with lavender infused; The delicious potato confit with mushroom ragout, zucchini ribbon, Parmesan cheese and basil oil.

kuala lumpur **malaysia**

pan-roasted lamb loin, pumpkin mashed potatoes in balsamic reduction with lavender infused

serves 4

4 x (150g) lamb tenderloin
8 medium-sized (500g) potatoes, peeled
500g pumpkin, peeled
500ml balsamic vinegar
400ml extra virgin olive oil
400ml whipping cream (36% fat)
300g unsalted butter
sea salt
cracked black pepper
ground white pepper
fresh mint leaves
organic lavender pulp

Lamb Tenderloin Method:

1. Marinate the lamb tenderloin lightly with olive oil, cracked black pepper and sea salt.
2. Pour a few drops of olive oil into a pan, just enough to coat the surface of the frying pan. Sear under high heat until the meat is lightly browned on all sides.
3. Cook the lamb to your desired doneness or complete cooking in an oven set at 350°C (660°F) for about 5 to 8 minutes.
4. Remove the lamb from the pan and allow to stand for about 3 to 5 minutes before slicing.

Mashed Potato Method:

1. Put the peeled pumpkins and potatoes in a deep pot filled with water, and add a little salt.
2. Bring the water to a boil and lower the heat to a simmer.
3. When the potatoes and pumpkins are tender, drain the water. You should be able use a small knife to poke all the way into the core.
4. Immediately put the drained potatoes and pumpkins into a mixer bowl with a paddle attachment.
5. Start the mixer at a low speed and add the small cubes of unsalted butter, whipping cream and salt.
6. Blend until all the ingredients become smooth and puffy in texture and adjust the seasoning with salt, ground white pepper and chopped fresh mint.

Balsamic Reduction Method:

1. Pour 250ml of balsamic vinegar into a small sauce pan.
2. Bring to a simmer over medium-low heat, making sure not to boil. Simmer until balsamic vinegar becomes thick. Remove from heat and cool, serve with lamb loin. Garnish with organic lavender pulp.

restaurant + address
NEO Restaurant & Luxe Lounge
19 Jalan Sultan Ismail
Kuala Lumpur, Malaysia
telephone: +60.3.2148 3700
email: neo@samadhi.com.my
website:
www.tamarindrestaurants.com

cuisine
international fusion with Indochinese/Southeast Asian influences

signature dishes
hot air agent—coke-glazed lamb loin • hot liquid agent—white cod, stewed mushroom with caramelised onion and veal stock reduction • blow torch agent—foie gras with mango purée, oven-dried watermelon, mint salt

signature drinks
selection from the mixology bar • single malt whiskey cellar

wine list
a comprehensive wine list with 400 labels • wine by the glass is available for more than 50 bottles and a sommelier is available for food and wine pairing

opening hours
6pm–1am daily except Sundays
happy hour 5–7pm daily except Sundays

what's nearby
Wisma KFC • Hotel Equatorial

sao nam

Vietnamese food is characterised by its strong flavours and generous use of herbs, and is enjoying a renaissance throughout the region. Although beef noodles and rice paper rolls were once the only known Vietnamese dishes, gourmands have recently developed interest in other aspects of this cuisine.

In Kuala Lumpur, the chefs at **Sao Nam** have been making waves in the local dining scene with their exemplary Vietnamese fare. Sao Nam has two branches, one in Sri Hartamas and the other in Bukit Bintang, both of which have won numerous awards. What is served here is not run-of-the-mill street food. Sao Nam's menus introduce diners to Vietnamese cooking at its best, from home kitchen to palace galley.

Sao Nam, which literally means "star of Vietnam"—is a fitting ambassador to the country, and enjoys widespread popularity in Kuala Lumpur. Housed in a pre-war building, the tongue-and-cheek décor and Pop Art paintings add to the stylish and trendy atmosphere of the restaurant.

This popular dining choice has been recognised by the top publications of the country, from airline magazines to high society glossies. In fact, it has consistently won Best Restaurant awards in the *Malaysia Tatler* for the past five years, and comes highly recommended by international gourmet magazines. Travel guides such as *Lonely Planet* and *Rough Guide* also regularly list Sao Nam as a must-visit restaurant. Credit must be attributed to Consultant Chef Madam Cam Van, who designed the menu, and Sao Nam's award-winning Chief Chef Phan Minh Thien from Vietnam. Chef Thien was head-hunted by Madam Cam Van and he quickly earned admiration in Kuala Lumpur and around the region. Many Michelin-starred chefs have sat at his table and enjoyed his cooking, marked by a balance of sharp and sweet, subtle and pungent flavours. His best-known creations are a unique mangosteen salad which has won the Sopexa award in Vietnam, and his vegetarian spring rolls, another dish that also won an award in Ho Chi Minh City.

Athough the chef has trained with the some of the best chefs in Vietnam, he cites his main inspiration as his grandmother's cooking. At Sao Nam, the dishes are refined in taste and presentation, while the authenticity of traditional flavours is preserved.

THIS PAGE (FROM TOP): *Pop Art on the walls are just some playful accents Sao Nam uses to create a contemporary setting; The iconic star is a fitting symbol that stands out here.*

OPPOSITE (FROM TOP): *Signature dish vit sot tom is a must-try; A casual dining table setting is perfect for a relaxed meal.*

kuala lumpur **malaysia**

vit sot tom (duck in tamarind sauce)

serves 4

4 boned duck breasts with skin
2 tbsp vegetable oil
150ml homemade chicken stock
1 tsp Vietnamese fish sauce
1 tsp five spice powder
juice of 2 young coconuts
1 carrot, sliced
20g tamarind pulp
4 shallots
50g sliced ginger
pinch of sugar
pinch of pink pepper
30 crushed peanuts for garnishing
4 sprigs holy basil

Method:

1. Pound the shallots, garlic, salt and sugar into a paste with a mortar and pestle.
2. Add the five spice powder, a pinch of pepper, fish sauce and 2 tablespoons of chicken stock. Stir the paste to mix well. Marinate the duck breast in this for at least 30 minutes.
3. Place the tamarind pulp in 120ml hot water to soften. Heat oil over medium heat in a heavy-based pan covered with a lid. Drain duck breasts from the marinade and fry until nicely browned on all sides. Pour away the excess oil from the pan.
4. Pour the coconut water over the duck breast and bring to a boil. This will help reduce the gamey taste.
5. Add sliced ginger together with the reserved marinade and chicken stock. Bring to a boil, then lower the heat and simmer for 15 minutes.
6. Add the strained tamarind liquid and the carrot slices. Continue cooking until the duck is tender and the carrots are cooked. Add salt and pepper according to taste.
7. Remove the duck and slice. Place on a serving plate, spoon the sauce over the duck and arrange the carrot slices attractively.
8. Garnish the duck with a sprinkling of crushed peanuts and a sprig of holy basil. Serve with rice or baguette.

Notes:

The Vietnamese especially treasure this recipe as one of their traditional dishes. In this recipe, two unusual ingredients stand out—coconut water and tamarind. Almost all duck recipes require a souring agent or the use of highly aromatic spices and herbs to cut through the richness of the meat.

restaurant + address
Sao Nam Bukit Bintang
25 Tengkat Tong Shin
Kuala Lumpur 50200, Malaysia
telephone: +60.1.2218 9743
                      +60.3.2144 1225
                      +60.3.2144 8225
email: pliao800@gmail.com
website: www.saonam.com.my

cuisine
fine Vietnamese cuisine

signature dishes
mangosteen salad • *bahn xeo* (Vietnamese pancake) • lamb in coconut sauce • eggplant in fish sauce

wine list
the wine list features both Old and New World wines, with a special emphasis on white wines that match dishes on the menu • wines are offered by the glass

opening hours
lunch 12.30–2.30pm daily, except Monday
dinner 7.30–10.30pm daily, except Monday
(drinks only after 10:30pm)

what's nearby
Petronas Twin Tower • KLCC • Bukit Bintang shopping and entertainment

tamarind springs

Kuala Lumpur's **Tamarind Springs** is a well-known restaurant that has consistently won awards at gourmet summits and food festivals. Its unique combination of thatched roofs, native art, wooden furniture and indigenous music playing in the background all conspire to make it a unique dining spot.

The concept touted here is "jungle-luxe dining", which its owners define as an intimate dining experience set close to nature and far removed from the city. This dining style obviously appeals to the top echelons of Malaysian society. It is not unusual to see glamorous patrons strolling down Tamarind Springs' red-stone walkway lit with flickering candles to enter the restaurant, which is set in a lush garden setting. Teak accents are generously used to create a luxurious yet rustic feel, and local art and artefacts embellish the dining area, making Tamarind Springs very inviting indeed.

The menu offers an array of dishes that is characterised by unique and unusual flavours. Designed by Executive Chef Somkuhan, the inspired menu combines the lesser-known Cambodian and Laotian influences alongside the more familiar Vietnamese flavours. The tantalising result is what the chef calls traditional Indochinese village cuisine.

Chef Somkuhan is the perfect candidate to run this kitchen—she was born in a remote village in Northern Thailand and comes from a family of chefs who worked in the royal Thai kitchens; her grandmother once cooked for the King of Siam. Since joining the group's first restaurant, Tamarind Hill, the chef has raised the bar and elevated her home-grown culinary skills to an international platform. Chef Somkuhan has played an integral role in helping Tamarind Springs win a string of epicurean awards, and most notably, a prestigious rating in the Miele Awards for Best Asian Dining 2008–09.

There are degustation sets to try, but what is truly unique here are its tried and tested Khmer-style seafood specialities.

THIS PAGE (FROM TOP): *The tropical and rustic Tamarind Springs is set in the midst of a luscious garden setting; The inviting ambience of the restaurant is created by warm lighting and traditional décor.*

OPPOSITE (FROM TOP): *The signature dish crispy snakehead; An elegant table setting, ideal for a perfect meal.*

kuala lumpur **malaysia**

crispy snakehead fish

serves 4

2 cloves garlic
1 piece coriander root
 (*akar ketumbar*)
1 snakehead fish
2 eggs
fish sauce and sugar to taste

For Garlic, Lime and Peanut Sauce
2 cloves garlic
2 tbsp toasted peanuts
juice and zest of 1 large lime
sugar and fish sauce to taste

Method :
1. Mince the garlic and the coriander root.
2. Clean the fish and carefully remove the skin, slowly peeling it back and making sure that there are no tears.
3. Keep the skin whole for stuffing later.
4. Scrape the fish meat off the bone, and mince the fish meat with the minced garlic and coriander root. Mix in the beaten egg, fish sauce and sugar according to taste.
5. Stuff the filling into the fish skin and mould it back into shape. Steam the stuffed fish for approximately 15 minutes.
6. Slice the fish into pieces and serve with mixed vegetables such as blanched long beans and a mix of salad greens.
7. Chop garlic and peanuts for the sauce. Add lime juice and zest, and season with sugar and fish sauce according to taste. Mix well and serve as a dipping sauce for the fish.

Notes:
Snakehead fish are a freshwater species native to Asia and Africa. The Chinese value the snakehead for its "curative" powers and often use it to make tonic soup for patients recuperating from surgery or a long illness. The snakehead fish is known for its tenacity for life as it can survive many hours out of the water. The fish gets its name because of its resemblance to the reptile, with a flat-topped head and sharp teeth. It is also a fierce predator and may swallow its prey whole, just as snakes do. In the wild, snakeheads can grow to an enormous size, and one-metre (three-feet) long specimens are commonly found.

The snakehead fish is popular in Southern China, Vietnam and most of Southeast Asia. Table-size snakeheads range from 25–60cm (10–24in), and the smaller fish are eaten deep-fried or stuffed. The larger fish sold as fillets are thinly sliced and popular in stir-fries.

restaurant + address
Tamarind Springs
Jalan 1 Taman TAR, Ampang, Malaysia
telephone: +60.3.4256 9300
email: tamarindsprings@samadhi.com.my
website : www.tamarindrestaurants.com

cuisine
traditional Indochinese village cuisine

signature dishes
Khmer *krom* stir-fried crab • Khmer *krom* shrimps with thick rich peanut green curry sauce and green papaya • Khmer stir-fried pumpkin with shrimps • stir-fried beef with lemongrass and pepper

wine list
a comprehensive wine list with 400 labels • wines by the glass are available from more than 50 bottles • a sommelier available for food and wine pairing

opening hours
lunch noon–2.30pm daily
dinner 6–10.30pm daily
bar noon–midnight daily

what's nearby
15 minutes drive from KL town • Menara Indah Condominium

top hat restaurant

Top Hat Restaurant is a charmingly eclectic restaurant in Kuala Lumpur named after its signature savoury appetiser. This is a crisp pastry shell shaped like an overturned top hat, piled with a mixture of shredded vegetables and garnished with chopped herbs and chilli. Its inspiration comes from the Nyonya *kueh pie-tee*, a popular festive snack.

While Top Hat's *kueh pie-tee* is understandably popular, it is the delicious mix of Western and Malaysian cuisine that keeps drawing its faithful back. This can be credited to the fact that the restaurant is constantly evolving, and it reinvents its menu every three months. The restaurant is located in the heart of town, in an elegant colonial bungalow just a stone's throw from Embassy Row, in the shadow of the Petronas Twin Towers.

At Top Hat, diners may choose from classic European or authentic Malaysian cuisine. The blend of East and West décor typifies Malaysian chic—with local art on its walls, luxurious drapes and comfortable seating accented by antique furniture. Soothing earth tones of brown and black are contrasted against hues of yellow and red, and complemented by warm lighting.

Malaysian Chef Richard R. Moreira runs the Western kitchen while Chef Ineh Bibi is in charge of the local dishes and desserts. Both cuisines enjoy equal popularity, and rave reviews have appeared in local publications. The restaurant has even earned recognition from foreign press such as *The New York Times*, *The Sunday Times* of London and renowned travel guides, *The Lonely Planet*.

Top Hat is famous for its international favourites such as oxtail stew and chicken pie, as well as local dishes like Nyonya *laksa* and the *nasi kerabu* platter. Home-made desserts enjoy popularity, and consist of tiramisu, *sago gula melaka*, *cendol* and ice cream. *Sago gula melaka* and *cendol* are both local desserts that are made using coconut milk and palm sugar, perfect for those with a sweet tooth.

There is a decent wine list, and diners can be initiated into the ceremonial art of champagne-opening using a sword, an ancient French tradition reserved for members of the Order of the Golden Sabre. If you have time to kill, relax by the Antique Bar for some delectable pre-dinner cocktails.

THIS PAGE (FROM TOP): The casual chic décor makes dining at Top Hat a relaxing experience; The restaurant is set amid lush greenery which creates the setting for a soothing meal.
OPPOSITE (FROM TOP): The signature chicken and mushroom pie; The oven-baked New Zealand cod with spicy tamarind sauce is another delicious option.

kuala lumpur **malaysia**

chicken and mushroom pie

serves 4–6

100g brown onion, sliced
1 bay leaf
100g butter
100g abalone mushrooms, sliced
100g fresh button mushrooms, sliced
30g black fungus, soaked in water, then sliced
50g flour
250g chicken meat, sliced
½ cup white wine (optional)
400ml fresh cream
salt and pepper to taste
2 x 375g packet puff pastry
1 egg, for egg wash

Method:

1. Sauté onions, bay leaf and butter in a pan. Add mushrooms and cook for about 2 minutes.
2. Add chicken slices and stir-fry for another 2 to 3 minutes.
3. Sprinkle flour over the mixture and stir for about 30 seconds. If desired, add the white wine.
4. Add fresh cream and simmer until cooked. Adjust seasoning according to taste.
5. Remove from heat and cool the cooked pie filling.
6. Divide the puff pastry into 12 portions. The bottom 6 must be larger than the top 6 pieces. Roll out the puff pastry into circles.
7. Grease the pie dishes with butter and place the larger pastry bottoms in the greased pie dishes. Fill the pie with the cooled filling.
8. Place the pie lids on. Press with a fork to seal the pastry on all sides.
9. Brush the egg wash over the top and on the rims of the pies.
10. Make little holes using cocktail picks and bake in the oven for about 30 to 45 minutes or till the pies are golden and the pastry has risen.

Notes:

Abalone mushrooms or oyster mushrooms are widely cultivated and increasingly used in professional kitchens. They are popular in Japan, Central Europe and Southeast Asia. The texture of the mushroom is chewy, smooth and tender and it is a good addition to stews, imparting its own buttery flavour and absorbing the scent of the accompanying meat.

Black fungus is a type of jelly mushroom, and is actually a deep, rich chocolate brown and not black. It is crunchy and its crispness stands up to long cooking. Black fungus has no significant flavour and it is used as a "texture" food, to add contrast rather than for its almost indiscernible woody scent.

restaurant + address
Top Hat Restaurant
3 Jalan Stonor
50459 Kuala Lumpur
Malaysia
telephone: +60.3.2142.8611/1863
email: info@top-hat-restaurants.com
website: www.top-hat-restaurants.com

cuisine
classical European and authentic Malaysian

signature dishes
Nyonya *laksa* • top hats • oxtail stew • roast rack of lamb • tiramisu • peach and banana crumble • crème brûlée • warm chocolate pudding • pear and ginger upside down pudding

wine list
fairly extensive list of both Old and New World wines and champagnes • house wines are served by the glass, wine dinners can be organised and a sommelier is available upon request

opening hours
noon–midnight daily

what's nearby
KL Convention Centre • Petronas Twin Towers • Suria KLCC • Malaysian Handicraft Centre • Malaysia Heritage Centre • Royale Chulan Hotel • Prince Hotel • Pavilion KL • Prince Medical Centre

indulgence restaurant + living

Indulgence Restaurant & Living is a restaurant that has been making waves in the local culinary scene. Here, what is served is unadulterated soul food that tantalises the senses. From its very humble beginnings, Indulgence has grown to an award-winning restaurant and boutique hotel housed in a sprawling colonial mansion. This can be attributed to the driving passion of its owner, chef-entrepreneur Julie Song.

Since opening in 1996, Indulgence has earned a reputation for serving some of the best food in town. The fame of the restaurant has now spread far beyond Ipoh, and attracts gourmets from all over the country. The chef's meticulous attention to detail and quest for perfection are recognised by the many diners who constantly flock back here. The operating philosophy is simple, and the focus is solely on the food and how it tastes—there are no pretentious trimmings or black ties here. Chef Song ensures that all her ingredients are of the best quality and for this reason, most of what is served to her tables is imported. She plans her menu based on what is in season, and her special menu is never the same.

The chef's motto is to keep her food and décor fresh, exciting and fun. What is served on her plates is appropriately matched by the restaurant's interior. Its theme can be described as modern eclectic, and the relaxing ambience allows the food to take centrestage, with no distractions. The menu can be best described as modern European cuisine, though the pride of the restaurant are the desserts, the part of the meal the Chef enjoys the most. There are 12 different varieties of brownies served here, all sinfully rich and absolutely decadent.

The boutique hotel houses seven rooms, each decorated according to a different theme. Guests can choose from three suites and four bedrooms according to their style and preference. This unique concept has won Indulgence many awards over the years, and it has been listed annually as *Malaysia Tatler*'s Top 100 Restaurants from 2008–10. Most recently, Indulgence was a finalist in the Malaysia Tourism Awards 2009–10. It is worthy to note that Chef Julie has recreated the menu for Malaysia Airlines Enrich Platinum members, a milestone in her career that points to her achievements both locally and regionally. Some recommended dishes at Indulgence are the foie gras and Hot Marie with chilli angel hair pasta and feta prawns.

THIS PAGE (FROM TOP): *Dine in complete comfort at Indulgence where the muted colours of the private rooms are perfect for dinner parties; The cool and eclectic décor sets the stage for a delicious and simple meal.*
OPPOSITE (FROM TOP) *Signature dish, cressy lamb tenderloin; Macaroon and fruits dessert to end the meal.*

ipoh malaysia

cressy lamb tenderloin
serves 4

For Mozzarella Balls
1 cup oil for frying
16 x 0.5cm cubes of mozzarella
flour for dusting
egg white, lightly beaten

For Cauliflower Froth
100g cauliflower (about a quarter of a head), roughly chopped
⅛ cup cream
1 tbsp butter

For Lamb Jus
300g lamb trimmings
50g butter
1 tbsp olive oil
100g onions, chopped
50g garlic, chopped
1 cup chicken stock

For Lamb Tenderloin
12 cherry tomatoes
8 pieces lamb tenderloin
olive oil to cook
salt and pepper

For Garnish
mesclun leaves
oven-dried cherry tomatoes
balsamico reduction

Mozzarella Balls Method:
1. Heat oil in a small pot. Coat cheese cubes with flour, dip into the egg white, and then toss in flour again.
2. Deep fry until golden brown. Set aside.

Cauliflower Froth Method:
1. Put the cauliflower into a saucepan with enough water to cover. Boil for about 10 minutes, drain and then purée in a blender.
2. Sieve and reserve the liquid. Add cream and butter to 1 cup of liquid.
3. Whisk the cauliflower cream mixture until it foams. Set aside.

Lamb Jus Method:
1. In a saucepan, brown the trimmings with butter and olive oil. Add onions and garlic and cook until browned.
2. Add stock, a ladle at a time, cooking until the mixture is reduced by half. Skim off any fat.
3. At this point you can infuse the jus with herbs or spices as you wish. Strain and reserve for use.

Lamb Tenderloin Method:
1. Slice the base of the cherry tomatoes slightly so that each tomato sits well on a flat surface. Plunge them in boiling water for about 10 seconds and run through with some cold water.
2. Peel the tomato skin from bottom up to the top of each tomato so that it looks like a flower. Set aside.
3. Heat the griddle pan. Drizzle lamb tenderloin with olive oil and season with salt and pepper. Sear meat on all sides for 3 minutes for medium rare. Remove from heat and allow to rest for 5 minutes.

Assembly:
1. Cut the lamb into 4cm (1.5in) lengths and stand them on 4 plates.
2. Place mozzarella balls alongside lamb, with some mesclun leaves, oven-dried tomatoes and tomato flowers.
3. Spoon on the cauliflower froth and then drizzle the lamb jus and balsamico reduction.

restaurant + address
Indulgence Restaurant & Living
14 Jalan Raja Dihilir
30350 Ipoh, Perak, Malaysia
telephone: +60.5.255 7051
email: indulge@indulgencerestaurant.com
website: www.indulgencerestaurant.com

cuisine
modern European

signature dishes
foie gras • wagyu or kobe beef • hot marie with chilli angel hair and feta prawns • Eryngli mushrooms and avocado on fire-toasted house bread

wine list
the wine list offers a selection from Italy, France, Spain, Chile and Australia, consisting both Old World and New World wines • Australian and French wines are available by the glass, and there is a sommelier who can recommend wine to complement your food

opening hours
9am–11.30pm Wednesday–Sunday

rooms
3 suites and 4 deluxe rooms

features
large LED TV • safe deposit box • wireless broadband internet access

what's nearby
Perak Turf Club • City Library • shopping malls

the view hotel equatorial penang

The View at **Hotel Equatorial Penang** lives up to its name by offering sweeping views of Penang's coastline with its floor to ceiling windows. As Equatorial's star feature and signature restaurant, The View is easily one of the island's top dining destinations.

Although the award-winning hotel houses a number of food and beverage outlets, The View's Provençal cuisine is the main attraction. French fine-dining at its best, American Chef Junious Dickerson heads the kitchen to create haute cuisine with the highest quality ingredients. With Chef Dickerson, the dining experience is a visceral one, not only impressing his guests with the taste of his food, but also amplifying the journey with the presentation of his dishes. As a widely travelled chef, he draws inspiration from his journeys, all the while preserving the bona fide flavours of French cuisine. The chef defines his own culinary style as French Mediterranean haute cuisine, a commitment reflected in a menu which consists of many innovative dishes. Monthly promotions highlight seasonal air-flown ingredients from around the world, including Alaskan crab, truffles and fresh foie gras.

An impressive wine list complements the menu. It boasts over 200 French wines of excellent pedigree, and The View also offers wine-pairing degustation dinners upon request. It comes as no surprise that the restaurant has played host to prestigious wine events including the Chaine Des Rotisseurs, or that it has been repeatedly won awards from *Malaysia Tatler*. It has also been listed as one of the finest restaurants in Asia, in the 2009–10 *Miele Guides* list.

THIS PAGE: *The breathtaking view of the island's coastline is the perfect backdrop for a delicious, world-class meal.*

OPPOSITE: *The View's signature dish, Mediterranean caesar salad on truffled Parmesan custard with olive tapenade and air-dried chicken floss.*

penang malaysia

mediterranean caesar salad on truffled parmesan custard with olive tapenade and air-dried chicken floss

serves 4

For Anchovy Dressing
1 clove garlic, skinned and chopped
1 shallot, skinned and chopped
4 tbsp balsamic vinegar
2 tbsp French mustard
1 tsp lemon juice
1 anchovy fillet
1 egg yolk
¼ cup extra virgin olive oil
¼ cup canola oil
4 tbsp grapeseed oil
1 tbsp white truffle oil
freshly ground white pepper

For Parmesan Custard
⅓ cup heavy cream
⅓ cup milk
50g Parmigiano Reggiano
1 egg plus ½ egg yolk
Kosher salt and ground white pepper
10g black truffles, chopped

For Parmesan Disc
¼ cup Parmesan, grated
1½ cups hearts of romaine, sliced
40g mixed micro greens
½ potato, finely shaved
150g chicken floss
4 quail eggs, soft-boiled
2 cherry tomatoes, cut into halves

For Tapenade
2 anchovy fillets
50g Nicoise olives, pitted
3–4 tomatoes, skinned and chopped
10g artichoke hearts, chopped
1 tbsp chopped parsley
1 tbsp extra virgin olive oil
juice from half a lemon

For Assembly
toasted baguette croutons
thinly sliced potato strips, deep-fried

Method:

1. Make the dressing by blending garlic, shallots, vinegar, mustard, lemon juice and anchovies until smooth. Transfer the purée to a bowl and beat in the egg yolk. Drizzle oil into the dressing while steadily beating all the time until it comes together like a mayonnaise. Adjust seasoning with white pepper.
2. Prepare the custard by pouring cream, milk, Parmigiano Reggiano and truffles in a saucepan. Bring to a simmer then turn off the heat, cover and allow flavours to infuse.
3. Whisk eggs and egg yolk together. Reheat the cream mixture until it is just below simmering point. Strain the hot cream mixture into the egg slowly, taking care not to scramble it. Season to taste.
4. Grease four 50g molds and pour the custard mixture in till three-quarters full. Place the molds into a deep baking dish and add hot water so that it covers the moulds halfway.
5. Cover the top of the molds with foil. Bake in an oven at 180°C (360°F) till the custard is set. A knife inserted in the custard will come out clean. Refrigerate them until ready for use.
6. For the tapenade, blend anchovy fillets, olives, chopped tomatoes and artichoke hearts. Turn the processor to its lowest setting and slowly drizzle olive oil into the mixture. Fold in chopped parsley and add lemon juice according to taste.
7. Make the Parmesan discs by spreading 2 teaspoons of cheese onto a greased baking tray. Shape into 5cm (2in) rounds. Bake in an oven at 180°C (360°F) until golden brown. They will harden as they cool.
8. Plate the caesar salad. Place 2 croutons on the plate and place the custards on top of the croutons.
9. Put a Parmesan disc on top of the custard. Toss hearts of romaine slices with dressing until just coated. Do the same with the micro greens. Place dressed romaine on top of the Parmesan disc.
10. Top with dressed micro greens. Put a quenelle of tapenade on the plate, and a soft-boiled quail egg and cherry tomato halves on top.
11. Place some deep-fried potato strips on the plate, and a garnish of chicken floss. Drizzle dressing around the plate for contrast.

restaurant + address
The View
Hotel Equatorial Penang
1 Jalan Bukit Jambul
11900 Bayan Lepas
Penang, Malaysia
telephone: +60.4.643 8111
email: info@pen.equatorial.com
website: www.equatorial.com

cuisine
French Mediterranean

signature dishes
tournedos de boeuf rossini (beef on truffle-infused polenta with seared foie gras and *perigueux* sauce) • *l'assiete de canard* (composition of smoked and braised duck confit) • *jarret de agneau* (braised lamb shank on ragout of French kidney beans with cumin)

wine list
a wine list of more than 200 labels, with a particular emphasis on premium French wines • there are both Old World and New World wines, champagnes, sparkling wines, with house pours available by the glass

opening hours
lunch noon–2.30pm Monday–Friday
dinner 6.30–10pm Monday–Saturday
closed on Sunday and public holidays

rooms
655 rooms

features
driving range and putting green • outdoor swimming pool with waterfall • Equinox Fitness Centre • reflexology path

other f + b outlets
Golden Phoenix • Kampachi • Coffee Garden • Blue Moon

what's nearby
Bukit Jambul Golf and Country Club • Queensbay Mall—Penang's largest retail, dining and entertainment complex

fish w retreat + spa - maldives

Enjoy the tranquility of being far away from maddening crowds at **FISH**, the signature seafood restaurant at the **W Retreat & Spa - Maldives**. The private island playground of W Retreat & Spa - Maldives is located on Fesdu Island, in North Ari Atoll in the Maldives, a 25-minute seaplane ride from the Male International Airport. FISH is set on the southern side of the island where shooting stars can be seen many nights of the year.

South African-born Chef Wicus Prinsloo exercises his creativity in the kitchen, and uses a palette of the freshest ingredients to create Asian inspired flavours. Diners can eat in an open-air area created by Singapore-based interior designer Ed Poole. He has dressed the show kitchen counters with blue-lit glass panels reminiscent of ocean waters. On the other side of the restaurant, displays of crustaceans and fish are just waiting to be transformed into the chef's signature sushi, sashimi and his seafood specials.

Chef Prinsloo is an international chef whose accolades include being inducted as a Les Disciples of d'Auguste Escoffier and Chef Rôtisseur of Confrerie de la Chaîne des Rôtisseurs. His culinary team also took home several medals in the Asia Culinary Challenge in 2008 and 2009.

FISH has organised its menu into "Raw" (sushi, sashimi, oysters, caviar), "Airy" (light starters) and "Plentiful" (mains). It is a thoughtful classification that allows diners to sample many items from the menu. A sample tasting menu may include pacific salmon sashimi, *ikura* sushi with caper berries and *kimchi* dressing, grilled deep-sea scallops and squid-ink noodles with a mild *tom yam* sauce. The restaurant also hosts a weekly food and wine pairing dinner for those spoilt for choice. There are Master Classes available for those who wish to learn how to make their own sushi, or for those who want to know the recipes behind the latest cocktails.

THIS PAGE (FROM TOP): **FISH is set over the water and under the stars; 15 Below, the only underground nightclub in the Maldives; The luxurious Ocean Haven suite at the resort.**

OPPOSITE: **Signature ikura sushi dish served at FISH, made with the freshest ingredients found on Fesdu island.**

fesdu island **maldives**

ikura salmon sushi

serves 1

5 slices salmon sashimi
30g sushi rice
10ml Japanese mayonnaise
1 tbsp salmon roe
1 tsp sour cream
1 tsp black *tobiko*
10ml *kimchi* dressing
1 egg
3 caper berries
kimchi salad
extra virgin olive oil
honey
salt and pepper to taste

Method:

1. Cook sushi rice and allow to cool (See page 42).
2. While the rice is cooking, make a smooth scrambled egg.
3. Slice salmon sashimi and set aside.
4. Mix the sushi rice with scrambled egg, salmon roe, salt and pepper and the Japanese mayonnaise together.
5. Shape the rice mixture and unmold on a square plate, arranging the salmon sashimi on top.
6. Drizzle the *kimchi* dressing on one corner of the plate and place the caper berries in the other corner.
7. Place a scoop of sour cream on top of the sashimi and heap the black *tobiko* over. Serve chilled.

Note

To make sushi rice, you need to temper the cooked short-grain rice with sweet sushi vinegar while it is still warm. Most Asian stores or supermarkets stock sushi vinegar but you can also use a mild vinegar with sugar dissolved in it. Cool the sushi rice with a fan as this helps the rice to absorb the flavours.

Tobiko comes from the Japanese flying fish and is a sparkling roe that is prized for its decorative value as well as its sweetness. You can substitute with lumpfish roe or caviar if you wish.

---

restaurant + address
FISH
W Retreat & Spa – Maldives
Fesdu Island, North Ari Atoll
Republic of Maldives
telephone: +960.666 2222
email: wmaldives.welcome@whotels.com
website: whotels.com/maldives

cuisine
seafood with an Asian flair

signature dishes
Pacific salmon sashimi • grilled deep sea scallops • grilled warm citrus salad with dried *miso* • pan seared wahoo • squid-ink noodles with mild *tom yam* sauce

wine list
an extensive wine list with more than 100 bottles to choose from • there is no sommelier on the island, but vintners and distributors often come as guests, and to train the restaurant staff

opening hours
dinner 6–11pm daily

rooms
78 retreats

features
Away Spa • Down Under dive centre • Wave water sports centre • Sweat, the 24-hour gymnasium • library

other f + b outlets
15 Below • Sip • Fire • Wet • Kitchen

what's nearby
the best house reef in the Ari Atoll • Gaathafushi—the island's own deserted island available for private rental • twenty dive spots within an hour's distance • local island tours • island snorkel hopping

vilu conrad maldives rangali island

THIS PAGE (FROM TOP): Ithaa, the world's first and only undersea restaurant is a unique dining choice; The wine cellar boasts a selection of over 10,000 bottles.

OPPOSITE: Chef Laval's signature dish of smoked salmon, crabmeat salad with pistachio, lime and argan oil dressing.

With miles of idyllic white-sand beaches, a coral reef and a lagoon as part of the natural landscape, it is no wonder that **Conrad Maldives Rangali Island** has been twice voted the "Best Hotel in the World". For the gourmet, however, it is the resort's restaurants which prove irresistible. This award-winning resort has a total of seven restaurants and a wine cellar that notably boasts over 10,000 bottles, making a holiday at Conrad Maldives an excursion of epicurean indulgence.

Vilu is the resort's signature restaurant serving contemporary Mediterranean fine-dining with an Asian twist. There is a special focus on wine pairing at Vilu, and a sommelier will gladly assist you with your wine selection. Dine beneath a blanket of stars as the waves lap on the beach beside your table.

Executive Chef David Laval has been collecting many international culinary awards for his innovative resort cuisine over the years, which recognise his unique ability to combine cuisines and cultures seamlessly. At Vilu, the degustation menu displays the chef's talent. The meal starts with fresh scallops in crispy *feuille de brick*, dusted with 12 spices and lemon fine sea salt, served with a side of tomato salsa and paired with a 2007 Austrian Gruner Veltliner. The main course is the best quality Black Angus, spiced with Sarawakian black pepper and served with foie gras. Again the wine pairing is impeccable, and the sommelier recommends an Argentinian Malbec.

Vilu's wine list is an extensive one, offering a collection of both Old World and New World wines. This comprehensive list is matched by the eclectic selection of meat and seafood used in the menu such as crocodile meat (not for the faint-hearted), Bresse poultry, Iberico pork, Wagyu beef and lobster.

rangali island **maldives**

smoked salmon, crabmeat salad with pistachio, lime and argan oil dressing

serves 4–6

For Dressing

1 tsp argan oil
4 tsp olive oil
dash of lime juice
salt and pepper to taste

For Crabmeat Salad

6 slices smoked wild salmon
500g crab meat
2 tbsp finely chopped purple onion
freshly chopped chives
juice of kaffir lime, to taste
1 tbsp fresh basil, shredded
70g smoked haddock, finely diced
50g whole macadamia and pistachio nuts, roasted and chopped
2 tbsp confit of red pepper, finely chopped
finely chopped garlic, to taste
3 tbsp homemade mayonnaise

Method:

1. Prepare the dressing. Whisk the oils and lime juice together and season with salt and pepper.
2. For the crabmeat salad, mix all the ingredients together, except the smoked salmon, adding the mayonnaise last. Do not use too much mayonnaise and adjust the seasoning as required. Place in moulds.
3. Lay a slice of the smoked salmon on a plate. Unmold the crabmeat salad on top of the salmon. Top with some green salad, grissini sticks, crispy capers, and a few edible flowers. Drizzle with dressing.
4. You may also like to add some finely sliced fresh fennel bulb or some caviar to the salad.

Notes:

A confit of red peppers is very useful to add to a tapas platter or to any salad. Although roasting the peppers may take some time and patience, once this is done, marinating the peppers and keeping them preserved in a jar of good olive oil is simple.

Roast the peppers over an open flame, either on the barbecue or on top of the gas fire on your stove. The pepper skins should get thoroughly charred. Toss the black-skinned peppers into a paper bag and allow them to steam and cool. After that, rub off the charred flakes with a dry kitchen towel. Rinse the peppers, remove the seeds and slice. Place peppers into a jar of seasoned olive oil and keep in a dark cool area. Do not keep in the fridge as the olive oil will mist over.

Argan oil is pressed from the nuts of the hardy argan tree, a desert plant that grows in Morocco. It is a rare oil, treasured for its nutritional and medicinal properties. The nuts are individually harvested and hand-pounded before being mashed and only then is the oil extracted.

---

restaurant + address
Vilu
Conrad Maldives Rangali Island
Rangali Island, 2034
Republic of Maldives
telephone: +960.6680 629
email: www.conradmaldives.com
website: www.conradmaldives.com

cuisine
Mediterranean fine-dining with an Asian twist

signature dishes
beef wagyu salad with tamarind and kumquat dressing • bonbons piment of lentils and prawns • Iberico pork with star anise and eucalyptus honey • *nori* crusted beef tenderloin

wine list
extensive wine list featuring Old World and New World vineyards such as Carruades de Lafite, Vega Sicilia, Barolo, Chateau Rayas, Chateau d' Y Quem, Barolo, Cloudy Bay Sauvignon Blanc and Dom Perignon 2000

opening hours
7am–11pm daily

rooms
150 villas • 55 Conrad suites

features
Jiwa Spa and Wellness Studio • 350-metre (1,150-feet) pristine beach • 33-metre (110-feet) swimming pool and lagoons • Infinity the magnificent beachfront wedding venue • water sports • cultural programmes • 25-metre (80-feet) spa pool

other f + b outlets
Atoll Market • Ithaa Undersea restaurant • Koko Grill restaurant • Mandhoo Spa restaurant • Sunset Bar and Grill • The Wine Cellar • Vilu Restaurant and Bar • Rangali Bar • The Wine Bar

what's nearby
islands, atolls and coral reefs

carousel royal plaza on scotts

The restaurant takes its name from the merry-go-round concept of its open kitchens, which serve up a cornucopia of Asian and Mediterranean dishes, a rotisserie and some seriously good pastries. Gathered here is one of the best Halal-certified buffets in Singapore. Seven satellite kitchens keep the tables laden with fresh seafood and meat selections. A dessert station offers a luscious chocolate fountain, authentic Asian sweets and little macaroons that look like they came straight out of the window display of a Parisian patisserie. The aroma of freshly baked dessert wafts through the restaurant all day, and few diners can resist leaving without a little box of fresh pastries.

Culinary Executive Chef Abraham Tan heads a team that has helped to cement Carousel's reputation as an award-winning buffet restaurant, and it goes without saying that he has collected accolades of his own for his culinary skills. Chef Tan was awarded the silver medal in the Gourmet Team Challenge for the FHA Culinary Challenge 2008, and has won gold in previous years.

His latest culinary project is Cookery Connection by Carousel, a cooking course for amateur cooks. The monthly class focuses on recipes from different cuisines, and the two-hour sessions led by Carousel's team of talented chefs offer everything one needs to know about cooking—from practical tips on shopping for ingredients, to creating the dishes as well as food presentation.

THIS PAGE: The bright colours of the furniture are a playful contrast for state-of-the-art open kitchens at Carousel.
OPPOSITE: Chef Tan's signature dish at Carousel, oven-roasted fillet of cod, celeriac mousseline with sautéed porcini, orange buerre blanc.

The appeal of big buffets has always been the abundant choices available at one table. **Carousel** has perfected buffet service to a fine art, serving up an array of dishes designed to suit every palate and taste bud.

Carousel is the signature restaurant of **Royal Plaza on Scotts**, and its prime location in the heart of Singapore's busiest shopping street is just another factor that adds to its popularity. The restaurant plays host to a large clientele ranging from businessmen meeting clients to ladies of leisure and tourists who wish to sample an assortment of local and international delights.

singapore

oven-roasted fillet of cod, celeriac mousseline with sautéed porcini, orange buerre blanc

serves 4

4 cod fillets, about 160g each
2 tbsp olive oil
salt and freshly crushed
  pepper to taste

For Celeriac Mousseline
200g celeriac, peeled and sliced
2–3 stalks celery, diced
½ large onion, diced
½ stalk leek, diced
½ potato, diced
200ml fresh cream
50g butter
50ml water

For Sautéed Porcini
250g porcini mushrooms
2 tbsp shallots, minced
1 tbsp parsley, chopped
salt and pepper to taste

For Orange Beurre Blanc
200ml orange juice
100ml water or fish stock
1 tbsp vinegar
100g softened butter
4 tbsp shallots, minced
salt and pepper to taste

Method:

1. Preheat the oven to 200°C (390°F).
2. Sauté diced onions, celery, leeks and potatoes in a stockpot with a little olive oil. Add the celeriac and continue stirring until the vegetables are soft.
3. Add water and fresh cream, and stir to blend. Purée the mixture in a blender with butter, salt and pepper to taste. Set aside.
4. Next, sauté the porcini mushrooms with olive oil and shallots, until golden. Add parsley, salt and pepper. Set aside.
5. Season the cod with salt and crushed pepper. Place fillets on a greased tray and bake for approximately 7 minutes.
6. Deglaze pan with the orange juice. Add water, vinegar, and shallots and reduce the mixture by half. Slowly whisk in butter, a little at a time. Add salt and pepper to taste.
7. Ladle a spoon of celeriac purée on a plate and pour sauce before placing the baked cod on top. Garnish with mushrooms and serve.

restaurant + address
Carousel
Royal Plaza on Scotts
25 Scotts Road
Singapore 228220
telephone: +65.6589 7799
email: carousel@royalplaza.com.sg
website: www.royalplaza.com.sg

cuisine
halal-certified international and asian cuisine

signature dishes
international • asian • mediterranean • seafood • rotisserie selections from seven satellite kitchens

wine list
a good selection of Old and New World wines, with house pour selections by the glass • wine and food pairing dinners are available on request

opening hours
breakfast 6.30–10am daily
lunch noon–2pm daily
high tea 3.30–5.30pm daily
dinner 6.30–10.30pm daily

rooms
511 rooms, including 29 suites

features
outdoor swimming pool • business centre facilities • gymnasium • club lounge • spa facilities • ballroom and function rooms

other f + b outlets
Gourmet Carousel • Heat Ultralounge

what's nearby
Orchard Road shopping

cherry garden mandarin oriental, singapore

THIS PAGE (FROM TOP): Magnificent doors in the style of an oriental courtyard residence welcome diners here; Cherry Garden's chinoiserie chic décor creates a sense of opulence and grandeur. *OPPOSITE:* Cherry Garden's delectable garlic-scented soya sauce king prawns.

Few restaurants manage to combine classic Cantonese cuisine and chinoiserie chic as effortlessly as **Cherry Garden** at **Mandarin Oriental, Singapore**. In a city where diners are self-professed aficionados, Cherry Garden manages to set itself apart by offering guests a truly memorable experience. From the rich hues of the interior to the ornate architecture, there is a true sense of opulence here. Needless to say, the food served is of the highest standard. The restaurant has won a string of accolades in recent years, and has earned a faithful following that includes stalwarts who fiercely guard its reputation.

The pride of the restaurant is Executive Chinese Chef Hiew Gun Khong. This young chef has a knack for concocting menus that are comfortably based on tradition, while incorporating surprising twists that make the dishes his own. His devotion to seasonal produce and the finest, freshest ingredients results in delightful creations such as a double-boiled superior shark's fin in shark's cartilage soup and an oven-baked fillet of sea perch in hawthorne herbal glaze, topped with spicy garlic-shallot crumbs.

He enjoys experimenting with new ingredients and unique flavours, often deconstructing classic dishes to create his own renditions. Chef Hiew was appointed Executive Chinese Chef at Cherry Garden in 2006. His relentless search for inspiration ensures that his culinary skills are constantly evolving, and this has quickly made him one of Asia's most innovative Chinese chefs. Some of his favourite ingredients to work with are seafood and exotic ingredients because Chef Hiew says they allow him more room for creativity—this is one chef who never stops pushing the envelope.

Some of Chef Hiew's wide-ranging recommendations include appetisers such as crisp-fried scallop with salted egg yolk and crispy Asian spice crumbs, a delightful duo of roast duck on crispy seasoned tofu wrap and soft shell crab. Chef Hiew's modern Cantonese creations are complemented by a wide selection of hand-picked Chinese teas and an extensive wine list, specially selected to match Asian cuisine.

garlic-scented soya sauce king prawns

serves 4

4 king prawns
9 cloves garlic
1 cup tempura flour

For Garlic-scented Soya Sauce

3 tbsp oyster sauce
4 tbsp light soya sauce
1 tsp Maggie seasoning sauce
1 tsp yeast extract
  (Marmite/Vegemite)
1 tbsp Chinese wine (*huadiao*) or
  cooking sherry
white pepper and sesame oil to taste

Method:

1. Mix sauce ingredients into a small saucepan and bring to a boil. Allow to cool so that the flavours infuse, and set aside.
2. Smash garlic cloves with the back of a knife and set aside.
3. Make a cut along the back of each king prawn and remove the central black vein. Rinse and pat dry.
4. Dust the king prawns with the tempura flour and gently lower into hot oil. Deep-fry until golden brown and just cooked. Drain the oil from the prawns on some kitchen paper.
5. Pour away the oil from the pan, leaving about a tablespoon to brown the garlic over high heat.
6. Add the ready-made soya and wine sauce to the fried garlic, toss to mix and adjust the seasoning with white pepper and sesame oil according to taste. Drizzle the sauce over the deep-fried king prawns. Garnish, and the dish is ready to serve.

Notes:

Tempura flour is a ready-made mixture of flour, corn flour, rice flour and powdered egg white. It makes for a very light and airy batter that gives the prawns a tasty crunch. It also creates a velvety coating which allows the prawns to absorb the flavours of the sauce, which may otherwise slip right off the naked shells.

The sauce itself combines the sweetness of oyster sauce, the saltiness of soya sauce and a surprising touch of yeast extract, which adds yet another layer of richness.

---

singapore

restaurant + address
Cherry Garden
Mandarin Oriental, Singapore
5 Raffles Avenue, Marina Square
Singapore 039797
telephone +65.6338 0066
email: mosin@mohg.com
website: www.mandarinoriental.com

cuisine
classic Cantonese cuisine with a contemporary twist

signature dishes
double-boiled superior shark's fin in shark's cartilage soup • oven-baked fillet of sea perch in hawthorne herbal glaze, topped with spicy garlic shallot crumbs

wine list
an exclusive wine list of both Old and New World wines, and a selection of Chinese wines

opening hours
lunch noon–2.30pm daily
dinner 6.30–10.30pm daily
weekend *dim sum* buffet 11am–3.30pm

rooms
452 guestrooms • 75 suites

features
spa facilities • fitness centre • 25-metre (80-feet) pool • wireless high speed internet access • conference facilities • banquet facilities

other f+b outlets
Dolce Vita • Axis Bar and Lounge • Melt~The World Café • Mortons, The Steakhouse • Wasabi Bistro

what's nearby
Marina Bay • Singapore Flyer • shopping • Esplanade—Theatres on the Bay

inagiku fairmont singapore

In every major city outside Japan, there are at least one or two restaurants Japanese expatriates head to when they crave the comfort of their home cuisine. In Singapore, that restaurant is **Inagiku** at **Fairmont Singapore**. This is one restaurant that believes that ambience is as much a part of the dining experience as the cuisine itself. It was renovated in 2007, and now the restaurant's enchanting ambience, impeccable service and exquisite food serve to provide a visceral experience that appeals to all the senses.

Inagiku prides itself on staying true to tradition, and offers classic Japanese cooking in a setting of timeless appeal. Warm lighting and a soothing colour scheme create a vibe of understated chic, while sturdy leather chairs in walnut are strong urban accents that make for an interesting contrast. Inagiku also commissioned artist Michael Ong for the works of art on its walls. He has created a very tactile collection of works by braiding, shredding, weaving and pleating. His pieces create a sense of the organic, which is in line with Inagiku's operating philosophy. It comes as no surprise that the restaurant's private dining rooms are decorated and appropriately christened after nature's inspiring elements of beauty—*sakura* (cherry blossom), *kiku* (chrysanthemum) and *ume* (plum).

The food at Inagiku boasts the freshest ingredients, often flown in daily from Japan. *Hirame* sashimi is "live" flounder sashimi with sea urchin and caviar, and Wagyu *ishiyaki* is thinly sliced Wagyu beef on a stone grill with *wasabi* and Japanese cress. Inagiku's desserts are something to leave room for, and the most popular way to end a good meal is with *anmitsu*, mixed fruit and jelly with red bean ice-cream, *wasabi* cherry sherbet, vanilla and *azuki* bean jelly. These dishes provide a sense of comfort while epitomising the height of good taste and indulgence.

Head Chef Shinji Morihara also creates *kaiseki* menus according to each season's ingredients. Diners may experience the culinary prowess of this Master Chef, who serves some of the finest delicacies in Singapore. This is a first-class dining opportunity that surely should not be missed.

THIS PAGE (FROM TOP): *Facade of the world-class Fairmont Singapore in the heart of the central business district; The spacious, modern design of Inagiku's private dining room.*

OPPOSITE (FROM TOP): *Signature dish hot pot with Kyoto winter radish and sweet miso; Inagiku's alluring sushi counter.*

singapore

hot pot with kyoto winter radish and sweet miso

serves 4

800g Kyoto winter radish, peeled
10cm piece *konbu*, soaked
2 tbsp Japanese short-grain rice
4 Japanese wheatcakes

For Broth
80g sweet *miso*
4 tbsp *mirin*
3 tbsp sugar
2 cups *dashi*
1 egg yolk

Method:
1. Trim the Kyoto winter radish into four thick slices and place in a pot of boiling water together with the soaked and drained *konbu*, and the short-grain rice.
2. Simmer until the radish is tender. This should take approximately an hour to 90 minutes.
3. Put the *dashi*, *mirin* and sugar in a pot. Pour the sweet *miso* in a sieve and slowly press it into the broth, stirring all the time.
4. Stir in the beaten egg yolk.
5. To serve, divide the broth into 4 bowls and place each bowl over a charcoal brazier.
6. Place a piece of Kyoto winter radish inside the hot pot, with wheat cake cubes on top.

Notes:
Radish are especially valued in the winter, when the cold weather sweetens the vegetable and intensifies the flavour. Radish, or *daikon*, are now easily available in supermarkets all year round. Choose those with unblemished skin and no cracks. To check if they are fresh, look at their green tops. They should be cleanly cut and not shrivelled, with robust shoots showing through.

Japanese *konbu* is salted seaweed, often used to sweeten soup stocks. The seaweed has natural monosodium glutamate in it and is a great flavour enhancer.

Dashi is soup stock made from dried *bonito* fish shavings. Good dried *bonito* fish is extremely costly, and the best Japanese chefs treasure their *bonito*, shaving them freshly each day to make stock.

restaurant + address
Inagiku
3rd Floor, Fairmont Singapore
80 Bras Basah Road
Singapore 189560
telephone: +65.6431 6156
email: singapore@fairmont.com
website: www.fairmont.com/singapore

cuisine
classical Japanese

signature dishes
hirame sushi (flounder sashimi with sea urchin and caviar) • iron chef course of *teppanyaki* • foie gras *chawanmushi* (steamed egg custard with foie gras)

wine list
sake and shochu selections

opening hours
lunch noon–2.30pm daily
dinner 6.30–10.30pm daily

rooms
769 rooms

features
Willow Stream Spa • swimming pool • six tennis courts • business centre

other f + b outlets
Alligator Pear • INK Club Bar • Plaza Market Café • Prego • Szechuan Court

what's nearby
Raffles City Shopping Centre

peach garden

Peach Garden is the name of a chain of restaurants in Singapore that is widely popular with locals and tourists alike—gourmets constantly flock to this restaurant which offers exquisite and unadulterated Cantonese cuisine in a modern setting. If you are looking to indulge in an epicurean feast that is characterised by crisp and refined flavours, this is the place to go.

The secret to Peach Garden's success is its prowess for offering authentic Cantonese food in a fine-dining atmosphere. The menu reflects a commitment to refinement while preserving traditional flavours. A wide variety of delicately crafted dishes is offered here, and it is no wonder that the restaurant has quickly earned industry acclaim and recognition. Since opening in 2002, Peach Garden has expanded, and there are now four branches situated in prime locations in Singapore.

One of the restaurant's most popular dishes is the timeless *wasabi* prawn in golden cup. Crisp-fried prawns are coated with a spicy *wasabi* mayonnaise that scintillates the tongue and offers a foil for the fresh sweetness of the seafood. It has defined the menu from day one, outlasting food fads and fickle trends, and is reason enough to pay a visit to the restaurant. Other classic favourites served here include fried rice with crabmeat, egg white and conpoy, and steamed fine noodles with baby lobster in Chinese wine and chicken sauce. Peach Garden's chefs have elevated these simple dishes to an art, and like the critics say, something simple is often the most difficult to perfect. As far as these chefs are concerned, they have most definitely passed the mark.

Some recommended cold dishes on the menu include the classic chilled pork shank with jellyfish, and a panacea for all ills, a Cantonese tonic soup with Chinese herbs. The double-boiled shark's bone cartilage soup with fish maw and bamboo pith is another popular dish that cannot be missed, and sets the benchmark for fine Cantonese cuisine. It is worthy to note that the restaurant also offers catering services, seminar and wedding banquet packages. The banquet packages often require bookings one year in advance.

THIS PAGE (FROM TOP): *A banquet setting that sets the mood for a blissful wedding celebration; The private dining room offers breathtaking views of the city.*

OPPOSITE (FROM TOP): *Signature dish baked fillet of sea perch with preserved duck egg yolk and scrambled egg white; The delicious double-boiled apricot with rock sugar and glutinous rice ball.*

singapore

baked fillet of sea perch with preserved duck egg yolk and scrambled egg white

serves 4

4 fillets of sea perch, about 100g each
4 salted duck egg yolks, cooked and mashed
1 small carrot, shredded and fried
a few curry leaves, for garnish
1 tbsp of olive oil
5g butter

For Scrambled Egg White
50g butter
30g almond powder
1 clove garlic, finely minced
1/8 large onion, finely minced
5ml cream
1 tsp parsley, chopped
1 tsp olive oil
1 tsp curry powder
4 egg whites
1 tbsp chicken powder or a chicken cube

Method:
1. Preheat the oven to 120°C (250°F) for about 10 minutes.
2. Pan-fry the sea perch fillets in the olive oil until fragrant.
3. Remove the sea perch and sauté the mashed salted duck egg yolks with butter until fragrant.
4. Lay out the sea perch fillets on a baking tray and coat the salted duck egg yolks over each one. Bake in the oven until golden brown. This should take approximately 20 minutes.
5. To make the scrambled egg white, beat the butter, almond powder, minced garlic, onions, cream, parsley, olive oil, curry powder and chicken powder together with the egg white. Sauté till the egg white is fluffy and then set on serving plates.
6. Place the baked sea perch on top of the scrambled egg white and garnish with fried shredded carrot and curry leaves.

Notes:
If sea perch is not readily available in the market, cod fish is a recommended substitute.

restaurant + address
Peach Garden
273 Thomson Road
#01-06 Novena Gardens
Singapore 307644
telephone: +65.6254 3383
             +65.6252 9833
email: banquet@peachgarden.com.sg
website: www.peachgarden.com.sg

cuisine
modern Cantonese cuisine

signature dishes
roasted golden suckling pig • double-boiled shark's bone cartilage soup with fish maw and bamboo pith • fried prawn with *wasabi* salad cream • chilled jelly royale in young coconut

wine list
a wine list featuring more than 60 labels of both Old and New World wines • wines are available by the glass, and food and wine pairing services are also offered

opening hours
lunch 11.30am–2.30pm daily
dinner 5.30–10.30pm daily

what's nearby
Novena Square • Velocity • Square 2 • United Square • Novena Church

the song of india

In Singapore, you can often discover rare gems just a few steps off the beaten path. **The Song of India** is one such jewel, located in a tiny historical enclave only a stone's throw away from the flurry of Orchard Road, the island's bustling shopping district.

The Song of India is housed in a colonial-style black-and-white bungalow that is nostalgic of a more romantic era, when each meal was almost ceremonial in nature and treated as an event in and of itself. The grandeur of the building is but a precursor to the quality of food served here, which is fit for Indian royalty. The carefully landscaped garden reflects the Kerala style with century-old wooden frames and an old frangipani tree. Inside, white walls and warm wooden fixtures create a welcoming ambience, and the fine art and sculptures adorning the walls add to the restaurant's old world charm.

A wine cellar housing a good collection of international vintages has been specially designed, while the open dining area allows guests to have a full view of the show kitchen. There are also two private dining areas available for those who wish to have a more intimate meal. The two rooms are the Upper Crust and Indigo Mist, which can seat groups of eight to 14, and are lavishly decorated, with gold finish on the walls. The same attention to detail is reflected in the menu designed by award-winning Master Chef Milind Sovani. Chef Sovani has cooked for prime ministers, dignitaries and royalties, and has even hosted his own television shows. He has consistently collected various awards at the World Gourmet Summit since 2004, including Chef of the Year in 2005, and Asian Ethnic Chef of the Year in 2005 and 2006.

The Song of India's cuisine will take guests on a journey through India, exploring traditional recipes, herbs and spices—all individually tailored by Chef Sovani's expert touch. The restaurant also features authentic Lucknavi cuisine, which consists of dishes that appear on the dining tables of the royal family in Lucknow. This cuisine is renowned for its artful blend of spices and herbs, and the slow marinating processes which give the dishes depth and complexity of flavours. Set courses, wine pairing and degustation menus during lunch and dinner are also available.

THIS PAGE (FROM TOP): The ornate décor and warm lighting create a comfortable setting for a delightful meal; Indulge in lavish luxury at Indigo Mist, the restaurant's private dining room.
OPPOSITE (FROM TOP): The delectable lahsooni jinga, a signature appetiser at The Song of India; The sumptuous dessert, gajar ka halwa.

singapore

lahsooni jhinga (jumbo prawns stuffed with spiced crayfish and shrimps in a tandoor marinade)

serves 4

400g tiger prawns
75g lentil flour (*besan*)
50ml cream
2 egg yolks
a pinch of saffron (about 8–10 threads)
salt to taste
1 tbsp chopped ginger and green chilli
120ml thick yoghurt
1 tbsp ginger and garlic paste
juice of a lemon
2 tbsp mustard oil

For Stuffing
1 crayfish, shelled and finely chopped
4–6 shrimps, shelled and finely chopped
1 tsp red chilli powder
1 tbsp fresh coriander leaves, roughly chopped
1 tsp *garam masala* powder
salt to taste

For Garnish
fresh coriander leaves, chopped
lemon wedges
1 onion, sliced into rings

Method:
1. Shell the tiger prawns and keep the tails intact. Remove the black veins and wash well.
2. Marinate the prawns with the chopped ginger and green chilli, ginger-garlic paste and lemon juice. Leave for half an hour.
3. Prepare the stuffing by mixing all the ingredients together. Slit each prawn and fill the pocket with the stuffing.
4. Prepare a thick marinade by mixing together the lentil flour, mustard oil, cream, egg yolks, saffron and salt. Combine and stir to mix well. Add the stuffed prawns to the marinade and set aside for at least 2 hours.
5. Arrange prawns on a skewer and cook in tandoor until they are done. Alternatively, you can grill the skewers or cook in a hot oven at 240°C (460°F) for about 8 to 10 minutes.
6. Finally, serve with chopped coriander leaves, lemon wedges and onion rings.

Notes:
Chef Milind Sovani, who is an expert in the coastal western cuisine of India, has specially created this dish for seafood-loving gourmands of Singapore. This dish is a beautiful collage of tastes and textures combining fresh crayfish and shrimp, which are lightly spiced and then stuffed in a jumbo prawn. Chef Sovani has given it a subtle North Indian touch by smoke-roasting it in a tandoor.

Tandoor refers both to the style of cooking and the clay oven used to cook this style of cuisine. The clay oven is usually tall and cylindrical and uses coal to generate the heat needed for cooking. Tandoor cuisine typically consists of meat or vegetables marinated in a rich red marinade using spices and herbs in a thick yoghurt base.

restaurant + address
The Song of India
33 Scotts Road
Singapore 228226
telephone: +65.6836 0055
email: namaste@songofindia.com.sg
website: www.thesongofindia.com

cuisine
modern Indian fine-dining

signature dishes
lahsooni jhingha (jumbo prawns stuffed with spiced crayfish and shrimps in a garlic-enhanced tandoor marinade) • *nalli gosht* (lamb shank) • lobster *moily*

wine list
an extensive award-winning wine list with an international selection of over 300 labels • wines by the glass come from eight house wines—four kinds of red and white wines

opening hours
lunch noon–3pm daily
dinner 6pm–11pm daily

what's nearby
Ministry of Environment • Newton MRT • Sheraton Towers • IndoCafé

yan ting the st regis singapore

THIS PAGE (FROM TOP): Classic grandeur is created by a neutral colour palette and red accents; The specially commissioned paintings of the Four Seasons form the perfect backdrop for a world-class, delicious meal.

OPPOSITE (FROM TOP): Yan Ting's signature dish dong po rou; The succulent roast pork is another appetising choice.

Yan Ting, the signature restaurant at **The St Regis Singapore**, offers some of the best Chinese fine-dining in the city. It follows a classical culinary tradition that can be traced back to the ancient Ming Dynasty, when gastronomic skills played a big part in culture.

Yan Ting—which means "palace of feasts"—stays true to the Chinese art of banqueting where colour, aroma, taste and form play equal roles in stimulating one's appetite. The restaurant is regally decorated with Chinese art and antiques, a befitting interior for one housed in a five-star hotel. Yan Ting is known for its top-notch service, and is one of the few Chinese restaurants in Singapore with a dedicated sommelier on call. This signature service that Yan Ting provides has become a key feature that differentiates it from other Chinese restaurants.

Yan Ting is the hotel's award-winning restaurant which showcases culinary excellence with an emphasis on authentic Cantonese heritage. The restaurant prides itself on its extensive a la carte menu, comprising traditional delicacies and exquisite *dim sum* selections. Elegantly decorated rooms offer private dining, and the ambience is dignified without being intimidating—an ideal setting for an unhurried and delicious meal.

The restaurant's dedication to detail can be seen in the original artwork that hang on its walls, which includes four specially commissioned panels featuring the Four Seasons by artists Joseph Lim, Phoebe Yang and Zhang Chunlei. These notable pieces create an ethereal backdrop for the luxurious food that is served here.

Classical Cantonese cuisine cannot do without its iconic *dim sum*, which consist of dumplings, Chinese buns and pastries served hot in bamboo baskets. The *dim sum* served here are delicately crafted so that no two buns taste the same. These delectable treats are served during the popular weekend brunch, an event that has gathered a faithful following because of the wide variety offered.

The lunch and dinner a la carte menus on the other hand, also feature an immense diversity of dishes to choose from. The overarching theme is the chef's commitment to bringing out the best natural flavours of the ingredients he chooses. Some of Yan Ting's noteworthy dishes include shark's fin and braised supreme abalone. Innovative tasting set menus are also available.

singapore

dong bo rou (pork belly stew)

serves 4

500g pork belly
1 cup *shaoxing* wine
3g rock sugar
3 tbsp mushroom-flavoured dark soya sauce
½ cup stock
½ litre water

Method:
1. Wash the pork belly and carefully remove any bristle that may remain. Rinse and set aside.
2. Bring a pot of water to the boil and plunge the pork belly in. Remove after about a minute and immediately place in cold water to stop the cooking process.
3. Cut the pork belly into large cubes.
4. Place pork belly and the rest of the ingredients in a clean pot, and bring to a boil. Lower the heat and allow to simmer for approximately 4 hours, or until pork is tender and the gravy thickens.
5. To serve, place pork belly squares in a bowl and drizzle the gravy over. Serve with freshly steamed white rice, buns or fried dough fritters.

Notes:
This simple pork belly stew is named after the Song Dynasty poet and court official Su Shi, better known as Su Dongbo, the "scholar of the eastern slopes". He was known for his passionate opinions, whether they were on palace politics, government reforms or the banquet table.

It was in Hangzhou that Su reputedly created this dish that was named after him. There are no written records of how, if ever he did, invent the dish, but this is one of the culinary legacies that bears the name of a poet beloved to his people.

One story that still circulates in Hangzhou says that Su Dongbo had put a piece of cheap fatty pork to stew, but was distracted by a visitor. By the time he remembered to check the stove, the meat had been cooked for a few hours, and had become deliciously tender.

restaurant + address
Yan Ting
Level 1U, The St Regis Singapore
29 Tanglin Road
Singapore 247911
telephone: +65.6506 6866
email: dining.singapore@stregis.com
website: www.stregisdiningsingapore.com

cuisine
classical Cantonese cuisine

signature dishes
dong po rou (pork belly stew) •
shark's fin • braised supreme abalone

wine list
there is a sommelier who will recommend wines to complement diners' choices of food

opening hours
lunch 11.45am–3pm daily
dinner 6–11pm daily

rooms
262 rooms • 37 suites

features
Remède Spa • 24-hour business centre • outdoor swimming pool • fitness centre

other f + b outlets
LaBrezza • Brasserie Les Saveurs • Decanter • The Drawing Room • Astor Bar

what's nearby
Orchard Road shopping

bed supperclub

THIS PAGE (FROM TOP): *The avant-garde exterior of the nightspot is both modern and sleek; The minimalist interior of pink and purple hues engenders a modern and warm ambience.*

OPPOSITE (FROM TOP): *The delicious almond daquoise with berries; A unique cocktail at Bed Supperclub, body beautiful.*

As one of Bangkok's most famous entertainment spots, **Bed Supperclub** has maintained its fashionable status by providing more than just music, food and drinks. Over the years, it has held its own, constantly offering fresh perspectives and modern twists with its inventive cuisine and unique cocktail menu.

Aptly described as a unique combination of upscale restaurant, club, art gallery and theatre, this hotspot has unmistakable edgy appeal. The white, minimalist interior of the restaurant was designed specifically to act as a three-dimensional canvas for the events hosted here, which include interactive performances and artistic installations.

The avant-garde interior is matched by its continuously evolving menu. From Sundays through Thursdays, three-course meals are served with choices of appetisers, mains and desserts. The food can be described as Western fusion with an occasional nod to Thai cuisine. Signature mains are the lamb with *miso*, pine nuts and blue cheese dressing, and the roast pumpkin and almond ravioli in butter lemon sauce and mustard fruits. Not to be missed are exotic desserts such as the raspberry, young coconut, pomegranate and white chocolate herb salad.

The man behind these gastronomic treats is Executive Chef Cameron Stuart, whose culinary portfolio boasts stints with Australia's Neil Perry and David Thompson, the man who single-handedly brought Thai cuisine to Michelin-star status in London and Sydney. Chef Stuart started his career with the Peppers Guesthouse chain in Australia, before joining Neil Perry at Rockpool and becoming the Head Chef in Perry's kitchen at Sydney's Museum of Contemporary Art.

Stuart's ability to redesign and recreate menus soon earned him a great following, many coveted awards and a desire to venture abroad to discover new flavours. He has found even more creative inspiration in his partnership with Bed Supperclub. The chef believes that Bed is the ideal platform to showcase his food, which he describes as modern eclectic—a mixture of everything, from Italian to Mediterranean cuisine.

bangkok **thailand**

almond daquoise with berries

serves 4

For Almond Daquoise (yields 8 pieces)
90g almond meal (ground almonds)
90g icing sugar
2 egg whites (from large 60g eggs)
1 tsp cream of tartar
1 tbsp castor sugar

For Pastry Cream
185ml milk
1 vanilla bean
1 tbsp sugar
1 egg yolk
1 tbsp plain flour
whipped cream

For Garnishing
200g raspberries
100g blueberries
2 tbsp Grand Marnier liqueur
castor sugar to taste
sprigs of mint to garnish

Almond Daquoise Method:
1. Whisk egg whites and cream of tartar together with an electric beater, slowly adding sugar until soft peaks form.
2. Mix icing sugar and almond meal together and fold gently into the egg white mixture.
3. Pipe batter onto parchment-lined baking sheets, forming small rounds about 10–12cm (4–5in) in diameter.
4. Bake in an oven at 160°C (320°F) for about 25–35 minutes.

Pastry Cream Method:
1. Slice vanilla bean lengthwise and scrape out the seeds.
2. Add vanilla seeds to the milk and bring to a boil. Allow to infuse.
3. Whisk egg yolk and sugar until it becomes pale and creamy.
4. Strain the egg yolk mixture. Slowly add the hot milk to the mixture, a little at a time, while continuing to whisk.
5. Return the egg and milk mixture to the stove and cook on low fire, stirring all the time so that it does not scramble. The mixture will thicken into a custard.
6. Sprinkle the flour onto the custard and whisk well to incorporate.
7. Remove the mixture from the heat and strain again into a bowl placed in a basin filled with ice cubes.
8. When cooled, fold through a small amount of whipped cream to lighten the mixture.

Assembly:
1. Place a round of almond daquoise in the centre of each plate.
2. Mix berries with the Grand Marnier and sprinkle sugar to taste.
3. Pipe pastry cream onto the almond daquoise and pile the macerated berries on top.
4. Finish with a dusting of icing sugar, and a sprig of mint.

restaurant + address
Bed Supperclub
26 Soi Sukhumvit 11
Sukhumvit Road
Klongtoey-nua, Wattana
Bangkok 10110, Thailand
telephone: +66.2.651 3537
email: info@bedsupperclub.com
website: www.bedsupperclub.com

cuisine
modern eclectic

signature dishes
check the website for their current menu

signature cocktails
gay lavender hissy fits martini • melting chocolate tart mojito • jinga

wine list
an extensive wine list—red wines are categorised into light-, medium- and full-bodied • whites are similarly classified, with an additional list for rosés

opening hours
7.30pm–2am nightly

what's nearby
prime residential area • Emporium mall

thailand 179

cotton shanghai mansion bangkok

Old Shanghai meets new Bangkok at **Cotton** in **Shanghai Mansion Bangkok**. Situated in the heart of the Thai capital's Chinatown is this luxurious boutique hotel, tucked away behind a row of bird's nest and sharks' fin shops. Once you enter the hotel's spacious lobby, you are immediately transported into another world and another time. Ornate spiral staircases dominate while Oriental lanterns hang from the ceiling above, and a shallow koi pond stretches out along the length of the narrow atrium.

All the mysticism of the Orient is encapsulated in Shanghai Mansion—Chinese calligraphy scrolls, sepia images of the Qing Empress Dowager and teak-panelled rooms named after classic Chinese blossoms set the stage for the recreation of Old Shanghai memories. In the rooms, the décor is characterised by lavish grandeur associated with the decadence of The Bund—brocade bedsheets, chaise longue and claw-foot tubs are all features that are reminiscient of a more romantic era.

The hotel's newest attraction is Cotton, a jazz bar which gets its name from the old Chicago Cotton Club days. Newly opened on the third level of the Mansion, Cotton features local jazz bands as well as international jazz acts. Cotton Club jazz, classical big-band standards and bebop are guaranteed nightly from 6.30pm till late. Cotton serves delicious food to complement the music. Updated counter favourites such as the signature sweet and sour pork ribs head the list, along with spicy skewers of chicken saté, grilled river prawns, steak frites and chicken curry. Cotton also offers a la carte dining and *kan tok*, which are traditional Thai set meals, for a taste of local flavour.

The drinks, of course, go with the music, and colorful names such as Shanghai Sunset, Shanghai Royale and Shanghai Golden Magarita, are a precursor for the burst of flavours you will experience with every sip. The typical classics are not forgotten, and reviews praise a defining Mai Tai and the Bond-inspired 007 Martini, shaken not stirred.

THIS PAGE (FROM TOP): *Spiral staircases and chinois décor bring guests back in time; Modernity meets antiquity in the hotel rooms which are decorated with the opulence and regality of Old Shanghai.*

OPPOSITE (LEFT TO RIGHT): *Cotton's signature cocktails—Shanghai Royale, Shanghai Cosmo and Shanghai Sunset—are forces to be reckoned with.*

bangkok **thailand**

cotton cocktails

Shanghai Royale
40ml crème de cassis
80ml cranberry juice
15ml lemon juice
15ml sugar syrup

Shanghai Cosmo
40ml vodka
15ml triple sec
80ml cranberry juice
15ml lemon juice
15ml sugar syrup

Shanghai Sunset
40ml rum
15ml galliano
80ml strawberry juice
15ml lemon juice
15ml sugar syrup

Shanghai Royale Method:
1. Pour the crème de cassis and combine all the ingredients.
2. Add crushed ice and shake well.
3. Pour into a glass and garnish with orchid or cantaloupe.

Shanghai Cosmo Method:
1. Chill a margarita glass well.
2. Pour vodka and combine all the ingredients.
3. Add crushed ice and shake well.
4. Strain and pour into the glass.
5. Garnish with lime and maraschino cherry.

Shanghai Sunset Method:
1. Mix rum and galliano together.
2. Combine all the remaining ingredients.
3. Add crushed ice and shake well.
4. Pour everything into a glass and garnish with pineapple.

restaurant + address
Cotton
Shanghai Mansion Bangkok
479-481 Yaowaraj Road
Samphantawong, Bangkok 10100
Thailand
telephone: +66.2.221 2121
email: rsvn@shanghaimansion.com
website: www.cotton.shanghaimansion.com

cuisine
comtemporary fusion cuisine with Thai and English influences

signature dishes
green chicken curry • sweet and sour pork ribs • fish and chips

signature cocktails
Shanghai royale • Shanghai cosmo • Shanghai sunset • Shanghai golden margarita • mai tai • 007 martini

wine list
a wine list featuring wines from six countries, with an equal mix of Old and New World wines • wines are also offered by the glass

opening hour
6.30–11.30pm daily

rooms
60 rooms • 16 suites

features
library • meeting room facilities • room service • wireless internet access • gallery shop • water garden

what's nearby
Chinatown district • Wat Traimit—Golden Buddha Temple • The Grand Palace • The Emerald Buddha • Erawan Shrine • Wat Benchamabopit—The Marble Temple

thailand 181

minibar royale

THIS PAGE (FROM TOP): The casual chic décor of Minibar Royale is reminiscent of a New York-style café or a brasserie; The bar offers some very unique cocktails to complement your meal.

OPPOSITE (FROM TOP): Croque with home-smoked salmon; The Minibar Royale cocktail.

Minibar Royale is a New York-style café located in the heart of Sukhumvit, an upmarket enclave in Bangkok. The café is the brainchild of close friends who decided they wanted to recreate the memories, taste and feel of their sojourn in New York. Their concept was to design a place that would immediately remind diners of the Big Apple, by serving home-style delicacies and drinks in a relaxing and trendy ambience.

Minibar Royale stands as a testament of how globalisation has influenced today's cross-cultural, cross-border migration of good food. On the menu you can find all the comforting café favourites, set against the unique backdrop of exotic Thailand. Bask in the balmy breeze as you sip on freshly brewed espresso, and watch as the world passes you by. The restaurant's signature sandwich, the French *croque*, is served many ways—from the classic ham and cheese to some more New York-styles such as black-pepper tuna or home-made Italian sausage. The brunch menu is the highlight at Minibar as it offers pure indulgence. Diners may choose to enjoy what are arguably the best eggs benedict in Bangkok, drenched in a tangy Hollandaise sauce. Otherwise, they can choose to order forgotten classics such as the corned beef hash. Other signature dishes in the daily menu include the timeless French onion soup and a gourmet-style mac and cheese, made with three types of cheeses. The deep-fried calamari with roasted bell pepper sauce is a must-try, a dish that exploits the freshness of seafood and the richness of bell peppers. Those with more robust appetites can choose the All-American hearty beef stew, a slab of baby back ribs and a very popular Gorgonzola Ed and Ted with grilled chicken breast and shitake mushrooms served in a truffle oil infused Gorgonzola sauce.

The overarching theme of both décor and menu is playful indulgence and creativity. The owners have taken great pains to recreate the casual chic vibe of a café or brasserie, while retaining the sophistication appropriate for a trendy area like Sukhumvit. Fun cocktails are available alongside a selection of wines, and patrons will definitely be enticed by signature concoctions such as the Minibar Royale, which is a mix of sparkling wine and pomegranate juice or the Bumble Bee, a mix of sparkling wine, gin and honey-lime juice.

bangkok **thailand**

croque with home-smoked salmon

serves 4

8 slices sandwich bread
4 tbsp clarified butter
salt and pepper to taste
320g smoked salmon, sliced
4 tsp capers
mayonnaise
2 tbsp chopped dill

For Mixed Salad

40g green oak lettuce
40g red oak lettuce
40g rocket leaves
40g *mizuna* leaves

For Salad Dressing

2 tbsp lemon juice
2 tbsp honey
8 tbsp extra virgin olive oil
salt and pepper to taste

Method:

1. Brush clarified butter on the bread and season with salt and pepper.
2. Mix the smoked salmon with the capers, mayonnaise and dill. Season with salt and pepper.
3. Place two pieces of bread on top of the sandwich maker. Place a large spoonful of smoked salmon on the toast and top with another piece of buttered bread.
4. Close the sandwich maker and cook until the bread is nicely toasted.
5. Cut the sandwich in half and serve with mixed salad and dressing.

Notes:

Croque simply means "crunch" in French and there are many variations to the basic *croque monsieur*—the original sandwich that has a filling of ham and cheese.

The *croque* sandwich is considered fast food in France, and more elaborate versions may come with a béchamel or mornay sauce. If the basic *croque* is served with an egg on top, it becomes a *Croque Madame*. A tomato filling turns it into a *Croque Provencal*. If the filling has blue cheese, it is called a *Croque Auvergnat*. Another variation is the *Croque Gagnet* which has gouda cheese and andouille sausage.

restaurant + address

Minibar Royale
Citadines Bangkok Sukhumvit 23
37/7 Sukhumvit 23
Bangkok 10110, Thailand
telephone: +66.2.261 5533
email: dining@minibarroyale.com
website: www.minibarroyale.com

cuisine

Western-style comfort food with mainly French and American influences

signature dishes

eggs benedict with citrus hollandaise • *croque* with home-smoked salmon • mussel royale • ribs de brooklyn • gorgonzola ed and ted • steak frites • banana pudding

wine list

signature cocktails are available, and a hand-picked wine list featuring both Old and New World wines • three different kinds of wines are available by the glass

opening hours

11am–midnight Sunday–Thursday
11am–1am Friday–Saturday
brunch 11am–2pm Monday–Friday
brunch 11am–3pm Saturday and Sunday

what's nearby

Queen Sirikit National Convention Center • Sukhumvit MRT station • Asoke BTS station

floyd's brasserie burasari

The late celebrity chef, Keith Floyd was one of the most prolific chefs on television, hosting a string of programmes in which he explored global cuisines from Alaska to Asia. He became famous for his adventurous approach to eating and cooking, and he introduced many to the exotic flavours in Indian, Chinese and Thai cuisines. It seems only fitting that he chose the tropical **Burasari** resort to open his first and only restaurant.

Burasari is named after a rare local flower and caters to an elite clientele looking for an exclusive stay at Patong Beach. It is home to **Floyd's Brasserie**, where diners can enjoy a menu personally designed by the celebrity chef, which comes complete with wine pairing. During his illustrious career, Floyd wrote more than 20 cookbooks and filmed multiple television series. With his exposure to international cuisines and a great sense of adventure, the chef was a true force to be reckoned with. At Floyd's Brasserie, he personally taught and mentored his staff, passing on his knowledge from fundamental basics to the most sophisticated techniques so as to ensure top quality and consistency.

Dining at Floyd's Brasserie has become a prime attraction for visitors to Phuket, an experience that is relished by the resort's international clientele and guests. Although the flamboyant chef is no longer with us, his legacy of good food and fine wines is a continuing tradition at the Brasserie. The restaurant is located in the heart of Phuket's exciting entertainment centre, and offers a reprieve for gourmet diners who can indulge with a meal in Burasari's scented garden, in the midst of the hustle and bustle of Patong.

Chef Floyd's signature approach to fine-dining is reflected in the elegant but simple preparation of dishes and a devotion to the freshest ingredients. Some of his most popular dishes include fresh Phuket lobster thermidor, aromatic crispy duck leg on herb salad and of course, the island's freshest seafood. The Brasserie also offers Floyd's Royal Thai Menu, one that was inspired by the chef's interpretation of Thai cuisine.

The Brasserie was recognised for its impeccable food and service when it was voted Best Restaurant by *Thailand Tatler* in 2008. If you wish to spoil yourself with some world-class cuisine, make a trip here to taste the best international and Thai food in town.

THIS PAGE (FROM TOP): The lobby of Burasari, an escape of peace and indulgence; A wide selection of the freshest seafood at Floyd's Seafood counter.

OPPOSITE (FROM TOP): Signature dish, lobster thermidor; The inviting exterior of the restaurant.

phuket **thailand**

lobster thermidor

serves 4

4 cooked lobsters, about 450g each
25g butter
1 shallot, peeled and finely chopped
150ml dry white wine
300ml béchamel sauce
1 tbsp chopped fresh parsley
1 stalk tarragon, chopped
90g grated Parmesan cheese
a pinch of mustard powder
a pinch of paprika
salt and pepper to taste

For Béchamel Sauce

5 tbsp all-purpose flour
5 tbsp clarified butter
4 cups milk
1 tsp nutmeg
1 sprig thyme
salt and pepper to taste

Method:
1. Lay the cooked lobsters belly down on a chopping board. With a sharp knife, split each lobster cleanly in half, piercing through the cross at the centre of the head.
2. Remove the tail meat and dice into 1cm (0.5in) chunks.
3. Melt butter in a pan and sauté the diced shallots for 5 minutes until soft but not browned. Add the white wine and let it bubble until the mixture is reduced by half.
4. Add the béchamel sauce. Simmer until it has a creamy consistency.
5. Add the lobster meat together with the chopped parsley, tarragon and about two-thirds of the grated Parmesan. Add salt and paprika according to taste.
6. Spoon the mixture into the lobster shells and sprinkle with the remaining cheese.
7. Grill to brown the top and then serve immediately.

Notes:
Béchamel sauce is a white sauce considered "the mother sauce" in French and Italian cooking. Béchamel is used on its own, but also forms the base of many other sauces. It is made traditionally by whisking scalded milk into a basic roux made with equal parts of flour and clarified butter, flavoured with thyme or nutmeg, pepper and salt.

Béchamel Sauce Method:
1. Pour milk into a saucepan and add a sprig of thyme. Scald and do not allow to boil. Remove the thyme sprig and set milk aside.
2. Heat up the butter in a separate saucepan and add the flour slowly, stirring all the time. Cook until the mixture starts smelling like toast and begins to turn a very light golden brown.
3. Add scalded milk slowly to the mixture, whisking in briskly so that no lumps form and the mixture becomes very smooth. Bring to a boil and simmer for about 10 minutes. Add nutmeg, salt and pepper according to taste. Set aside until ready for use.

restaurant + address
Floyd's Brasserie
Burasari
18/110 Ruamjai Road, Tambon Patong
Amphur Kathu Phuket 83150, Thailand
telephone: +66.7.637 0000
email: rsvn@burasari.com
website: www.keithfloyds.com

cuisine
international and Thai cuisine

signature dishes
aromatic crispy duck leg on herb salad • *tournedos rossini* (tournedos of fillet steak, foie gras, truffle or cepes and Madeira) • seafood selection

wine list
a wide selection of both Old and New World wines • wine by the glass is available, and food and wine pairing can be recommended by trained staff

opening hours
6.30–11.30pm daily

rooms
186 rooms

features
two swimming pools • spa facilities • wireless internet access

other f+b outlets
Kantok • Misty's Bar

what's nearby
beach • shopping area • nightlife

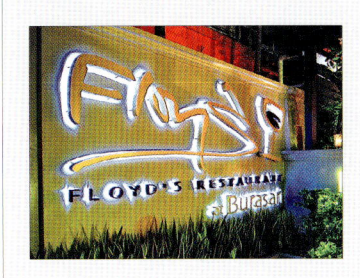

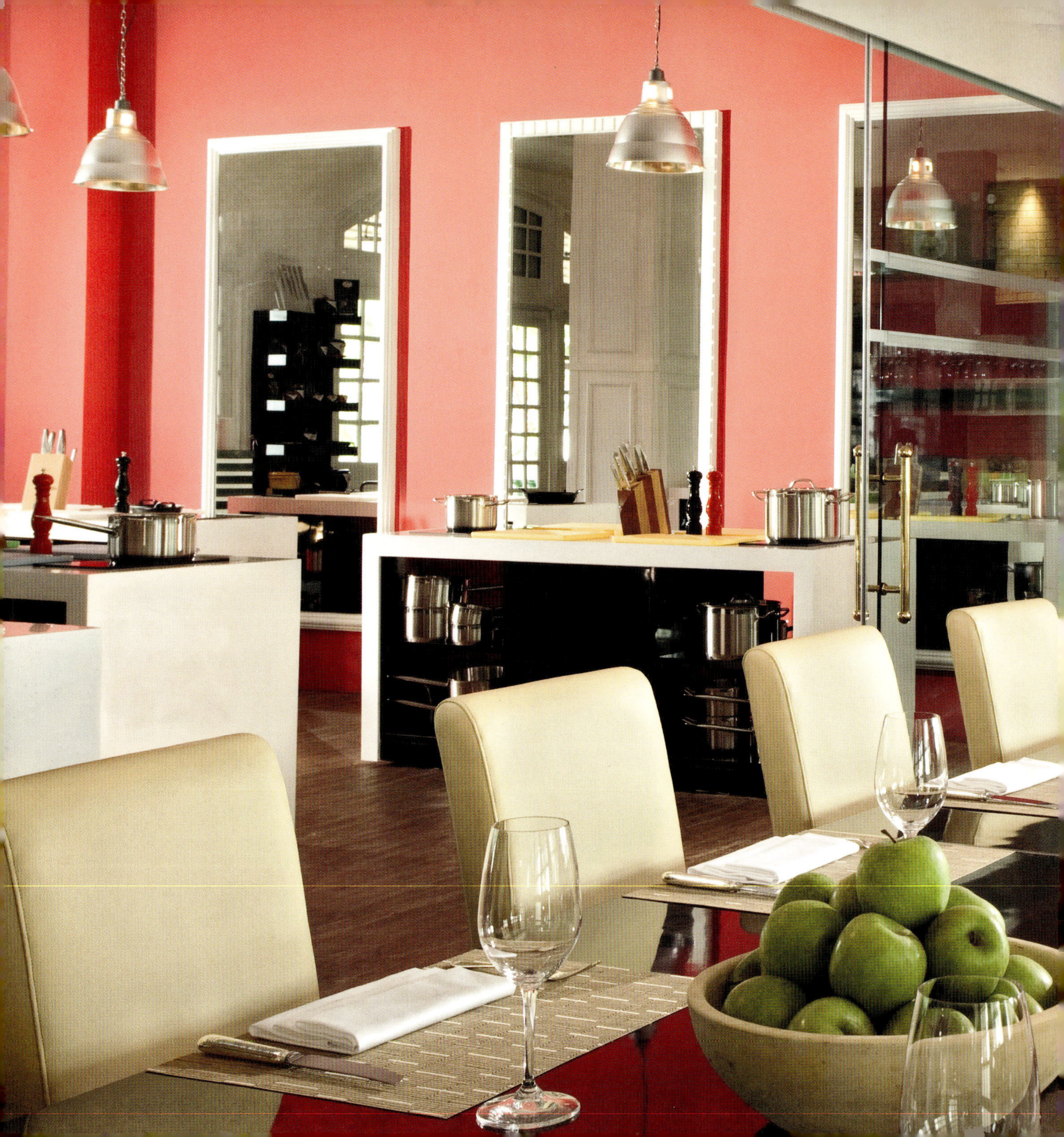

THE ASIAN KITCHEN
herb
discovering WINE
RICE
Home Baking
MODERN THAI FOOD
hot & spicy asian cooking
asian stir fries
SPICE

picture credits + acknowledgements

The publisher would like to thank the following for permission to reproduce their photographs:

ABC via Getty Images 23 (Jamie Oliver)
AFP/Getty Images 23 (Gordon Ramsay), 89 (bottom left), 92 (top)
Alison Miksch/Getty Images 21 (bottom)
Allison Dinner/Getty Images 16 (bottom)
Anders Ryman/Corbis 15 (bottom)
Andre Baranowski/Getty Images 44 (top)
Andrew Geiger/Getty Images 45 (bottom left)
Angelo Cavalli/Robert Harding World Imagery/Corbis 59 (top left)
Photos by Anson Smart 75 (top, left and right)
Atlantide Phototravel/Corbis 92 (bottom right)
Au Jardin 37 (left)
Picture by Banyan Tree Hotels and Resorts front cover (dining on beach), front flap (bottom), 4, 52, 57, 60, 61 (top), 96 (bottom, left and right)
Bed Supperclub 178–179
Bijan Bar & Restaurant 71 (bottom right), 140–141
Bloch Lainé/photocuisine/Corbis 42 (bottom)
Brian Hagiwara/Getty Images back cover (gingerbread), 47 (top)
Brent T Madison/Corbis 58
Bumbu Cooking School 83 (bottom)
Burasari 184–185
Café Gray Deluxe back cover (steak tartar), 29 (top, left and right)
Cépage 29 (bottom, left and right)
Charles O'Rear/Corbis 92 (bottom left)
Chiva-Som 67 (top; bottom, left and right)
Citabria 138–139
The Club at the Saujana 148–149
COMO Shambhala Estate 31 (top and bottom), 66 (top), 120–121
Conrad Bali back cover (serving at table), 72 (bottom right), 132–133, 192
Conrad Maldives Rangali Island 53 (top), 164–165
Coriander Leaf 78 (bottom)
Dale Wilson/Getty Images 64
David Sacks/Getty Images 13 (top)
Derek Cooper Photography Inc/Getty Images 18
Dorling Kindersley/Getty Images 44 (bottom), 45 (top left)
Emmanuel Stroobant 24 (top)
Fairmont Singapore 34, 71 (top), 170–171

The Farm 65 (bottom left)
Foodcollection/Getty Images 42 (top left)
Four Seasons Hotel Hong Kong 37 (right), 39 (top)
Four Seasons Hotel Singapore 65 (Chef Bruno)
Four Seasons Resort Chiang Mai 81 (top and bottom)
Gene Mok 24 (bottom)
Getty Images front cover (restaurant interior), 12, 23 (Nigella Lawson and Anthony Bourdain)
Glow Juice Bar and Café, Singapore 65 (top, left and right)
Hall/SoFood/Corbis 45 (bottom right)
Hammond/SoFood/Corbis 42 (top right)
Hong Kong Tourism Board 77 (bottom)
Hongkong-Asia Exhibition (Holdings) Ltd 77 (top)
Hotel Equatorial Penang 160–161
Hotel New Otani Tokyo 56 (bottom)
Hotel Tugu Bali 51 (top and bottom), 116–117
Hyatt on the Bund 49 (bottom)
Image Studios/Getty Images 13 (bottom)
IMAGEMORE Co Ltd/Corbis 54
IMAGEMORE Co Ltd/Getty Images 20
Indulgence Restaurant & Living 158–159
Inmagine Asia/Corbis 74
InterContinental Hong Kong 27 (top and bottom), 35 (bottom), 38
J Sudres/photocuisine/Corbis 46 (bottom right)
JW Marriott Phuket 17, 82, 83 (top)
Jetta Productions/David Atkinson/Getty Images 46 (top)
Jimbaran Puri Bali 126–127
John Anthony Rizzo/Getty Images 42 (top middle)
Joerg Lehmann/Getty Images 85 (bottom left)
Jones The Grocer 86 (middle and bottom)
Judd Pilossof/Getty Images front cover (flavoured salts), 40
Kate Kunz/Corbis 47 (bottom)
Kathleen's 5 Rooftop Restaurant & Bar 112–113
The Langham Hong Kong 28 (top and bottom), 71 (bottom left), 108–109
The Legian 136–137
Lilli Day/Getty Images 22 (bottom)
Lisa Romerein/Getty Images 43 (bottom)
Luca Trovato/Getty Images front cover (crab, tuna, caviar, mango and avocado timbale), 5

Mandarin Oriental Bangkok 26 (top and bottom), 72 (top), 76 (all), 80 (top and middle)
Mandarin Oriental Hong Kong 106–107
Mandarin Oriental Sanya 110–111
Mandarin Oriental Singapore 168–169
Mascarucci/Corbis back cover (chef plating), 10–11
Matahari Beach Resort & Spa 134–135
Maya Ubud Resort & Spa 66 (middle and bottom), 124–125
Minibar Royale 182–183
Mr & Mrs Bund 32 (bottom right)
Mozaic back flap (dessert), 30 (top, left and right)
Nacivet/Getty Images 19 (top right)
NEO Restaurant & Luxe Lounge 150–151
Nicolas Loran/Getty Images 41 (top right)
Nicoloso/photocuisine/Corbis front cover (three glasses), 15 (top)
Nikolai Buroh/Getty Images 68
Nusa Dua Beach Hotel & Spa 41 (top left), 130–131
nutmegs restaurant – dining at hu'u 72 (bottom left), 128–129
PB Valley Khao Yai Winery 89 (top and bottom right)
Palate Sensations 79 (top and bottom)
Park Hyatt Beijing 55 (top and bottom)
Park Hyatt Shanghai 56 (top)
Paul Chesley/Getty Images 14
Paul Poplis/Getty Images front flap (chocolate truffles), 84
Paula Bronstein/Getty Images 69
Pauline D Loh 90 (top, left and right)
Peach Garden 172–173
Penina/Getty Images 21 (top)
The Peninsula Tokyo 97 (top; bottom, left and right)
Peter Knipp Holdings Pte Ltd front cover (chocolate dessert "Orient Express")
Prismapix/Getty Images 41 (pesto sauce)
Pudong Shangri-La, Shanghai 32 (top, left and right)
The PuLi Hotel & Spa 39 (bottom)
Radius Images/Corbis 93
Raffles Hotel Singapore 30 (middle, bottom, left and right), 33 (top and bottom), 78 (top), 95 (bottom), 186–187
Royal Plaza on Scotts 166–167

Ryman Cabannes/SoFood/Corbis 43 (top), 45 (top right)
Saint Pierre 35 (top)
Sam+Yvonne/Getty Images 22 (top left)
Sao Nam 53 (bottom), 152–153
The Saujana Hotel, Kuala Lumpur 146–147
Scott Wright 32 (bottom left)
Shanghai Mansion Bangkok 180–181
Shangri-La Hotel, Beijing 100–103
Siam Paragon Development Co Ltd 85 (top and middle)
Simply Thai 96 (top), 114–115
Six Senses Resorts & Spas front cover (forks)
The St Regis Singapore back cover (cocktail), 176–177
Stuart Fox/Getty Images 19 (top left)
Studio Eye/Corbis 46 (bottom left)
Sofitel Metropole Hanoi 80 (bottom)
The Song of India back cover (kulfi dessert), 75 (bottom), 174-175
Swissôtel The Stamford 16 (top), 25 (bottom, left and right), 59 (top right and bottom)
Tamarind Springs 154–155
Thilo Mueller/AB/Corbis 2
ThreeSixty MARKET PLACE 86 (top)
Tippling Club front flap (mixologist), back flap (cocktails), 94, 95 (top and middle)
Tohoku Color Agency/Getty Images 85 (bottom left)
Top Hat Restaurant 156–157
Traders Hotel, Kuala Lumpur 142–145
Travel Ink/Getty Images 91
Tung Lok Group front cover ("The Passion that Lasts, Knows No Bounds"), back cover (oysters), 25 (top, left and right), 36, 70
Tuul/Hemis/Corbis 88
Ubud Hanging Gardens 61 (middle and bottom), 118–110
Uma Ubud back cover (pots of tea), 122–123
Valerie Janssen/Getty Images 22 (top right)
Vom Fass Singapore 87 (top, left and right)
W Retreat & Spa – Maldives 1, 63 (top and bottom), 162–163
The Westin Beijing Financial Street 41 (bottom), 50, 73, 104–105
Whampoa Club 48, 49 (top, left and right), 62
Yadid Levy/Robert Harding World Imagery/Corbis 90 (bottom)
Ying Kee Tea House 87 (middle and bottom)

188 gourmetchic

index

Numbers in *italics* denote pages where pictures appear. Numbers in **bold** denote profile pages.

100 Century Avenue Bar, Park Hyatt Shanghai (China) 95–6
100 Century Avenue Restaurant, Park Hyatt Shanghai (China) 13, 54, 55, 56

A

abalone mushrooms 157
Akashi, Shigeru, Meritus Mandarin Singapore 43, 46
Alive!, Batangas (Philippines) 65
almond daquoise with berries 179
Ananda Spa, Ananda-in-the-Himalayas (India) 67–8
anti-oxidants 20
aphrodisiacs 63
Asian spices 18–19
L'Atelier by Joel Robuchon, Hong Kong (China) 47
Atoll Market, Conrad Maldives Rangali Island 53
Au Jardin (Singapore) 35, 37
Australia 18–9
Ayurvedic system 68, 120

B

Babah Peranakan cuisine 52, 116
bagna cauda (anchovy and garlic dip with *miso*) 139
baked fillet of sea perch with preserved duck egg yolk and scrambled egg white 173
Bakerzin (Singapore) 47
Bale Sutra, Hotel Tugu Bali (Indonesia) 51, 52, **116–7**
Bali (Indonesia)
  cookery schools 83
  leading chefs 30–1
  organic food and spa cuisine 66
  restaurant interiors 51–2
  restaurants **116–37**
  romantic escapades 60–1
  wines 88
Balinese *bebek betutu* (roasted duck) 131
Balinese vanilla, coconut and kaffir lime-scented pannacotta with brûléed mango and coconut wafers 125
Bangkok (Thailand)
  cookery schools 80
  gourmet cocktails 96
  high-altitude dining 57–8
  leading chefs 27
  restaurant interiors 52–3
  restaurants **178–84**
  romantic escapades 60, 62
Banyan Tree Bangkok (Thailand) 52, 57, 58–9, 96
Banyan Tree Bintan (Indonesia) 60–1, 62
Bax, Matthew, Tippling Club, Singapore 94, 95
Béchamel sauce 185
Bed Supperclub, Bangkok (Thailand) 60, 62, **178–9**
Bedmar, Ernesto 48
Bedrock Bar & Grill (Singapore) 43, 46

"Beds on the Beach" 61
Beduur, Ubud Hanging Gardens, Bali (Indonesia) **118–9**
Beijing (China)
  cookery schools 83
  high-altitude dining 54–5
  restaurant interiors 50–1
  restaurants **100–5**
Bhumibol Adulyadej, King 27
Bigi, Fabrizio, Prego, The Westin Beijing, Financial Street 43, 73
Bijan Bar & Restaurant, Kuala Lumpur (Malaysia) 40–1, 71, **140–1**
Bintan (Indonesia) 60–1, 62
biscuits 46–7
blood types 68
Blumer, Bob 75
Bo Innovation, Hong Kong (China) 16, 29, 30
Bourdain, Anthony 22, 23, 85
Bowles, Graham Elliot 76
braised lamb shanks with gremolata 113
BreadTalk (Singapore) 85
Bumbu Bali Restaurant & Cooking School 83
Burasari (Thailand) **184–5**

C

cable cars (Singapore) 59, 62
Café Cha, Shangri-La Hotel, Beijing (China) **100–1**
Café Gray Deluxe, Hong Kong (China) 28, 29
Calamari Index 22
Californian food revolution 19
Caprice, Four Seasons Hong Kong (China) 37
caramelised sea scallops on organic English spinach purée with sour cream and crispy Parma ham 127
Caravelle Hotel, Ho Chi Minh City (Vietnam) 96
Carousel, Royal Plaza on Scotts (Singapore) **166–7**
Carrefour (China) 84
celebrity chefs 13, 16, 26
Central Food Hall, Siam Paragon, Bangkok (Thailand) 86
Cépage, Hong Kong (China) 29, 38
Cooking School at Four Seasons Resort Chiang Mai (Thailand) 81
Cepe, Beijing (China) 51
Chan, Alan 49
Chan Yan Tak, Lung King Heen, Four Seasons Hotel Hong Kong 38
Chang, David 21–2
char kway teow (fried rice noodles) 143
Chateau Indage (India) 93
Chau Oi Fong, Nishimura, Shangri-La Hotel, Beijing **102–3**
chefs
  celebrity 13, 16, 26
  leading 24–33
  television 13, 18, 22, 23
  tips and secrets 40–7
Cherry Garden, Mandarin Oriental (Singapore) **168–9**
Chiang, Andre, Jaan par André, Swissotel The Stamford, Singapore 25, 26, 47
Chiang Mai (Thailand) 81

Chiba, Kazuto, Citabria, Tokyo (sommelier) 138
chicken 37, 44
  chicken and mushroom pie 157
  tori teriyaki (chicken *teriyaki*) 147
  coriander chicken with pineapple fried rice in red *sambal* coconut sauce 129
  green curry chicken 115
China
  gourmet cocktails 95–6
  gourmet foods and speciality shops 84–5
  major cuisines 22
  restaurants **100–15**
  wines 88, 90–1, 92
  see also Beijing; Hong Kong; Sanya; Shanghai
China Grill, Beijing (China) 13, 54, 55
Chinese herbs 20
Chiva-Som, Hua Hin (Thailand) 67, 81
Chow, Alex 75
Citabria, Tokyo (Japan) **138–9**
Clift, Ryan, Tippling Club, Singapore 95
Clouston, Dane, Jing'An, PuLi Hotel & Spa, Shanghai 38–9, 47
The Club at the Saujana, Kuala Lumpur (Malaysia) **148–9**
cocktails 94–7
  Kiwitini 145
  Lychee Rose 145
  Mata D'or 145
  origins of 97
  Selangor Sling 145
  Shanghai Cosmo 181
  Shanghai Royale 181
  Shanghai Sunset 181
  Singapore Sling 95
  Tokyo Joe 97
Collins, Grant, Lotus Restaurant & Cocktail Lounge, Hong Kong 97
COMO Shambhala Estate, Bali (Indonesia) 15, 31, 66, **120–1**
Conrad Bali (Indonesia) 45, 73, **132–3**
Conrad Maldives Rangali Island 53, **164–5**
Conran, Sir Terence 106
cookery schools 15–6, 78–83
Cooking School at Four Seasons Resort Chiang Mai (Thailand) 81
coriander chicken with pineapple fried rice in red *sambal* coconut sauce 129
Coriander Leaf (Singapore) 78, 79
Correa, Bruno, Four Seasons Singapore 65
Cotton, Shanghai Mansion Bangkok (Thailand) **180–1**
crème brulée 47, 119
cressy lamb tenderloin 159
crispy snakehead fish 155
croque with home-cooked salmon 183
culinary heritage 19
culinary summits 14, 74–7

D

D'Adamo, Dr Peter 68
design, restaurant 48–53
desserts
  almond daquoise with berries 179

Balinese vanilla, coconut and kaffir lime-scented pannacotta with brûléed mango and coconut wafers 125
passion fruit crème brûlée 119
sake kasu pannacotta 133
detox treatment 66
Dickerson, Junious, The View, Hotel Equatorial Penang 44, **160–1**
digestive system 68
dining trends, Asian 13–6
Doyle, Greg 75
Duc, Philippe, Spoon, Hong Kong 38
Ducasse, Alain 31, 37, 38, 106, 118
duck 43
  Balinese *bebek betutu* (roasted duck) 131
  vit sot tom (duck in tamarind sauce) 153

E

eggs
  baked fillet of sea perch with preserved duck egg yolk and scrambled egg white 173
  purple 44
Empress Jade (Singapore) 62
Endo, Tsutomu, Citabria, Tokyo **138–9**
Equinox Restaurant, Swissotel The Stamford (Singapore) 13, 46, 47, 59
ESpa, Krabi (Thailand) 68

F

Fairmont Singapore 41, 45, 46, 71, **170–1**
The Farm, Batangas (Philippines) 15, 65, 66
fast food franchises 18
Fearnley-Whittingstall, Hugh 22, 23
feng shui 53
fish
  bagna cauda (anchovy and garlic dip with *miso*) 139
  baked fillet of sea perch with preserved duck egg yolk and scrambled egg white 173
  crispy snakehead fish 155
  croque with home-cooked salmon 183
  ikura salmon sushi 163
  marinated barracuda in beetroot with capsicum flan 135
  marinated salmon with orange and Sichuan peppers 105
  oven-roasted fillet of cod, celeriac mousseline with sautéed porcini, orange *buerre blanc* 167
  slow-cooked petuna ocean trout with marinated fennel and parsley oil 137
  smoked salmon, crabmeat salad with pistachio, lime and argan oil dressing 165
  torched *nigiri* sushi 103
FISH, W Retreat & Spa – Maldives 63, **162–3**
flavoured salts 40
fleur de sel 127
Floyd, Keith 184

Floyd's Brasserie, Burasari (Thailand) **184–5**
foie gras 43
food awareness 22
Food and Hotel Asia, Hong Kong (China) 77
food festivals 14, 74–7
food miles 19
food tourism 15
food trends 18–23
Four Seasons Hong Kong (China) 37, 38
Four Seasons Resort Bali at Jimbaran Bay 60, 61
Four Seasons Resort Chiang Mai (Thailand) 81
Four Seasons Singapore 15, 65
Fratelli Fresh, Mumbai (India) 39
free radicals 20
free-range animals 14
Fresh, Mandarin Oriental, Sanya (China) **110–1**
fruit cake 47
functional foods 20
fusion 34

G

Gale, Amanda, glow, COMO Shambhala Estate, Bali **120–1**
garlic-scented soya sauce king prawns 169
Gehry, Frank 49
Ginga Cook Cooking School, JW Marriott Phuket Resort & Spa (Thailand) 17, **82–3**
gingerbread 47
gingko biloba 20
ginseng 20
Giraud, Fabrice, Jade on 36, Pudong Shangri-La, Shanghai 32, 44, 46
globalisation 14, 18, 85
glow, COMO Shambhala Estate, Bali (Indonesia) 31, **120–1**
Glow Juice Bar and Café (Singapore) 65
Gobo Chit Chat, Traders Hotel, Kuala Lumpur (Malaysia) **142–3**
goji berries 20
gourmet cocktails 94–7
gourmet foods 84–7
Gourmet Market, Siam Paragon, Bangkok (Thailand) 85, 86
green curry chicken 115
gremolata 113
Grover Vineyards (India) 92, 93

H

Hanoi (Vietnam) 80
Hatten Wines (Bali) 88
health and wellness 20–1, 38, 64–9
heirloom vegetables 14, 26, 47
herbs 20, 40–1
heritage recipes 15, 19
Hiew Gun Khong, Cherry Garden, Mandarin Oriental, Singapore **168–9**
high-altitude dining 13, 54–9
Hirsch Bedner Associates 51
Ho Chi Minh City (Vietnam)
  cookery schools 79–80
  gourmet cocktails 96
holistic healing 65, 67
homestyle food 21–2

index

Hong Kong
  food festivals and summits 77
  gourmet cocktails 97
  gourmet foods and speciality shops 87
  high-altitude dining 56
  leading chefs 27–30
  restaurant interiors 51
  restaurants 106–9
  signature dishes 36–8
Hong Kong Food Festival 14, 77
Hong Kong Food and Wine Year 77
Hong Kong International Wines and Spirits Fair 77
hot pot with Kyoto winter radish and sweet *miso* 171
hot-air balloons 59
Hotel Equatorial Penang (Malaysia) 44, 160–1
Hotel New Otani, Tokyo (Japan) 56
Hotel Tugu Bali (Indonesia) 51, 116–7
Hua Hin (Thailand) 67, 81
Huebner, Ebony, Kathleen's 5 Rooftop Restaurant & Bar, Shanghai 40
Hutong, Hong Kong (China) 54, 56
Hutong Cuisine, Beijing (China) 83

I
Ibrahim Salim 76
ice 94
Iggy's (Singapore) 48
ihealth 38
Ikebuchi, Koichiro 120, 122
ikura salmon sushi 163
Inagiku, Fairmont Singapore 34, 35, 41, 71, 170–1
India
  gourmet cocktails 95
  high-altitude dining 59
  organic food and spa cuisine 67–8
  wines 92–3
Indulge Restaurant & Living, Ipoh (Malaysia) 158–9
InterContinental Hong Kong (China) 27, 37, 38, 70
Ipoh (Malaysia), restaurants 158–9
Ithaa Undersea Restaurant, Conrad Maldives Rangali Island 53, 164

J
Jaan par André, Swissotel The Stamford, Singapore 25, 47
Jade on 36, Pudong Shangri-La, Shanghai (China) 32, 44, 46
Jaipur (India) 59
Japan
  gourmet cocktails 97
  high-altitude dining 56
  leading chefs 33
  restaurants 138–9
Jenny Lou's, Beijing (China) 84–5
The Jewel Box (Singapore) 62
Jewel, The Westin Beijing Financial Street (China) 50, 73
Jimbaran Puri Bali 126–7
Jing'An, PuLi Hotel & Spa, Shanghai (China) 38, 39, 47
Jones the Grocer (Singapore) 86, 87
JW Marriott Phuket Resort & Spa (Thailand) 82–3

K
Kamata, Mari 97
Kathleen's 5 Rooftop Restaurant & Bar, Shanghai (China) 40, 112–3
Keller, Thomas 21, 30
Kemiri, Uma Ubud, Bali (Indonesia) 31, 122–3
Khairul Ghazali 76
Kikunoi, Tokyo and Kyoto (Japan) 33
Kinchela, Nancy, The Restaurant, The Club at the Saujana 148–9
King, Grant 75
king prawn, orange and pomelo salad 123
Kishida, Shuzo, Restaurant Quintessence, Tokyo 33
Kiwitini 145
Kogetsu, The Saujana Hotel, Kuala Lumpur (Malaysia) 146–7
Kong, Kenny, Fairmont Singapore & Swissotel The Stamford 46–7
Kostner, Norbert, Mandarin Oriental, Bangkok 26, 27, 72
Krabi (Thailand) 68, 82
Kuala Lumpur (Malaysia) 40–1
  food festivals and summits 75–6
  restaurant interiors 52
  restaurants 140–57
Kudus House, COMO Shambhala Estate, Bali (Indonesia) 31
Kunz, Gray, Café Gray Deluxe, Hong Kong 28, 29
Kwong Wai Keung, Langham Hotels International 28

L
lahsooni jhinga (jumbo prawns with spiced crayfish and shrimps in a tandoori marinade) 175
lamb
  braised lamb shanks with gremolata 113
  cressy lamb tenderloin 159
  pan-roasted lamb loin, pumpkin mashed potatoes in balsamic reduction with lavender infused 151
The Langham Hong Kong (China) 16, 28, 46, 51, 70, 108–9
Lau Yiu Fai, Yan Toh Heen, InterContinental Hong Kong 27, 28, 38, 44, 70
Lauder, Darren, Nusa Dua Beach Hotel & Spa, Bali 41, 72–3
Laval, David, Vilu, Conrad Maldives Rangali Island 164–5
Lavis, David 84
Lawson, Nigella 22, 23
Le Rasle, Renaud, Beduur, Ubud Hanging Gardens, Bali 118–9
The Legian, Bali (Indonesia) 136–7
Leong, Sam, Tung Lok Group 16, 24, 25, 36, 70, 75
Leung, Jereme 84
Leung, Alvin, Bo Innovation, Hong Kong 16, 29, 30
Lim, Galvin, Au Jardin, Singapore 35, 36
Liu Biju, Beijing (China) 85
lobster 46

lobster custard, butter poached lobster and cauliflower purée 149
lobster thermidor 185
localvores 19
Long Bar, Raffles Hotel Singapore 95
Lotus Restaurant & Cocktail Lounge, Hong Kong (China) 97
Luise, Enrico, Fratelli Fresh, Renaissance Mumbai Conference Centre Hotel 39
Lung King Heen, Four Seasons Hong Kong (China) 38, 39
Lychee Rose 145

M
Malaysia
  food festivals and summits 75–6
  restaurant interiors 52
  restaurants 140–61
  see also Ipoh; Kuala Lumpur; Penang
Malaysian International Gourmet Festival (Malaysia) 76
Maldives 42
  restaurant interiors 53
  restaurants 162–5
  romantic escapades 63
Mandarin Grill + Bar, Mandarin Oriental, Hong Kong (China) 106–7
Mandarin Oriental, Bangkok (Thailand) 27, 72, 80
Mandarin Oriental, Hong Kong (China) 106–7
Mandarin Oriental, Sanya (China) 110–1
Mandarin Oriental, Singapore 168–9
Mansfield, Christine 76
Marina Bay Sands casino (Singapore) 54
marinated barracuda in beetroot with capsicum flan 135
marinated blue-shelled yabbies 111
marinated salmon with orange and Sichuan peppers 105
markets, organic 64
masak lemak udang dengan nenas (prawns and pineapple in spicy coconut milk) 141
Mata D'or 145
Matahari Beach Resort & Spa, Bali (Indonesia) 134–5
Maya Sari Mas Restaurant, Maya Ubud Resort & Spa, Bali (Indonesia) 124–5
Maya Ubud Resort & Spa, Bali (Indonesia) 15, 66, 124–5
Mayr, Thomas, Cépage, Hong Kong 29, 38
meats
  accountability 20–1
  tips and secrets 43–4
  see also lamb; pork; poultry
meditation 66
Mediterranean Caesar salad on truffled Parmesan custard with olive tapenade and air-dried chicken floss 161
menu-reading 13
Meritus Mandarin (Singapore) 43, 46
Meyrick, Will, Lotus Restaurant & Cocktail Lounge, Hong Kong 97
micro-greens 14, 15, 19
microbiotic cooking 15, 20

Mile Yunnan Hong Vineyard (China) 91
Millar, Richard, RIN, Conrad Bali 45, 73, 132–3
Miller, Chris, Kemiri, Uma Ubud, Bali 31, 122–3
Mimbimi, Philip, nutmegs restaurant – dining at hu'u, Bali 41, 43, 72, 128–9
Minibar Royale, Bangkok (Thailand) 182–3
minimalist décor 53
"miracle" foods 20, 21
molecular gastronomy 15, 16, 21, 106
Moreira, Richard R, Top Hat Restaurant, Kuala Lumpur 156
Morihara, Shinji, Inagiku, Fairmont Singapore 35, 41–2, 71–2, 170–1
Mozaic, Bali (Indonesia) 30, 31, 43, 44–5, 73
Mr & Mrs Bund, Shanghai (China) 31, 32
Muller, Michael, Fairmont Singapore 45
Mumbai (India) 39
Murata, Yoshihiro, Kikunoi, Tokyo and Kyoto 33
My Humble House (Singapore) 12, 16, 24, 36

N
Nelayan Restaurant, Jimbaran Puri Bali (Indonesia) 126–7
NEO Restaurant and Luxe Lounge, Kuala Lumpur (Malaysia) 150–1
Nepal 69
New Australian cuisine 18–9
New Delhi, gourmet cocktails 95
New Latitude wines 13, 77, 88–93
Ngan, Ronald, Jewel, The Westin Beijing Financial Street 73
Ngiam Tong Boon 95
Nishimura, Shangri-La Hotel, Beijing (China) 102–3
noodles
  char kway teow (fried rice noodles) 143
  slow-braised *udon* noodles with soya sauce 101
nouvelle cuisine 15, 25–6
Nusa Dua Beach Hotel & Spa, Bali (Indonesia) 41, 72, 130–1
nutmegs restaurant – dining at hu'u, Bali (Indonesia) 128–9

O
Old World wines 13, 88
Oliver, Jamie 22, 23
One Degree North, Bintan (Indonesia) 61
Ong, Christina, Glow Juice Bar and Café chain 65
Ono, Jino, Sukiyabashi Jiro, Tokyo 33
Opocensky, Uwe, Mandarin Grill & Bar, Mandarin Oriental, Hong Kong 106–7
organic food 14–5, 19, 21, 23, 64–9
Organic Himalaya Pvt Ltd, Phulbari (Nepal) 69
Oriental Thai Cooking School, Mandarin Oriental Bangkok (Thailand) 80
oven-roasted fillet of cod, celeriac mousseline with sautéed porcini,

orange *beurre blanc* 167
oysters 63

P
PB Valley Khao Yai Winery (Thailand) 89, 90
Pairet, Paul, Mr and Mrs Bund, Shanghai 31, 32
Palate Sensations (Singapore) 79
pan-fried crab claw with celery and bell peppers 109
pan-roasted lamb loin, pumpkin mashed potatoes in balsamic reduction with lavender infused 151
Park Hyatt Beijing (China) 54, 55
Park Hyatt Saigon (Vietnam) 79–80
Park Hyatt Shanghai (China) 13, 54, 55, 56, 95–6
parsnips 167
passion fruit crème brûlée 119
pasta 42, 43
pastries 46–7
Payard, François 76
Peach Garden (Singapore) 172–3
Penang (Malaysia), restaurants 160–1
The Peninsula Tokyo (Japan) 97
pepper 41
peppers, roast 165
Perry, Neil 18
Peter, The Peninsula Tokyo (Japan) 97
Petrini, Carlo 19
Philippines, organic food and spa cuisine 65, 66
Phuket (Thailand)
  cookery schools 82–3
  restaurants 184–5
Phulay Bay, a Ritz-Carlton Reserve, Krabi (Thailand)
  cookery schools 82
  organic food and spa cuisine 68
Phulbari (Nepal) 69
Pier 59, Banyan Tree Bangkok (Thailand) 52, 53
plating and food styling 15, 26, 70–3
  trends in 73
pork
  dong bo rou (pork belly stew) 19, 177
  pork loin with croqueta, apple jelly and mushroom quinoa 107
Pot, Bertjan 49
poultry
  tips and secrets 43–4
  see also chicken; duck; foie gras
prawn bisque 43
Prayut Piangbunta 88
Prego, The Westin Beijing, Financial Street (China) 43, 73
Prinsloo, Wicus, FISH, W Retreat and Spa – Maldives 42–3, 162–3
The Private Room, Park Hyatt Beijing (China) 55
produce supply chains 18
Pudong Shangri-La, Shanghai (China) 32, 44, 46
The PuLi Hotel & Spa, Shanghai (China) 39, 47

Q
Quek, Justin 75

R

radish
  hot pot with Kyoto winter radish and sweet *miso* 171
Raffles Culinary Academy, Raffles Hotel Singapore 78, *186–7*
Raffles Hotel Singapore 78, *95*, **186–7**
Raja's, Nusa Dua Beach Hotel & Spa, Bali (Indonesia) **130–1**
Ramsay, Gordon 23
raw green curry 121
RAW, Phulay Bay, a Ritz-Carlton Resort, Krabi (Thailand) 68, 82
raw-food philosophy 15, 65, 66, 79, 120
reality shows 13, 23
Renaissance Mumbai Conference Centre Hotel (India) 39
Restaurant Dewi Ramona, Matahari Beach Resort & Spa, Bali (Indonesia) **134–5**
restaurant interiors 48–53
Restaurant Quintessence, Tokyo (Japan) *33*
The Restaurant, The Club at the Saujana, Kuala Lumpur (Malaysia) **148–9**
The Restaurant, The Legian, Bali (Indonesia) **136–7**
Rick's, Taj Mahal Hotel, New Delhi (India) 95
RIN, Conrad Bali (Indonesia) **132–3**
Ritz-Carlton Beijing, Financial Street (China) 51
River Café, Maya Ubud Resort & Spa, Bali (Indonesia) 66
romantic escapades 60–3
Royal Plaza on Scotts (Singapore) 46, **166–7**

S

sable bases 119
Saigon Saigon Bar, Caravelle Hotel, Ho Chi Minh City (Vietnam) 96
Saint Pierre (Singapore) 24, 34, *35*
The St Regis Singapore **176–7**
sake kasu pannacotta *133*
salads 44–6
  king prawn, orange and pomelo salad *123*
  Mediterranean Caesar salad on truffled Parmesan custard with olive tapenade and air-dried chicken floss *161*
  smoked salmon, crabmeat salad with pistachio, lime and argan oil dressing *165*
Salans, Chris, Mozaic, Bali *30*, 31, 43, 44–5, 73
Salim, Ibrahim 76
salt and sugar curing 105
salts, finishing *40*
Sao Nam, Kuala Lumpur (Malaysia) 52, **152–3**
The Saujana Hotel, Kuala Lumpur (Malaysia) **146–7**
Schuster, Dorin, The Restaurant, The Legian, Bali **136–7**
seafood
  caramelised sea scallops on organic English spinach purée with sour cream and crispy Parma ham *127*
  char kway teow (fried rice noodles) *143*
  garlic-scented soya sauce king prawns *169*
  king prawn, orange and pomelo salad *123*
  lahsooni jhinga (jumbo prawns with spiced crayfish and shrimps in a tandoor marinade) *175*
  lobster custard, butter poached lobster and cauliflower purée *149*
  lobster thermidor *185*
  marinated blue-shelled yabbies *111*
  masak lemak udang dengan nenas (prawns and pineapple in spicy coconut milk) *141*
  pan-fried crab claw with celery and bell peppers *109*
  prawn bisque 43
  sesame-coated crab claws *117*
  slow-braised *udon* noodles with soya sauce *101*
  smoked salmon, crabmeat salad with pistachio, lime and argan oil dressing *165*
  tips and secrets 46
Selangor Sling *145*
Senses, The Westin Beijing, Financial Street (China) *50*, *51*, **104–5**
sesame-coated crab claws *117*
Setjadibrata, Anhar 51
Shanghai (China)
  gourmet cocktails 95–6
  high-altitude dining 54–6
  leading chefs 31–2
  restaurant interiors 49–50
  restaurants **112–15**
  romantic escapades 62
  signature dishes 38–9
Shanghai Cosmo *181*
Shanghai Mansion Bangkok (Thailand) **180–1**
Shanghai Royale *181*
Shanghai Sunset *181*
Shanghai World Financial Centre (China) 54
Shangri-La Hotel, Beijing (China) **100–3**
Shinyeh 101, Taipei (Taiwan) 13, *54*, 56–7
shops, speciality 84–7
Siam Paragon, Bangkok (Thailand) *85*, 86
Siam Winery (Thailand) 90
signature dishes 34–9
Simply Thai, Shanghai (China) *96*, **114–5**
Singapore
  cookery schools 79
  food festivals and summits 74–5
  gourmet cocktails 95
  gourmet foods and speciality shops 86–7
  high-altitude dining 59
  leading chefs 24–6
  restaurants **166–77**
  romantic escapades 62–3
  signature dishes 34–6
Singapore Flyer 59
Singapore Food Festival 75
Singapore Sling 95
Singapore Tourism Board 74–5
Sip (Maldives) *63*
Sirocco, Bangkok (Thailand) 13, *54*, 57, *58–9*
Siu Hin Chi, T'ang Court, The Langham Hong Kong 16, *28*, 37, 46, 70–1, **108–9**
sky dining 59, 62–3
The Sky, Hotel New Otani, Tokyo (Japan) 56
Skybar, Bangkok (Thailand) *57*, *58*
Skybar, Traders Hotel, Kuala Lumpur (Malaysia) **144–5**
skyscrapers 54–9
Slow Food movement 19, 20
slow-braised *udon* noodles with soya sauce *101*
slow-cooked petuna ocean trout with marinated fennel and parsley oil *137*
smoked salmon, crabmeat salad with pistachio, lime and argan oil dressing *165*
Snickers dessert *25*, 26
Sofitel Metropole Hanoi (Vietnam) 80
Somkuhan, Tamarind Springs **154–5**
The Song of India (Singapore) **174–5**
Song, Julie, Indulgence Restaurant & Living **158–9**
soups 46
sous vide 44
Sovani, Milind, The Song of India *75*, **174–5**
Spa at Maya, Bali (Indonesia) 66
spa cuisine 15, 64–9
Space@My Humble House (Singapore) 16, 24
spices *40*, *41*
Spoon, Hong Kong (China) *35*, 37–8
Sri Trang, Phulay Bay, a Ritz-Carlton Reserve, Krabi (Thailand) 82
The St Regis, Singapore **176–7**
Star Bar Ginza, Tokyo (Japan) *94*
Starck, Philippe 49
Steingarten, Jeffrey 22
stocks 46
storytelling experiences 61
Stroobant, Emmanuel, Saint Pierre 24, 34, *35*
Stuart, Cameron, Bed Supperclub **178–9**
Styles, Hugh, Equinox Restaurant, Swissotel The Stamford, Singapore 59
sugar substitutes 20
Sukit Niramitcharoenwong, Simply Thai **114–15**
Sukiyabashi Jiro, Tokyo (Japan) *33*
Sula Wines (India) *93*
super foods 20
Super Potato 49
sushi *103*
sushi rice 42–3, *163*
sustainable farming 19
sweeteners, natural 20
Swissotel The Stamford (Singapore) 46, *47*, 59

T

Taipei (Taiwan), high-altitude dining 13, *54*, 56–7
Taiwan, high-altitude dining 13, *54*, 56–7
Taketoshi, Minami, Kogetsu, The Saujana Hotel, Kuala Lumpur **146–7**
Tamarind Springs, Kuala Lumpur (Malaysia) **154–5**
Tan, Abraham, Carousel, Royal Plaza on Scotts, Singapore 46, **166–7**
Tan, Cassian, Equinox Complex, Swissotel The Stamford, Singapore 47
Tan, Nabil Taufiq, Bedrock Bar & Grill, Singapore 43, 46
tandoor cuisine *175*
T'ang Court, The Langham Hong Kong (China) *28*, 36–7, 51, 70, **108–9**
Tay, Daniel, Bakerzin, Singapore 47
television chefs 13, 18, 22, *23*
temperatures, cooking and eating 47
tempura *45* 169
teppanyaki 43
teriyaki technique *147*
Thailand
  cookery schools 80–3
  food festivals and summits 76–7
  gourmet cocktails 96
  gourmet foods and speciality shops 85–6
  organic food and spa cuisine 67, 68
  restaurants **178–85**
  wines 88–90
  see also Bangkok; Chiang Mai; Hua Hin; Krabi; Phuket
themed dinners 60–1
Thien, Phan Minh, Sao Nam, Kuala Lumpur 53, **152–3**
Thierry, Vincent, Caprice, Four Seasons Hong Kong 37
Thiti Thammanatr, NEO Restaurant and Luxe Lounge, Kuala Lumpur **150–1**
Thompson, David 76–7
ThreeSixty MARKET PLACE (Singapore) 86
Tippling Club (Singapore) **94–5**
Tokyo (Japan)
  gourmet cocktails 97
  high-altitude dining 56
  leading chefs 33
  restaurants **138–9**
Tokyo Joe 97
Top Hat Restaurant, Kuala Lumpur (Malaysia) **156–7**
tori teriyaki (chicken *teriyaki*) *147*
tourism, food 15
Townsend, Kath, Maya Sari Mas Restaurant, Maya Ubud Resort & Spa **124–5**
Traders Hotel, Kuala Lumpur (Malaysia) **142–3**
Tremblay, Stéphane, Senses, The Westin Beijing, Financial Street **104–5**
Trotter, Charlie 75
tuna 46
Tung Lok Group (Singapore) 16, 24, 70

U

Ubud Hanging Gardens, Bali (Indonesia) 60, *61*, **118–9**
Ueno, Hidetsugu, Star Bar Ginza, Tokyo 94
ULTRAVIOLET, Shanghai (China) 31
Uma Ubud, Bali (Indonesia) 31, 122
Uttaranchal (India) 67–8

V

vegetables, tips and secrets 44–6
vegetarian diets 21, 44–5
Vertigo Grill & Moon Bar, Banyan Tree Bangkok (Thailand) *57*, *58–9*, 96
Vietnam
  cookery schools 79–80
  gourmet cocktails 96
The View, Hotel Equatorial Penang (Malaysia) **160–1**
Vilu, Conrad Maldives Rangali Island **164–5**
viticulture 13, 89
vit sot tom (duck in tamarind sauce) *153*
Vom Fass (Singapore) 86, *87*
Vongerichten, Georges 84
Vue Restaurant, Hyatt on the Bund, Shanghai (China) *49*, 50

W

W Retreat & Spa – Maldives 42, *63*, **162–3**
Wakuda, Tetsuya 75, 94
Walmart (China) 84
Wanders, Marcel 49
The Westin Beijing, Financial Street (China) 43, 50, *53*, **104–5**
Whampoa Club (China) *48*, *49*, 62
Wine For Asia, Hong Kong (China) 77
Wines & Spirits Asia, Hong Kong (China) 77
wines, New Latitude 13, 77, 88–93
World Gourmet Festival, Bangkok (Thailand) 14, 76–7
World Gourmet Summit (Singapore) 14, 74–5, 136

X

"X-treme Chinese" cuisine 16, 30

Y

Yan, Martin 75
Yan Ting, The St Regis Singapore **176–7**
Yan Toh Heen, InterContinental Hong Kong (China) *27*, *38*, 44, 70
Ying Kee Tea House, Hong Kong (China) 87
Yung Kee Restaurant, Hong Kong (China) 87
Yunnan Gaoyuan Wine Co Ltd (China) 91
Yunnan Hong Wine Co Ltd (China) 91
Yunnan Shenquan Wine Co Ltd (China) 91

Z

Zimmern, Andrew 23
Zulkifli Razali, Bijan Bar & Restaurant, Kuala Lumpur 40–1, 71, **140–1**

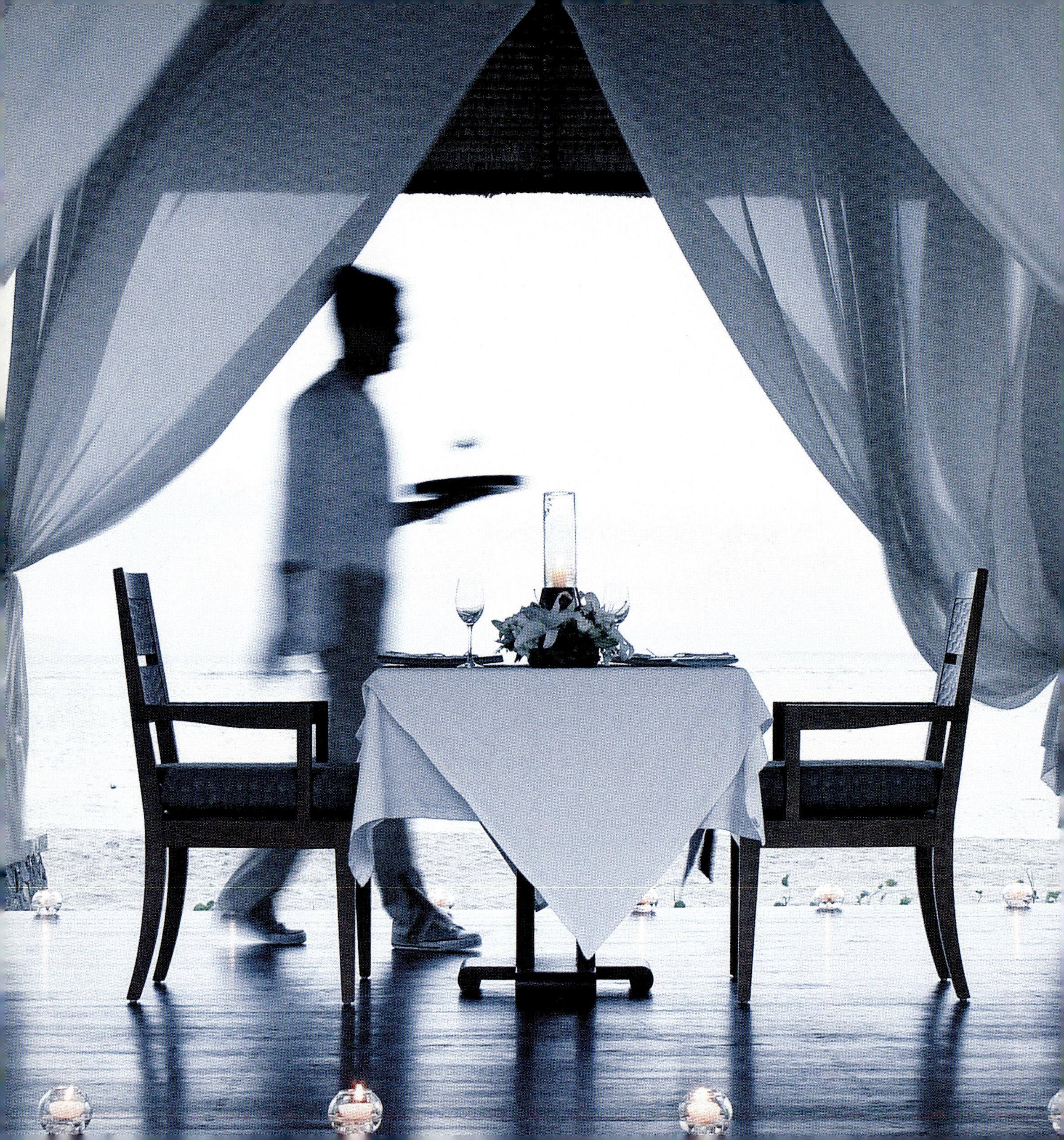